AUSTRALIAN HEIST

AUSTRALIAN HEIST

JAMES PHELPS

HarperCollins*Publishers*

HarperCollins*Publishers*

First published in Australia in 2018
by HarperCollins*Publishers* Australia Pty Limited
ABN 36 009 913 517
harpercollins.com.au

Copyright © James Phelps 2018

HarperCollins*Publishers*
Level 13, 201 Elizabeth Street, Sydney NSW 2000, Australia
Unit D1, 63 Apollo Drive, Rosedale, Auckland 0632, New Zealand
A 53, Sector 57, Noida, UP, India
1 London Bridge Street, London SE1 9GF, United Kingdom
Bay Adelaide Centre, East Tower, 22 Adelaide Street West, 41st floor, Toronto,
    Ontario M5H 4E3, Canada
195 Broadway, New York NY 10007, USA

A catalogue record for this book is available from the National Library of Australia

ISBN: 978 1 4607 5623 2 (hardback)
ISBN: 978 1 4607 1023 4 (ebook)

Cover design by Darren Holt, HarperCollins Design Studio
Case image: Colt's Patent Firearms Manufacturing Company, 1850 [Ben Hall's revolver],
nla.obj-139630731, courtesy National Library of Australia
Jacket images: Eugowra Rocks by Bluedawe/Wikimedia Commons; figures by shutterstock.com;
Ben Hall courtesy State Library of Queensland; detail of original portrait of Frank Gardiner 1864
by Freeman Brothers, carte de visite albumen photograph, Collection: National Portrait Gallery,
Canberra, purchased 2008 (reproduced in full detail below)

Typeset in Bembo Std by Kirby Jones
Printed and bound in Australia by McPherson's Printing Group
The papers used by HarperCollins in the manufacture of this book are a natural, recyclable
product made from wood grown in sustainable plantation forests. The fibre source and
manufacturing processes meet recognised international environmental standards, and carry
certification.

For Peter Phelps,
the Baryulgil Bushwhacker

AUTHOR'S NOTE

I spent part of my childhood in a place called Baryulgil, a tiny Aboriginal settlement located 72 kilometres north-west of Grafton in northern New South Wales. I was a bush boy. I swam in creeks with my mates, shot fruit bats with my dad and roamed the wild. The Australian bush was always alive, full of wonder and seemingly infinite. My backyard was brimming with life: kangaroos bouncing, red-bellied blacksnakes lurking, kookaburras singing. And there were four bushrangers living in my house.

Each morning I would grab my breakfast – mostly jam on toast – and stare at them. They lived above the fireplace in a painting. One was leaning over his horse, gun pointed at the ground. Was he asleep? Another was pointing his revolver, at no one apparently. Or was he? The third was having a casual conversation with a woman sitting in a horse-drawn cart, a shotgun dangling between his legs. What were they talking about? The fourth had his back turned. I could never see his face. I always wondered who these men were and what they were doing.

Recently, while searching for my latest non-fiction project, I stumbled across a story about a stick-up in an old newspaper clipping. It was an epic tale of gold and guns, of heroes and villains, of love and hate. And at the bottom of the story there was a picture of a painting: *Bailed Up,* by Tom Roberts. I was once again looking at the four bushrangers who had lived on my wall. With the print long lost in a house move, I had not seen the Tom Roberts masterpiece since I was eight. The caption on the article said that one of the many tales that inspired the 1895 painting was a gold heist that had occurred in western New South Wales in 1862. A gang of bushrangers, which included the infamous Ben Hall and Frank Gardiner, had stolen 77 kilograms of gold. When I read that, I had my next book. All my childhood questions would soon be answered.

Six months later, I'd got to know a group of men just like the ones who'd lived on my wall. And now, after digging up every available resource on what is known as the Eugowra Rocks Heist, I am able to tell the full and complete story of Australia's biggest-ever robbery for the first time.

The events in the following pages have been pieced together from primary and secondary sources, including court records, police reports, newspaper articles and eyewitness accounts. I have also drawn on a number of previously published books, which I have listed in the bibliography. I have taken few liberties with the narrative – the places, people, dates and events are all accurate according to the resources available. Where there were conflicting reports, I went with the most plausible version. I have also used and re-created historically accurate dialogue, based on court transcripts and police reports where available. Some details and scenes have, however, been re-imagined, with a deliberately modern spin.

So now it's time to learn about the gold and the guns, the heroes and the villains, the love and the hate. Welcome to *Australian Heist*.

James Phelps, 2018

Contents

Author's Note   *vii*

Prologue   *1*

1. The Plan   5

2. The Robbery   34

3. The Getaway   56

4. The Chase   69

5. The Arrests   85

6. The Trial: Day One   114

7. The Trial: Day Two   143

8. The Trial: Day Three   157

9. The Trial Ends   166

10. The Wanted   173

11. The Second Trial   184

12. The Hanging   204

13. The Gang   218

14. The Fugitive   242

15. The Accused   258

16. The Prison   288

17. The Cop   300

18. The Execution   313
19. The Damned   324
20. The Exile   335

Epilogue   345

Select Bibliography   349
Acknowledgements   351

Prologue

Southern Colorado, 1903

The old man turned his head, the simple movement a strain. Frail and fading fast, he now found speaking an effort.

'Get the boys,' he said. 'I need to tell them about the gold.'

Order issued, he closed his eyes, and his mind, mostly muddled these days, went to wondering.

Gold. Guns and gold. Australia.

He smiled, sunshine on a storm-ravaged face. He opened his eyes and looked towards the open window, the freshly cleaned curtains already collecting desert dirt.

'King of the Road,' he said. 'You know that's what they used to call me? Prince of Thieves …'

'I've heard stories,' said the elderly woman, moving towards his bed. 'We all have. And I have no doubt they are all true.' She leaned down and gave him a kiss. 'I'll go fetch the twins.'

He closed his eyes again.

Yep. King of the Road. Prince of Thieves. Australia's greatest bushranger.

And again he smiled, for now this old man was young. Frank 'Darkie' Gardiner was back in Forbes, no longer seventy-two, no longer on his Nevada deathbed. Frank was thirty-three, gun in hand, bum in saddle, galloping through gum trees after losing the law. On his way to drink beer at the sly shanty, bounty divided, bellies full. A hero's welcome in wait.

A coughing fit brought him back to San Luis Valley.

A young man rushed into the room. 'Dad, are you okay?'

He wasn't. Gardiner hacked, heaved and spat. His throat smoked, his lungs burnt.

Gardiner's son smacked him twice in the middle of his back. The coughing continued.

'What's wrong with him?' Lilburn looked to his mother. 'You didn't tell us he was sick.'

She didn't have to answer.

'It's the old man's friend,' said Gardiner, gritted teeth and a gulp of hot air killing the cough. 'He has come to take me home.'

At that moment Lilburn's twin brother entered the cramped room. 'Pneumonia?' William asked. 'The captain of death?'

Gardiner nodded before slumping back into his pillows. 'Should have been a bullet, boy,' he said. 'I have been bloody blessed. Always thought it would be a bullet …'

Cough subdued, Gardiner summoned his strength. He grabbed William's elbow, his hand a vice.

'Boys,' he said, looking first at William, then Lilburn. 'You might have heard a thing or two about me over the years. You know what they would say back in San Francisco?'

His sons nodded.

'Well, it's true,' he said. 'All of it. And then there is more. Some of it, well, you might struggle to believe. But you have to. It's my legacy and your future.'

And then Frank Gardiner, the King of the Road, Prince of Thieves, told his boys a tale of treasure. Of stagecoaches, shotguns and saddles. Of bandits called bushrangers, a bloke called Ben Hall, and a bounty that has never been beaten.

'It was Australia's biggest heist,' he said. 'Gold. Cash. Banknotes. And most of it was lost. Or so they say.'

And then he gave them a map.

Chapter 1

THE PLAN

Sandy Creek, south of Forbes, New South Wales, 11 June 1862

Gardiner sat in the corner, feet up, holding a book. With a gas lantern by his side, unlit but ready and waiting, he repositioned the page to find the setting sun, the winter rays now limping through the frosted window above the wood stove.

John McGuire walked through the open door and pulled out a chair beside the two men already seated at his kitchen table before turning towards Gardiner. 'What time are the rest of them coming?' he asked.

Gardiner did not take his eyes away from the page, a study of concentration. 'Soon,' he said.

McGuire stared at the book being read by the man who had sequestered his house for this 'meeting', squinting in the fading light until the title became clear: *Dream Book and Fortune Teller*. The book had an orange cover and looked old and tattered.

On the front cover an old woman in a cap pointed her finger at a girl wearing her hair in a bun while a gentleman in a suit looked on.

'What's your future like, Frank?' McGuire asked. 'You going to live long and be happy? Is it going to be suits and sheilas, or just hags pointing fingers?'

Gardiner looked up from the book and raised his eyebrows, the one on the left parted by a lumpy red scar. 'I'm going to be rich,' he said. 'And I'll run off with the girl of my dreams. A girl called Kitty.'

The two men sitting at the kitchen table with McGuire laughed knowingly.

Johnny Gilbert had been the first to arrive, at about seven that evening. Gilbert was a famed horse thief, born in Canada before moving to Australia to be raised by conmen. McGuire knew Gilbert and had been told by his brother-in-law, Ben Hall, to let him and a few other boys in for a meeting, just a chat and a drink. Worth your while, he'd said.

McGuire loved Hall. Everyone did. And he would do anything for the man who had married his sister and become co-owner of Sandy Creek Cattle Station with him. But Ben was breaking bad. He had just spent five weeks in gaol after being accused by police inspector Sir Frederick Pottinger of assisting Gilbert and Gardiner in the robbery of one William Bacon, but had been acquitted. During that time, though, Sandy Creek had gone to ruin. McGuire couldn't tend the cattle on his own, and he couldn't pay for the feed. Half of his cows were now dead.

'We are going to make it up to you,' Hall had said. 'That is what it is all about. We will get the station running again, just wait and see.'

So McGuire had got himself ready, stocked his kitchen with gin, made spare beds and pitched tents.

'You know Bow, right?' Gilbert had inquired as he walked through the door.

McGuire did. An accomplished stockman who could both read and write, the Penrith-born kid had met Gardiner when he was just fourteen. Wowed by Gardiner's charisma and Robin Hood–like tales of stealing from the rich to give to the poor, John 'Jack' Bow became a 'bush telegraph' for the outlaw, tipping Gardiner off about the movements of police and vouching for him where he could. Now, at twenty, he was a fully-fledged member of Gardiner's gang, and a heavy drinker with a temper and a gun.

'G'day,' he'd said. 'Where's the plonk? I'm as parched as a parrot.'

Gardiner had been third to arrive, letting himself in. He needed no introduction.

'G'day gents,' he'd said, tipping his hat. That was all. He'd just walked to the kitchen and unbuckled his belt to dump a python-sized serving of leather on the table, complete with holster and revolver, then taken his book to the chair.

He did not look up again until a stranger emerged from one of McGuire's guestrooms.

'And who is this?' Gardiner asked as the man walked to greet McGuire.

'You know Thomas, don't you?' he asked. 'Thomas Richards? The lemonade seller from Forbes?'

Gardiner studied the man.

'He is stopping here a few nights,' McGuire said. 'We have a little business to do.'

Gardiner put down his book, his fortune apparently foretold. 'Well, I have some business of my own to do here tonight,' he said, 'so you better be back off to your room, Mr Richards.'

Looking at the kitchen table, at the guns and gin, Thomas turned back to the man he knew as 'Darkie' and did not argue. 'Goodnight it is then,' he said. He turned and left the room.

And then Ben Hall walked in, handsome and tall.

'Here he is,' Gardiner said. 'The man of the moment. Free. And he is no outlaw.' Gardiner threw his book to the floor and walked over to embrace Hall.

'Not guilty in the eyes of the law, at least,' Hall said.

Hall laughed. Gardiner laughed harder.

'But did they ever catch that Gardiner,' Frank asked, 'the bloke you just happened to bump into at the time he was bailing them up?'

'Gardiner?' Hall echoed. 'Name doesn't ring a bell …'

Gardiner released Hall from his embrace and turned to the men who had walked in behind him.

'Lads,' he said. 'Let's have a drink.'

John O'Meally went straight to the table and poured himself a gin while Dan Charters stood back. Alexander Fordyce, a local barman, and an ex-convict named Henry Manns completed the kitchen crew. Gardiner walked around the room. Book forgotten, charisma found, he was once again the Prince of Thieves, the King of the Road.

'Take a look at this, lads,' he said as he slapped a folded broadsheet on the kitchen table.

Hall sent a puff of fresh smoke from his pipe into the air before putting his head down to study it. 'Ten thousand ounces,' he said. 'Are you kidding me? That's almost forty thousand pounds worth of gold. We could buy the whole damn Empire.'

The mob rushed in.

'What does it say?' demanded Manns.

'Yeah, read it,' said Fordyce.

Gardiner picked up the broadsheet, now damp with spirits. '"The Bathurst Free Press and Mining Journal, eleventh of June 1862,"' he began. '"The escort from Bathurst last night took down the following quantities of gold: Bathurst, 326 ounces; Lachlan, 8366 ounces; Turon, 1640 ounces; Orange, 48 ounces. Total, 10,380."' Gardiner slammed the grog-stained paper back on the table. 'My god – 10,380 ounces,' he said. 'And there it is. Written in print.'

Gardiner had been considering robbing an escort ever since the Lambing Flat gold rush had begun. It was nicknamed the Aussie El Dorado. In March 1860, on the squatting station called Burrangong, gold had been found on a horse's hoof at an afternoon muster. The find had sparked a search and soon gold was also located in a creek. The *Sydney Morning Herald* ran a story and with that thirty thousand men stormed the region, all hoping to make a fortune. Most didn't. But some did.

Gardiner had watched from his shop as 160,000 ounces of gold was gathered from the Lambing Flat goldfields over the next two years. He'd had a butcher's at Spring Creek – mostly a front for his real business of cattle stealing – and he'd stood outside it on Sundays when the gold was loaded into boxes and put in a wagon to be dragged to Sydney. The traps would boast about the size of the load, the crowd hanging on their every word, while the returns were even published in the paper every week. And Gardiner would watch on.

Only four traps? That much gold and just four traps?

'Some of you know that I have been planning this for a while,' Gardiner said, looking at Gilbert and Bow, his loyal lieutenants. 'Some of you don't. Anyway, I am going to bail up the gold escort. And I am going to do it this Sunday.'

The room was suddenly quiet, all eyes on Gardiner.

'I followed the escort last week,' Gardiner said. 'It was guarded by only four traps: that Condell, Moran, Haviland and some fresh bloke. Two of them rode in the wagon, two on top. They had no forward flank, nor a rear.' Gardiner winked. 'It gets better,' he beamed. 'The only horses they had were the ones pulling the wagon. Old mules. They couldn't catch a cold.'

There was laughter around the table.

Gardiner lost the smirk. 'But they were armed,' Gardiner continued. 'Shotguns, rifles and revolvers. And they will shoot.'

Gilbert slapped Gardiner on the back. 'Not if we shoot them first,' he yelled, 'and I never miss. Let's kill us some traps.' He laughed and then sculled, his drink slammed down in a second.

'There won't be any killing, you lunatic,' Gardiner said as he gave Gilbert a playful slap. 'It will be an ambush. They won't stand a chance.'

Hall stood up. 'Where you thinking, Frank?' he asked. 'Somewhere in the Blue Mountains?'

Gardiner shook his head. 'No, we'd get lost and starve. There is no taming those mountains. But Eugowra? That's our land. And have you seen Eugowra Rocks? There's a boulder the size of a hut, and the escort passes right by. Behind is the Nangar Ranges, a perfect getaway. It's rough, steep and hard riding – perfect for us, terrible for them.'

Gardiner laid out his plan. Eight men, two groups. Blacked-out faces and shotguns. Horses, and heels loaded with spurs.

'We shoot to scare,' he said, 'not to kill. We hit hard and fast. We get the gold and go to Wheogo.' Gardiner looked around the room, the faces now lit only by the flaming fire. 'Who is in?'

The room became a roar of agreement.

'We leave in the morning,' Gardiner said, grabbing his book from the floor and walking out the door.

'Where you off to, Frank?' Hall asked.

Gardiner raised his book. 'Apparently I am getting lucky tonight,' Gardiner said. 'I'm off to see Mrs Kitty Brown.'

And with that it was decided. The biggest heist in Australian history was about to go down.

* * *

Sandy Creek, 12 June 1862

They were still asleep when Gardiner returned, some in the house, some on the porch and some in the tents. He boiled tea in a billy and sat on his saddle, watching the winter sunrise. And he thought, *This is it. The big score. Me and Kitty. A new life.*

Gardiner's reign as Australia's greatest bushranger was coming to an end. The writing was on the wall. He had been on the run for a year. Arrested under suspicion of theft in 1861, he'd used an alias and been granted bail. He would have been locked up for life if they'd known any of his other names …

And they soon would. With the gold rush came people, wealth and the police. Once inept, the police were slowly becoming a formidable force. The new *Police Regulation Act* had been passed that year at the request of Colonial Secretary Charles Cowper and an eight-hundred-strong force assembled under the central control of Sydney-based Inspector General John McLerie. A once-haphazard approach to policing had been militarised. The colony was now divided into twelve districts, each under the control of a superintendent. And the police were trained. Before being sent bush, the officers were schooled in shooting, horse riding and tracking. They still weren't a match for the bush-born men, but they were bunches better than before.

Gardiner knew it was only a matter of time until he got caught. They would work out who he really was, and what he had done. So he'd skipped bail and become a full-time bushranger, turning exclusively to stealing. Unable to earn a legitimate income, Gardiner had formed a gang and led a reign of terror. He owned the roads of western New South Wales: Abercrombie, Goulburn,

Cowra, Grenfell, Lambing Flat and Forbes. In just a year he'd become Australia's most notorious outlaw.

Handsome, charismatic and now infamous, he had no trouble convincing young men to join his gang. The lure of the open road and riches was all it took. Drought, flood and thieves made farming a slog. Honest labour would get you nowhere, a mug's game. So Gardiner and his gang hit the road and became the traveller's terror, holding up anyone and everyone. They stole money, food, clothes, horses, guns – whatever they could use or sell. 'This is a bail up,' he would scream, gun drawn, eyes as empty as his gun holster. 'Your money or your life.'

Soon it was Gardiner's life that was on the line. In fact, he had even tried to take it himself after a shoot-out with the law. It had started as he was proposing, toasting and crystal-balling with William Fogg, his former butcher's business partner and owner of the grog joint he was in.

'Another!' he said to Fogg. 'I'll keep on stealing the cows, you keep on selling the meat. You are going to be rich. I am going to be richer.'

And then there was a knock on the door.

'Shit,' said Fogg. 'Nobody knocks. Mary! *Mary!* Go see who it is.'

Fogg's wife obeyed, walking towards the already wide-open door. Mary screamed and threw her hands in the air before hitting the floor. Detective Middleton, pistol in hand, war in his eyes, stood in the doorway.

'He's here!' he screamed. 'Gardiner is fucking here! The tip-off was good.'

They started to shoot, Gardiner first, jumping through a door to unload his Colt Navy revolver, the first of the .36-calibre balls almost hitting Middleton's head. Next Middleton with his single-shot percussion pistol.

Boom!

The bigger bullet ripped the door from the frame, splinters flying, hinges turned to skin-splitting shrapnel. Mary screamed again as a piece of hot metal tore through her forearm, then grabbed her children and headed for the yard. Middleton took cover to reload while Gardiner took aim.

Bang!

Gardiner hit Middleton, the officer's face torn open as the metal slug seared through flesh and smashed teeth and bone. The copper screamed as the blow sent him to the floor. Face fucked, all blood and shattered bone, he brought his hand up to meet the mess. Middleton loaded his gun and thrust his head through the frame to fire again. But confused, face hanging from jaw, life on the line, he'd loaded powder only, not ball, and so the gun shot only soot.

Gardiner fired again, this time hitting Middleton in the back of the hand.

The detective was done. His hand flayed flesh, he couldn't reload, so his only option was to retreat back outside. 'Go round the back,' he screamed at his colleague, Hosie, behind him. 'Don't let him get out.'

Hosie bolted, gun first, bullets before brain, and ran to the back of the hut. *Shit!* There was no back door. He went back the way he had come.

'There,' Middleton said as he pointed towards the front door. 'He is still in there.'

Hosie checked his gun; it was locked and loaded. He held it proud and high and walked towards the void.

Bang!

Boom!

Two shots, almost simultaneous. Both men were hit, a metal ball blasting Gardiner in the face and a lead slug hitting Trooper Hosie in the temple.

And with that Gardiner welcomed death.

'Poison,' he'd said, looking towards Mary. 'You got strychnine? Get me strychnine.'

She just might have had she not been scared stiff and sheltering her kids.

'Surrender or die,' Hosie said, a ball freshly loaded, end of the barrel pressed against Gardiner's head.

'Who?' Gardiner asked. 'Who gave me up?'

'Surrender and you might find out,' Hosie said.

They tied Gardiner to a horse. All bloodied and bruised, at least two of them – Gardiner and Middleton – in danger of dying, the trio set out for Bigga, the nearest town with a doctor, an hour away.

'Twenty pounds,' Gardiner said. 'I'll give you twenty pounds if you let me go.' He was met with silence. 'I'm probably going to die anyway,' he said. 'Look at me.'

Trooper Hosie stopped in his tracks. 'Fifty,' he said. 'Give me fifty. You shot me in the head.'

Gardiner smiled. 'Done,' he said.

'Not quite,' Hosie said. 'Another fifty if this one lives.' He pointed to his colleague slumped on a horse, fingers gone, face blood and bone. 'And fifty to his family if he doesn't,' he continued.

Gardiner agreed. 'Drop me here,' he said. 'I'll bring you the cash if I live. My word. If I don't, go and see Johnny Gilbert. Tell him what went down.'

Hosie shook Gardiner's hand before pulling him from the back of the horse and dumping him on the ground.

'I'll tell 'em you're dead,' he said. 'That you did the runner while I was bringing you in. That I shot you just before you disappeared into the bush. Yep, you was as good as gone.'

* * *

So Gardiner had survived. He'd paid his debt and moved on. Now he was looking at the sun, big, brilliant and rising fast. It was a day he easily could have been denied. Probably should have been denied. And now he was in love.

Kitty. Mrs Catherine 'Kitty' Brown.

The daughter of John Walsh, sister of Biddy and wife of John Brown, Kitty had grabbed him one night while he was talking to her brother in-law, Ben Hall.

'Kiss me,' she'd said. 'It's you I love, not John Brown. I was a fool for marrying so young. A fool because I'd never met you. Kiss me. Take me. Do what you want.'

Ah, Kitty. I'll take you. I'll take you away from all of this.

O'Meally woke next.

'What the fuck are you looking at?' he asked.

'Just dreaming about gold and girls,' Gardiner said.

The rest of the gang were soon up. They had breakfast, Mrs McGuire cooking bacon and eggs.

'Righto,' Gardiner said. 'Time to go.'

* * *

Forbes, 13 June 1862

Hooves thundered, dust rose and animals scattered from the side of the trail as the gang of eight made their way to Forbes. Tracking true north, the forty-mile trip took eight hours. Soon they were on the outskirts of the booming town, smoke rising from chimneys, the noise of industry filling the air.

'Forbes,' Gardiner said. He smiled.

Consisting of a single hut until 1861, the town had exploded to a city of thirty thousand when gold was found, and now it was the centre of the colony of New South Wales's wild west. Wooden huts had been erected. Shops slapped up. Tents littered the landscape.

The town's biggest building was a stone pub called the Albion Hotel. It was not only a place to drink but the travelling stop for the coaches of Ford & Co. – the Court House Hotel on the Lachlan River was another popular spot, usually full of drinkers, workers and the occasional woman. The Albion took up to a hundred pounds over the bar on a good day, more than any other hotel in the colony. But Gardiner wasn't there to spend his money on girls or grog. He was there for guns. He gave Johnny Gilbert a bag full of coins.

'Take one of the lads into town,' he said. 'I need you to get supplies. It might be best to pay someone to go and get the stuff for you so you are not seen.'

Gilbert nodded. 'I'll take Charters,' he said. 'No one will recognise him. What do we need?'

Gardiner had thought of everything. 'Get six shotguns,' he said. 'I have a couple but we will need one per man. We'll also need percussion caps and gunpowder. Buy a tomahawk or an axe too. We'll need something to smash open the gold boxes. You getting all this?'

Gilbert nodded.

'Get some scarves and some black for our faces,' Gardiner said. 'We are going to disguise ourselves. A lot of you aren't wanted men and we want to keep it like that. And get food and grog. As much as you can load on the horse.'

Gardiner knew he could count on Johnny Gilbert. The pair had met during a stint at Cockatoo Island, the infamous convict prison. Both were doing time for horse stealing. But as for Dan Charters, well, Gardiner was not so sure about him.

'Keep an eye on him, Johnny,' he said. 'He is a bit green that one.'

Charters had been recruited to the gang on the recommendation of Hall, the pair becoming close after Charters moved into the region to run a cattle station he took over from his father, who had died in 1858 when a wild horse jammed him into a tree. Just twenty at the time, Daniel, who immigrated to Australia from Ireland when he was three, was left part-owner of five cattle stations. One of them, The Pinnacle, was close to the Sandy Creek

Cattle Station run by Hall and McGuire. Ben took Dan under his wing, showing him the cattle business first – then the crime game.

'This your first job, boy?' Gardiner asked.

Charters nodded.

'You'll be fine,' he said. 'Just remember to keep your mouth shut and all will be well.'

Gilbert jumped on his horse and, with a flick of his wrist, rein slapping horse, he set off. Charters followed his dust.

Soon they were in the heaving town centre. Horses hitched and walking towards the Albion Hotel, Gilbert came up with a plan.

'You go and buy the food and grog,' Gilbert said. 'There is nothing suspicious about that. Also get the black for our faces and the scarves.'

Again Charters was nodding. 'Easy,' he said. 'Give me some coin and I'll find a store. You getting the guns?'

Gilbert shook his head. 'Not me,' he said. 'You think I want to be seen buying six guns a few days before hitting an escort? I'll get someone else to buy them.' Gilbert slapped Charters on the back after handing him the cash. 'I'll see you back here in half an hour,' he said.

Gilbert looked towards the Albion: now it was past five o'clock, it was packed. The prospectors had stopped their digging and started their drinking. The balcony threatened to break under the weight of a boisterous bunch singing, shouting and sinking gin.

Gilbert knew he could find someone to do his shopping in the Albion but he couldn't risk being seen by so many people.

The Albion was also a place popular with the traps. He kept himself in the shadows as he walked past the pub and soon he was standing outside the Harp of Erin Hotel. The pub was quiet, at least compared to the Albion, and right across the road from a gun store.

Perfect.

He walked into the saloon and studied the room. He saw two men he knew, both scoundrels.

Perfect.

'Darcy,' Gilbert said, tipping his hat. 'Foster. How would you lads like to make a bit of coin?'

'Do the Chinese like gold?' Darcy replied.

Darcy and Foster headed across the road to William Baldwin's store with a fistful of money and instructions to buy six shotguns, gunpowder, caps and an axe.

'I said six guns, you galahs,' Gilbert said when Darcy and Foster came back. 'Six. Did you hear me say two?'

Darcy handed him the guns and change. 'He only had two,' Darcy deadpanned. 'You will have to get the rest down the road.'

'What about the axe?' Gilbert fired. 'Surely he had an axe?'

Foster produced a tomahawk: compact but big enough to hack open a lockbox.

'Well thank the Lord for small miracles,' Gilbert said. He handed them a handful of coins. 'Don't say a word,' he warned. 'I wasn't here. You didn't see me. Right?'

They nodded in unison.

Gilbert walked back to his horse. 'More guns,' he said to Charters. 'We need another four.' He handed the man known as 'Flash Dan' the change.

'Got 'em,' Charters said when he returned.

List ticked off, they headed back to camp. Gardiner's gang was now all geared up and ready to rob.

* * *

Eugowra, 13 June 1862

Gardiner and his gang were on the outskirts of Eugowra by nightfall. They travelled in stealth off the beaten path, single file and laying low. Located twenty-four miles east of Forbes, Eugowra could not be called a town, just a cattle station with a river crossing that formed part of the gold rush highway, an increasingly worn trail that linked Sydney to Forbes.

'We'll make camp here tonight,' said Gardiner. 'I've made us a reservation at the Starlight Hotel.'

A fire was lit and gin produced. The gang sat on their saddles, talking gold and future fortunes.

'I am going straight after this,' Hall said, looking at Gardiner's battle-scarred faced in the firelight. 'It will be enough to get the station up and going again. Maybe even enough to get Biddy and the boy back. I don't want to live like this. All I ever wanted was a family and a farm.'

Hall was not on the run. He had escaped punishment for his role in robbing William Bacon, but his prospects were now almost as painful as prison. The charge, and the five weeks he had spent in prison during the trial, had left him busted and broke. Cattle dead, the twenty-pound-a-year lease on the Sandy Creek Cattle Station that he shared with McGuire soon to be revoked.

'Yep,' Gardiner said, 'you'll be able to buy all the cattle in the colony. And Biddy, well, she'll come to her wits soon enough. And even if she doesn't, you have Henry. He will always be your boy.'

Hall's wife had left him. Grabbed his kid and gone.

'And there is always a bullet for her bloke,' Gardiner said sternly.

Hall had married Bridget Walsh in 1856 at St Michael's at Bathurst. Then only nineteen, he was already an expert stockman and a skilled bushman. He was a man on the rise. In 1859, shortly after the birth of his son, Henry, Hall had co-leased the ten thousand acres of land at Sandy Creek with John McGuire, built a slab-walled, bark-roofed hut and moved his young family in. With the land cleared and fenced, the country was ideal for cattle.

Enter the gold rush.

Suddenly the demand for cattle went through the roof. Down the road in Forbes, the miners, builders, bakers and storekeepers all needed their meat. And, of course, so did the butchers. That was how Hall had first met Gardiner.

'I can never get enough cattle,' Gardiner had said. 'And I won't mind if they are not legally yours. No one will know. I'll cut 'em up nice and quick. A T-bone looks like a T-bone, right?'

'Have you spoken to Kitty about my missus?' Hall asked now, staring into the fire. 'Has she said anything about Biddy?'

Gardiner shrugged. 'Haven't asked,' he said.

Hall shook his head. 'What a mess,' he said. 'How did it get to this?'

Hall's descent had begun earlier in the year, when he'd come home to an empty house. He had spent the week driving his cattle to Forbes, the weekend getting shitfaced in the pub. He'd pushed at the door, hoping to be met with kisses and kindness, hopefully more …

'Biddy,' he had yelled. 'I'm home.'

The creaking door was his only answer. Bridget Hall was gone. Baby Henry too.

'Biddy?' Hall had yelled again. 'Henry?' Nothing. No one.

'Taylor,' McGuire had said when Hall came rushing to his house. 'They left with James Taylor.'

Hall was shattered. And then he found out this Taylor was a former cop. 'A damn trap,' Hall said. 'I'll … I'll …' Hall didn't know what he would do.

Fast-forward six months and Hall was about to lose it all. Wife and kid gone, his cattle station was next.

He held his hands over the fire. 'Yep,' he said, 'this will get me back on track. Money. Station. Biddy. Henry. So what about you? You already got your next job lined up?'

Gardiner tilted his head back to reveal an ear-to-ear smile. 'Next? The Bank of New South Wales? No, Ben. This is the end of the road. I'm done too. I either finish now or I'll wind up dead. I am going to take your sister-in-law and move to

Queensland. Going to disappear with gold and a girl. What could be better? Me, Kitty and all the money I could need.'

Frank Gardiner meant it. He was finished. Out. This was the score that would set him straight and end the twelve-year crime spree that had started when he'd stolen a cow.

* * *

Frank Gardiner had begun his life in 1830 as Francis Christie. Though some said he was half Aboriginal and raised in the Australian bush, the reality was that the soon-to-be terror of the roads had in fact been born in Scotland, to a white mother and father. There was nothing remarkable about his upbringing, nothing to suggest he would go on to become Australia's greatest thief.

Mr and Mrs Christie had arrived in Australia on 17 November 1834, as free settlers, on the three-master *James*. They'd wanted to escape the bleak, harsh, even hellish life they'd had in Scotland. They'd moved to Sydney wanting better, but the only thing better was the climate. They'd travelled 10,500 miles for a hotter kind of hell.

Still, they hoped their son, Francis, would make himself a name. Four when he arrived in Sydney, he was already learning to read and write. They continued his education and gave him a chance, and Francis Christie took it. In fact Christie took it all, even if he wasn't really entitled to what he took.

First it was cattle: in 1850 the young stockman turned cow thief. And then it was horses: Francis stole a mob from Goulburn and rode to Port Phillip to sell them. On the way, in the border town of Albury, he came across another mob of mares, thirty-seven of them, apparently unattended. So he took them too. And off he went, dozens of horses in tow, gun by his side. He decided to head to Portland, a whaling centre, where he would turn his crime into cash.

He didn't get there.

The man he'd stolen the horses from was an expert tracker. Two weeks after his thirty-seven horses went missing, Victorian stockman William Lockhart Morton caught up with Christie, finding the young thief fast asleep in bed. He might have belted a man, but a kid? Well, Morton just handcuffed him and turned him over to the police.

Christie was gaoled for five years, becoming one of the very first residents of Pentridge Prison.

Christie didn't like Pentridge. Sent out in a chain gang to work on the road, with just five weeks of his five years served, Christie thumped a guard and bolted for the bush. And with that, Francis Christie was gone. Francis Christie became Francis Clarke: new name, same game.

For four years he was free, stealing, stooping and sneaking in Goulburn. But in March 1854 he was arrested for horse stealing in Young and sent to a place worse than Pentridge. They called it Cockatoo Island, but it was commonly known as hell. Francis Clarke was sentenced to seven years' hard labour in Australia's worst prison, once a convict-only gaol where men were chained to blocks and starved to death.

It could have been worse, though. Because he had a fake name and a fake story, Gardiner's previous charges and his prison escape were not known: if he'd said he was Francis Christie, he would have been hanged. But he said he was Clarke, and this Clarke became a prison pet – 'A cut above the convicts: well spoken, hard-working and polite', as his release papers put it – and he was set free after serving five years. He walked out of that forty-acre harbour hell in March 1859. And a legend was born. For Francis Clarke became a bushranging butcher called Frank Gardiner, who was soon Australia's most famous outlaw.

* * *

Eugowra, 14 June 1862

Charters led the way, the ring-in going first. Soon they would be at the ambush site. 'Not far now,' he said. 'No more than five miles.'

They had just crossed the Lachlan River.

'All we have to do is follow this creek upstream,' Charters said.

The slowly rising terrain, now strewn with granite, was proving a challenge.

'Shhh,' Charters said, holding up a palm. 'Stop.'

Gardiner walked forward and put his hand on Charters' shoulder. 'What?' he whispered. 'What's going on?'

Charters pointed towards the road about a hundred yards away. Gardiner squinted and stared, the midday sun blazing.

There was a dust cloud in the distance. Dirt rising. 'Somebody is coming,' he said.

Gardiner turned to his gang. 'Make yourself scarce, lads,' he said. 'We are about to have company. Lay low and keep the horses quiet.'

The motley crew took cover in a creek bed, steep banks hiding them from the road. Gardiner grabbed at a thick root, more branch than riverweed, and pulled himself to the top of the bank. He peered across the plain, a scrubby bush providing adequate cover and camouflage.

He watched. And waited. 'Two riders,' he whispered. 'No wagon. Shhh.'

On any other day the approaching riders would have been perfect targets for Gardiner and his gang. But not today – Gardiner had bigger fish to fry.

Heart rates rose as the hooves thundered, metal shoes hitting gravel. Closer. Closer. Here.

'Shhh,' Gardiner whispered again. 'We will have to shoot them if they see us.'

The gang remained silent and unseen. Gardiner watched as the riders went past, waiting until they were a speck in the distance.

'Holy shit,' Gardiner finally said. 'Do you know who that was?'

'Nup,' Hall replied. 'We couldn't see a thing from down here.'

'Well, we have dodged a bullet there, my boy,' Gardiner said. 'That was the police magistrate and the goldfields commissioner.'

Disaster averted, a chance meeting with the law avoided, the gang continued along the side of the creek till Gardiner said, 'This is it. This is the spot.'

The men left the cover of the creek and cut through the scrub to an open plain littered with boulders. Granite chunks were strewn across the ground, most the size of cricket balls but some wrecking-ball big. And one, well, one was as big as a house.

'There it is,' Gardiner said. 'Coonbong Rock. Look at the size of it.'

Ten yards long and more than three high, the granite boulder jutted out of the side of a hill about twenty paces away from the road. Its name translated as 'dead man', and Coonbong was said to hold the spirit of a great Aboriginal warrior. It was an ancient site of ceremony and the landscape was almost alien. Behind the rock were a steep hill, pebbles, rocks and scattered boulders, more surface-of-the-moon than a typical western range.

'Look at this,' Gardiner said as he walked around the rock. 'Perfect. This is it. Set up camp, men.' He looked upstream and across the fertile flat to the Eugowra Station homestead. 'Best we stick to the scrub,' Gardiner said. 'Just to be safe.'

That night they feasted on tinned lobster and sardines, stolen from a station storeroom the day before, whisky and gin warming their bellies, while the small campfire warmed their faces and fingers. Freed from their saddlebags, the horses roamed, chewing on oats and drinking from the stream.

* * *

Eugowra, 15 June 1862, 6 am

Gardiner was again first to rise, springing from his swag as the first rays of sun hit the hill. He went straight to work, pulling out a box of .36–calibre balls and then inspecting each and every gun, checking bolts, barrels and stocks. He loaded all of them with gunpowder and balls himself. This wasn't something he would leave to anyone else.

Weapons ready, Gardiner summoned his gang. Time to rehearse.

'Get up,' he said. 'Rise and shine.'

He walked towards the trail, away from the shadow of the hill and the boulder, and pointed directly at Daniel Charters.

'You first, Charters,' Gardiner said. 'Your job is easy. You are going to take all the horses into the gully. Tie them up, feed them and keep them quiet. You are going to keep yourself and our gear hidden. You won't even have to fire a shot.'

Gardiner suspected Charters was not the shooting type. There was no way he was going to trust Hall's friend with his life. Best to keep him out of the way, just in case.

Charters did not complain. He figured he'd been given the job because of his expertise with stock.

'Now?' Charters asked. 'You want me to take the horses now?'

'No,' Gardiner snapped. 'We will move into position at one o'clock. The escort isn't expected until three, but we can't take a chance.' Gardiner pointed towards the shotguns, freshly cleaned, loaded and lined up against the rock, military precise. 'Get a gun, lads,' he said. 'There is one per man and they are locked and loaded, so don't go pulling the trigger.'

Hall grabbed a gun first, then O'Meally, then Gilbert. Soon they were all packing heat and waiting for their next command.

'We are going to split up into two groups,' Gardiner continued. 'We will hit them from two sides. Hall, O'Meally and Fordyce, you will be behind the rock with me. The rest of you will wait by the creek, over there in the scrub. You'll be taking orders from Gilbert.'

The men, guns slung across shoulders, nodded.

'That's all there is to it,' Gardiner said. 'Off you go. Take your marks. Let's do a run through.'

Gardiner pointed, pushed and pulled until he had every man exactly where he wanted them. He walked out onto the road, first looking towards the rock.

'Good,' he said. 'You are bloody ghosts. They won't see a thing.' He looked towards the creek. 'A bit to the left,' he said. 'Johnny, use that tree for cover.'

Gardiner walked back to the rock.

'Charters,' he barked. 'Run on up the road about a hundred yards and then walk back. You are going to be the coach.' Gardiner stood beside the rock, raised his gun and waited. 'Keep on coming,' he shouted as Charters neared. 'A little more. Okay, stop.'

Charters was about twenty yards from the end of Gardiner's gun.

'Good,' Gardiner said. 'Perfect, that's the spot.'

Gardiner put down his gun and measured the distance between himself and his target, his steps providing the count. He then stepped out the distance to the men in the bush.

'Okay, we are all in firing range,' Gardiner said. 'It isn't perfect. You guys in the scrub have a better range than us behind the rock, but it will do.' He pointed to the men at the rock. 'We might have to come out from our cover and close the gap,' he said, 'unless we can get them off the trail and closer to the rock.'

The men gathered again and their leader continued his briefing.

'I'll jump out and fire a warning shot,' Gardiner said, 'and I'll tell 'em to drop their weapons. Hopefully they will surrender and the rest of you won't have to do squat.' Gardiner shook his head. 'But not likely.' He looked to Hall, O'Meally and Fordyce.

'If they shoot,' Gardiner said, 'you shoot. Come out and unleash hell.' He pointed to the other four. 'They won't know what hit them when you spring from the creek. It'll be an all-out assault until they surrender. When we reload, the blokes in the scrub will shoot. Continuous fire. Unbeatable.'

Gardiner continued with the instruction, assigning horse-packing, box-busting and hostage-tying duties.

'And then we will make off over the hills,' Gardiner said. 'I have a camp stocked, set up and waiting. Now, time to calm our nerves.' He pulled out a case of gin. 'Looks like you could use a drink, Fordyce,' he grinned. 'You're blooming shaking already.'

At forty-two, Alexander Fordyce was the group's senior citizen, ten years older than Gardiner. A barman at Paddy O'Meally's makeshift inn, Fordyce was untried and untested, and only included out of necessity. Gardiner had walked into O'Meally's looking for a drink and walked out with a hired gun.

Fordyce grabbed a bottle and took a swig. 'A few of these and I'll be right as rain,' he said.

Now it was time to wait.

Charters came bursting out of the scrub. 'Quick, Frank,' he said. 'Over there – the escort is coming!'

Gardiner grabbed his gun and sprinted out from the rock. He held onto the shotgun with his right hand and used his left to shield his eyes from the midday sun.

'It's not the escort,' Gardiner said. 'Just a couple of bullock drays.' He cracked a smile as bright as the sun. 'Take cover and follow my lead,' he said. 'That book told me it was going to be my lucky day.'

As the bullocks came around the bend, Fordyce was a mess, but Gardiner was patient.

Closer. A little closer.

Gardiner sprang from his rock, out from the cover and into the open. 'Bail up!' he screamed.

The driver threw his arms into the air. 'Take whatever you want,' he stuttered. 'Don't shoot. I'm unarmed.' He stared down the barrel of Gardiner's gun, slow recognition dawning. Suddenly the bushranger was no longer a story. 'Take the horses,' he said. 'The produce. There is plenty of feed.'

John Burgess was making his first trip to the goldfields. With demand for produce through the roof, the Molong publican could get double the Sydney price in Forbes. He had three bullock teams dragging grain, four horses and his thirteen-year-old son for help.

Gardiner shook his head. 'Nah, we aren't going to rob you,' he said. 'We just need to borrow your bullocks for a bit. I want you fellows to come along with me.'

Gardiner had found a way to get the escort closer to the rock: a roadblock. He directed Burgess to bring his bullocks to the edge of the path and then told him to upend the carts.

'Perfect,' Gardiner said after Burgess tipped them over, spilling grain all over the road.

The escort would now be forced to the right – there was a gully on the left – and straight towards the rock. Dead man's rock.

Burgess and his son were tied up and made to lie face down in the scrub. A passing teamster and a swagman soon joined them, hats over eyes, hands behind backs.

At quarter to one, Gardiner addressed his gang.

'Time to get ready,' he said. 'Black out your faces and put on your scarves.' He looked at Fordyce. 'And put down that gin,' he said. 'You are fucking legless. I said calm yourself, not drown yourself. Wake up and look sharp or I will cut you off.'

White breeches, faces as black as their coats, and red scarves tied across noses, the Gardiner gang grabbed their guns and split into their groups. They were ready. They were waiting.

Chapter 2

THE ROBBERY

Eugowra, 15 June 1862, 2.45 pm

The trap stared at the scenery. It never changed. Pine-clad ridges lined a winding road of rough dirt. Grass fields, still green after a kind autumn and a warm and wet winter so far, touched the horizon. The fields were alive, endless and oblivious to the freeze that would come.

Constable William Haviland was fresh to the job, a trooper in the newly reorganised New South Wales police. He had a badge, a gun and a licence to shoot anyone who shot at him first.

He also had a sore arse.

'How far to go?' Haviland asked.

'Ha,' drawled Senior Constable Henry Moran. 'Six hours. Well, unless a horse dies.'

Haviland, dressed in his newly issued uniform of blue tunic, waistcoat, kepi cap, cord pantaloons and knee-high riding boots, laughed.

'That's not a joke,' said Moran. The senior constable stuck his head out of the stagecoach and pointed. 'Have a look at these nags,' he said, the four black horses heaving. 'They look like racehorses to you? They are the cheapest nags in the goddamn colony. Look at that one. I think it has the plague.'

The weathered driver, a man called John Fegan, shouted down at them from his perch. 'Would you two shut up? These bloody horses are smarter than the pair of you.'

'Pipe down, old man,' Haviland said, 'or you might have yourself an accident.'

Sergeant Condell, riding shotgun, intervened. 'Oh would all of you just shut up,' said the boss as he slammed the butt of his ten-gauge Remington shotgun into the floor of the Ford & Co. coach.

Fegan flinched, expecting a blast. 'Fucking watch it with that thing,' he said. 'That would kill a bloody elephant.'

The sergeant pointed the eighteen-inch barrel at the driver's face. 'Just fucking get us there. Let's go.'

Fegan cracked his whip and the horses jumped ahead, the metal-rimmed wooden wheels hitting rock. The Ford & Co. jolted, rattled and nearly rolled. The force was not dulled by the wagon's state-of-the-art suspension. Back in the cabin, Haviland's shoulder was sent smacking into steel.

'Ahh!' he cried, as his deltoid rammed a metal box. 'Jeez, that hurt. What's in that thing – lead?'

Moran shook his head. 'Gold, you idiot,' he said. 'You think we would be guarding lead?'

The four boxes of gold were being transported from Forbes to Orange under the command of Sergeant Condell.

That morning, pistols drawn, the constables had watched on as Chinese workers had filled the wagon with riches, Fegan smoking nearby. By the time Condell arrived, elephant gun and all, they had put 170 pounds of gold in the wagon, most belonging to the Oriental Bank and the rest to prospectors and other banks. There was also cash – 3,700 pounds in all.

It was a fortune, but the officers were oblivious to the load and to the threat. They were flat-out bored. Around them was nothing but green grass and ghost gums, though an early swooping magpie gave Fegan a fright.

'Oh, shoot that winged wretch,' he cried, the driver looking towards Condell's behemoth blasting gun. 'It's not even spring, it doesn't even have any young to protect yet. It is just after blood. A flying demon.'

They had been on the road for about four hours when the man with the big gun saw something he didn't like.

'What's up there?' Condell asked. 'Can you see that?'

Fegan nodded, his eyes squinting against the afternoon glare. 'Mmm,' he said. 'Cattle?' He applied pressure to the rein and the horses slowed.

'It's a bullock team,' the sergeant said. 'They've come a cropper. Keep on moving.'

The coach pressed on, the bending trail slowly revealing the rest of the road. Ahead, in the winding rough, bulls grazed, their bullock carts all busted and broken. Hay, at least a ton, baled by stringed bark, had spewed onto the trail. The biggest bull was pushing its snout into a pile of pulverised potatoes.

The driver shrugged. 'Righto,' he said, 'we will have to go over there. The only way around is by that big rock.'

* * *

Hall jammed the freshly oiled teak into his shoulder.

Breathe …

He gulped, a short hard suck sending frost into his lungs. The frigid air, stained by wet eucalyptus and green grass, forced him to grab at his chest. *Heart attack? No. Panic attack? Oh shit …*

Australia's newest outlaw issued himself an order. *Pull yourself together.*

Hall dragged his left hand from his heart and pulled his fingers into a fist. He watched as the red rushed away, his knuckles turning white. His hand shook.

Again he spoke to himself. *This is the only way to get it all back.*

He leaned his head to the right and his cheek hit steel. The barrel of his double-barrelled percussion shotgun was frozen, the weakened winter sun bouncing off the machined metal. He was no longer shaking.

'Soon,' cautioned Gardiner, squatting behind the sun-scorched rock. 'Not long now.'

Face blackened, everything but his eyes covered by a red scarf, Hall looked down the length of his gun, closing his left eye and focusing his right. Loaded with gunpowder and metal balls, the gun was locked, loaded and ready to kill. Soon he would be a finger-pull away from delivering death.

This is the only way to get them back.

He stood behind the rock with Gardiner, O'Meally and Fordyce, all disguised by red scarves and black polish. They were silent, but the crickets chirped, the birds tweeted and the falling foliage rustled.

'Shhh,' Gardiner said, more directed at crickets than his already silent men. 'Nobody say a word. Here they come. Fordyce, straighten up.'

Gardiner studied his mark and then nodded. 'Now!' came the cry, Gardiner launching from behind the boulder to confront the coach, aiming the shotgun up into the air.

Bang!

The blast silenced the crickets.

'Bail up!' Gardiner cried through drifting gun smoke. 'This is a stick-up. Stand and put your guns down. No one has to get hurt.'

The driver stuck his hands up before diving for cover. 'Don't shoot,' he cried.

But another man, dressed in police-issue black and blue, took aim.

Bang!

The earth shook like a cannonball had struck, the force of the blast sending the trap in the coach crashing back into the leather upholstery that lined the seat.

Hall peered out from his hiding place then instantly ducked. The buckshot smashed only rock, pieces of the boulder turned into splayed sand.

Then Ben Hall pulled the trigger and officially became a bushranger.

Crack! He fired off his first shot, his shotgun spewing steel. *Boom!*

Like lightning, he flicked out his powder flask and filled his barrel with powder. Next he shoved in balls.

Bang!

Again.

The first two shots struck the wagon. The next hit a human.

* * *

'Ahhh!' screamed Senior Constable Moran, the third shot tearing into his testicle. 'Jesus save me! My balls – he hit me in the bloody balls!' Moran jumped from the wagon and found cover behind the cart. 'Ahhh!' he screamed again, the pain of the wound on landing reaching a whole other level. Blood exploded from his lap like a geyser, his groin a busted water pipe, rushing a river of red.

The sight of his wounded colleague horrified Sargeant Condell – and then it angered him.

'Shoot these wretches,' Condell shouted.

'Kill them all!'

Haviland jumped out of the wagon and took cover at the back of the cart next to Moran. He looked down at his colleague's bloodied lap.

'Crap,' said Haviland. 'We don't get paid enough to die.'

The shooting was relentless. Bullets tore the wagon apart, smoke and splinters spewing into the air. The pair hugged their .53-calibre single-shot carbines like teddy bears. They would have just one shot – if they were crazy enough to take it.

'Wait till they reload,' screamed Condell, attempting to be heard over the gunfire, as he positioned himself at the front of the wagon. 'We will jump out and hit them when they are spent.'

But the shooting did not stop.

'How bad is it?' Haviland asked, again looking at the blood. 'Can you fight?'

Moran took a deep breath and steeled himself, the trap ignoring the agony of the bullet fragment in his balls. He then lifted himself from the floor.

'What choice do I have?' Moran replied. 'I'll cry about it later.' He took another deep breath, summoned all his mental strength to turn the bush blaze in his lap into a campfire. 'There must be two groups,' he said. 'One by the rocks and another on the other side. The second group is firing while the first reload.'

'We're screwed,' Haviland said.

The shooting from the open stopped and a new barrage from behind the rock began. Moran dared to sneak a peek at the attackers, who were now reloading. He stuck his head out of the cover of the cart to see what they were up against, knowing full well he could be shot again.

'There are three scamps out in the open,' he said. 'They are reloading.'

The bandits were heavily armed and their disguises were almost as frightening as their weapons: faces painted black, red scarves over their mouths. This was no friendly stick-up. These bushrangers were prepared to kill.

'Let's just run,' Haviland said. 'I don't want to die.'

'Really?' said Moran. 'Leave the Sergeant?'

Haviland shrugged. 'Better being a deserter than dead,' he said.

Moran looked down at his wound. He wondered if he could even run ...

'I said shoot these wretches,' screamed Sergeant Condell. 'Shoot them or I will shoot you.'

Moran sprang into action, his brief flirtation with fleeing shattered by the shouting sergeant. He leaped from cover, carbine in hand, and, defying the agony of his wound, ran towards the reloading bushrangers. He squeezed off his one and only round. He also had a revolver, an American Colt six shot, but with a .36-calibre handgun he might as well have spat at them from there.

Haviland followed and also fired, but the panicked pair missed their men. They stopped in their tracks as they heard the Sergeant scream.

'I am hit!' yelled Sergeant Condell. A bullet, launched from behind the rock, had torn into his side. 'Run!' he screamed. 'Go before this lot opens fire.' Condell and Haviland took off into the bush.

'Yeah, run, you chicken shits!' O'Meally screamed.

'You damn cowards!' Gilbert added.

Hall cheered before launching his own victory shot into the air.

Gardiner edged forward, gun raised and two of his men on his tail.

The stagecoach had been upended. Two of the horses had bolted, scared by the blasts and just missed by bullets. A wheel had been smashed free and the metal boxes were on the ground.

The driver was lying face down on the ground, his hands behind his head. The senior constable was resting against the upturned coach. His hands were firmly in his lap.

'Don't shoot,' said the trap. 'I am unarmed. And I need help. Look. My balls.'

Hall had now moved from his rock and edged towards Gardiner and the metal boxes, the lucky dip sprawled on the ground.

'Well, if you aim that cock of yours like your gun they wouldn't be any use to you now anyway,' Gardiner said. He pointed the barrel of his 1849 Colt revolver at the officer's face. 'But I might let you keep your head,' he said. 'Okay, what we are going to do now is tie you fellas up.' He looked down at the trap's wound. 'Ouch,' he said.

The man with testicles turned to minced meat gave him a painful nod. The bearded bushranger winced before turning to the lump on his right.

'You,' Gardiner said to O'Meally, 'tie them both up.' Next he looked to Gilbert and said, 'Get Charters to bring the horses.' Finally he nodded at Hall. 'Let's see what we've got,' he said, pointing to the score.

Hall looked at the four steel boxes sitting in the red dirt next to the upturned cart. His mind wandered.

Gold. Farm. Family. Biddy. Henry.

Hall heaved a box upright, back straining as he made the lift; it was far heavier than he'd imagined.

Gardiner stood behind him. 'Let's open 'er up,' he said. He pulled out the tomahawk and with a swing had smashed apart the lock. 'Woohoo,' Gardiner cried as he lifted the lid. 'Would you look at that? You fucking beauty! That's gold, my lads.'

Hall moved in to inspect the bounty.

'There is a quid or two here,' he said as he looked at the gold – freshly mined nuggets of all shape and size, some mere shavings, others the size of a fist.

Gardiner beamed. 'I told you this would be a score,' he said. 'Just have a look at what we've got here.' The experienced thief tempered his excitement then; they still had a job to do. 'Alright, let's get this all loaded up,' he said. 'Grab their horses. We will use their nags to carry the load.'

Gardiner did not want to tire his own horses. He suspected he would need them fresh to outpace the law. And the law would come.

'Are we going to open the other boxes first?' asked Hall.

'No time,' Gardiner said. 'Got to move.'

O'Meally had secured the driver and the trap with blasted balls. 'What about the mail?' he asked. 'Are we taking it?'

This time it was Hall who spoke. 'Let's leave it,' he said. 'That belongs to people like you and me.'

O'Meally snorted. 'But there could be a load of cash,' he said. 'People sending their wages to their family.'

'And their families should get it,' Hall said. 'We have plenty enough from the banks. Stealing from the rich is one thing. From the poor? Well, that's another.'

'He's right,' Gardiner said. 'No good getting the common folk offside. We are going to need all the help we can get. If they turn on us then we are done.'

O'Meally nodded. A bushranger was nothing without the protection of his people.

The gang secured the load then Gardiner grabbed at a rein, the tug starting the horse.

'Let's go, men,' he said.

The posse of black-faced bandits started heading over the hill, getaway begun.

* * *

Eugowra, 15 June 1862, 3.30 pm

'I'm going to die,' yelped Moran, the full extent of his wound becoming apparent now the adrenaline secreted during the attack had subsided. 'You need to find help.'

Fegan lifted his face from the dirt and looked around. The bushrangers seemed to have disappeared, so he started pulling his cramped body onto his knees. Now standing, his hands fastened firm behind his back, he looked down at the sergeant. He did not like what he saw. Moran was bleeding out; it didn't look like he had too long.

'Okay,' Fegan said, 'there's a station just over there. I'll go for help.'

The men from the bullock team had vanished too.

'I'll be back soon,' said Fegan. 'Keep pressure on the wound and you will be fine. I have seen worse.'

Fegan turned and walked. 'Ouch,' he whispered before shaking his head.

* * *

A little later, Fegan heard hooves.

'Here!' he shouted, every ounce of his breath used to send his voice as far as his lungs would allow. 'Over here!'

The rider spotted the man in his field and turned to gallop his way.

'What's going on?' he asked. 'I'm Hanbury Clements, owner of Eugowra Station. I was out with my cattle and I heard the shots. It sounded like war.'

Fegan looked up at the squatter. 'Escort coach, we were robbed,' said the driver. 'Bushrangers. They came from nowhere. Eight of them, maybe more. We never stood a chance.'

'Where are they now?' Clements asked, waving his shotgun. 'Did you get any of them?'

Fegan shook his head. 'No, but the senior constable copped one in the nuts,' he said. 'He is in a bad way. The sergeant and the other constable went for help.'

Fegan shrugged. 'I didn't even have a gun. There was nothing I could have done. It was an ambush.'

Clements raised an eyebrow. 'What about your lookouts?' he asked. 'What about your forward flank?'

Fegan shook his head. 'No, it was just us,' he said. 'No lookouts.'

The police inspector, Sir Frederick Pottinger, had laughed when Fegan had suggested the escort's security was lax.

'For a load like this we might want an advanced flank,' Fegan had said when he'd learned of the job. 'I would also suggest a rear flank.'

'Ridiculous,' Pottinger had said. 'Bushrangers attack the escort? How absurd. No one would dare attack the Crown and risk being hunted down and hanged.'

Fegan could handle arrogance, but not ignorance. 'Well, surely the other two officers will be mounted?' Fegan had inquired. 'They will be able to move both ahead and back?'

'How many horses do you think the police force owns?' Pottinger had replied. 'The horses are for pulling and nothing else. That would be a misuse of Crown resources, an unnecessary excess.'

Fegan had been beating a dead horse.

Clements shook his head. 'What's done is done,' he said. 'You point me to where the senior constable is and I will go fetch him. You are useless to me without a horse. Go back to the house and rest. Tell my wife what has happened and she will take you in. There will be a hot meal and a bed.'

Clements rode on and soon reached the crime scene: an upturned wagon, bullocks grazing on the produce they were supposed to cart, and a copper lying in a pool of spent bullet shells and blood.

Moran was out cold.

Clements hauled the senior constable onto his horse. He saw the wound but had nothing to stop the blood. He dug his heels into his horse and began the journey back to his house. He suspected the big man would die on the way.

Not far from home, the makeshift ambulance was stopped by a cry.

'Help! Over here!'

Haviland was holding up Condell, his arm tucked under a rib and using his right leg to kick him along.

'How bad is it?' Clements asked, looking at the sergeant. 'You look a little better than this one.'

Condell opened his jacket to show off his wound.

'Well, maybe just,' Clements said. 'Rest here. I'll take this one back to the house for help and then come fetch you. I'll be less than an hour.'

* * *

Condell was standing over Moran when the senior constable came to. He was tucked up in a bed, his scrotum having been cleaned, stitched and wrapped by Clements' wife.

'You need to go get help,' Moran said. 'We have to get these sons of bitches.'

Condell agreed, but he could not go himself. He again opened his jacket to look at his wound: now cleaned and bandaged, but just as sore. He called out for Clements.

'Can we ask just one more thing?'

Clements agreed. He then mounted his horse and rode into the night.

* * *

Nangar Range, 15 June 1862, 5 pm
Hall hitched his horse to a ghost gum. Only John O'Meally had beaten him to camp and was already pulling wooden boxes from shallow holes.

'There is enough food to feed Sydney,' O'Meally said. 'How long does he think we are going to be hiding out?'

Hall was now poking kindling into gaps between the stacks of wood, having been assigned to start the fire. 'Probably depends on how much we stole,' he said. 'They will send the entire force after us if there is as much gold in those other boxes as the first one. I might end up having to eat you.'

The sun had not quite set but the mountain floor five miles from the scene of their crime was in darkness. The rows of pines, gums and scrub that would hide them from the law kept out the dying breath of the sun.

Bow, Manns and Fordyce soon arrived.

'You got that fire going yet, Hall?' Manns demanded. 'We will freeze to death if the traps don't get us first.'

The loot followed, strapped to tired horses that had been urged on by equally exhausted men. Charters was dripping with sweat, the perspiration cutting skin-coloured rivers into his blackened face when he lobbed in. O'Meally leaped from his perch beside the firepit and tripped on a box of food as he rushed towards the bushrangers' bounty.

'Watch it,' yelped Charters. 'You will ruin the food. I'd rather be shot than starve.'

'Just don't break the grog,' said Gardiner, the leader appearing with the knockabout Gilbert at his side. 'We have some celebrating to do.'

The gang cheered and slapped each other's backs, the relief of having made it this far sinking in.

'Now let's see what we have,' Gardiner said.

The celebrations continued as the other three metal boxes were busted open. Inside were piles of gold and cash. It would later be established that the first box contained 521 ounces, the second another 129 ounces and the last held 3,700 pounds in cash. The box they had already opened contained 2,719 ounces. In total the men had seized 170 pounds of gold, now piled into potato sacks.

'Holy shit,' Charters said. 'That's more than the Victorian boys got from the bank.'

The robbery of the Ballarat branch of the Bank of Victoria was legendary. Four bold, brazen and armed-to-the-teeth bushrangers had stormed into the branch on the afternoon of 16 October 1854 and stuck up the bank. Storing riches from the nearby goldfields, the bank was an apple ready to be picked. The four gunmen had escaped with thirteen thousand pounds in cash and 330 ounces of gold. It was the biggest robbery in Australian history.

Until now …

Hall continued to work on the fire and finally a spark took to the tinder. He imagined his face on a wanted poster as he looked into the rising flame. A two-hundred-pound reward just for information about the Victorian bandits had been put up following their heist, and that was half the size of this one. He turned to look at the gold, now glittering thanks to his fire. Gardiner went about dividing the haul into piles, eight mostly even shares. He weighed the lots, but no doubt kept a little more for himself.

'Righto, lads,' Gardiner said. 'Here it is.' He hurled a bag to O'Meally. 'They are all the same, lads,' he said. 'You won't be able to spend any of them piles in four lifetimes.'

There was laughter from around the fire.

Gardiner pulled his red scarf from his pocket and threw it into the flames. 'You too, gents,' he said. 'Let's burn anything that will connect us to the crime. Well, everything except the gold.'

The rest followed suit.

'We leave for Mount Wheogo in the morning,' Gardiner said.

* * *

Forbes, 15 June 1862, 11 pm

Hanbury Clements burst into the police station.

'Where's the inspector?' he asked. 'I need to speak to the inspector. There has been a stick-up. Two officers have been shot.'

The squatter had made the thirty-mile journey to Forbes in just three hours. A man on a mission, the moon his only light, Clements had ridden his horse to breaking point. Lash after lash, the crack of his whip sending the creature speeding headfirst into darkness.

'Now,' Clements demanded. 'Your senior constable has had his balls shot off.'

Clements had their attention.

'Settle down, mate,' said the junior officer, 'we hear you. We'll go get the boss but for your sake I hope you're not telling porkies. We are going to have to drag him from bed.'

Sir Frederick Pottinger was standing in front of Clements fifteen minutes later. Having dressed fast, eyes red and crusty, he demanded answers.

'Balls, you say?' Pottinger asked. 'Shot in the testicles?'

Clements nodded and Pottinger shook his head.

'And this was my senior constable?'

'Yes,' Clements said. 'Moran. We stitched him up and he is at my station on the mend. The sergeant, Condell, gave me this.'

Sir,

About five o'clock we were attacked by a party from twelve to fifteen armed men, dressed in red jumpers, red scarves, and blackened faces. The road being blocked up with several drays, so that we had to pass close to a rock, where they were concealed, and as the coach was passing, six or seven men fired into the coach, and drew back.

Then six or seven others fired. We then returned the fire, two of the horses got wounded and started off with the coach, capsizing it and turning the escort out.

I received four bullets through the coat, one entering my left side. Senior Constable Moran received two balls, one which wounded him in the groin. The coachman receiving also two bullets but was not hurt.

The men then rushed to the coach, taking the gold boxes out, and also the mail bags, which they cut open, opening several of the letters.

I and two of the escort got to Mr Clements' station. I requested of him to proceed to Forbes and give information.

The bushrangers were commanded by one man, who gave them orders to fire and load. I believe it to have been the voice of

Gardiner, as I know his voice well. The bushrangers took two of the men's rifles, and three cloaks which remained in the coach after it was capsized, and they also cut open my carpet bag, taking from it two shirts, three pairs of socks. I cannot identify any of them with the exception of the voice heard.
JAMES CONDELL, Sergeant

Pottinger raged.

'Frank Gardiner,' he screamed. 'He has robbed the gold escort. That lunatic has shot Condell. And you can bet that Ben Hall was with him.'

Pottinger paused, attempting to collect himself. He couldn't.

'This is a disgrace,' he shouted. 'Incompetence. These cowards let Gardiner take the escort? This is unheard of. Moran is lucky his balls have been taken already.'

Pottinger bludgeoned the rest of the details from Clements.

'We need Billy Dargin,' Pottinger said. 'Go and get him. I don't care what he is doing. Just drag him in now.'

Dargin was an Aboriginal tracker. The best. He was also a precision shot and a level head. In another time Dargin would have been the inspector and Pottinger the help.

'And go get every officer in town,' Pottinger said. 'We are all going. These outlaws need to be hunted down. It will be the end of us if word reaches Sydney and we haven't locked them up. We need to get the gold.'

* * *

Sir Frederick Pottinger had rocketed through the policing ranks with a series of rapid-fire promotions that some would say he had not earned. Born in India in 1831, second son of Lieutenant General Sir Henry Pottinger of the East India Company, Pottinger landed in a life of privilege and wealth. Educated at Eton, he would go on to succeed his father and inherit his wealth. But Pottinger had a weakness. He liked a punt.

After losing his family fortune at the racetrack, his mother even sold all her jewellery to help him try to pay off his debt. He was rumoured to have lost over a hundred thousand pounds. Disgraced and still in debt, Pottinger was forced to flee England for Australia in 1856. Pottinger laid low and avoided the Sydney social set. He was determined to enter high society again, but not until he redeemed himself and made back his money.

He tried his hand at another type of gambling: gold. But as a prospector he also failed. So Pottinger joined the New South Wales police force as a lowly trooper. And there he remained until a mystery letter arrived on the desk of police captain John McLerie. Addressed to 'Sir Frederick William Pottinger', care of the New South Wales police. A quick search revealed Pottinger was stationed on the Burrangong goldfield.

'Bring him to Sydney,' ordered McLerie. 'Now! We have a noble in out midst. A baronet can't be a trooper.'

Pottinger – Sir Frederick Pottinger – was immediately promoted to clerk of petty sessions at Dubbo. Later that year he became the assistant superintendent of the Southern Mounted Patrol. Pottinger was a shooting star and scheduled to be promoted again, until a drunken brawl in 1861 stalled his climb.

Full of booze and arrogance, he belted a bloke in the Great Eastern Hotel, Young.

'You're a swindler,' shouted Henry Cohen, slamming down his pool cue. 'You have ripped me off.'

Cohen had just lost a game of pool to Pottinger, the renowned gambler finally winning a bet.

Pottinger cast aside his glass and picked up his pool cue. 'Swindler?' he shouted. 'How dare you!'

The blow knocked Cohen to the ground. Pottinger had used the thin end of the stick, the cue more whip than sledgehammer. Cohen was dazed, his head cut and bleeding. Pottinger then hurled the man through a window.

Cohen went on to successfully sue Pottinger for assault. He was fined a hundred pounds for the incident, but the very public affair also earned Pottinger a very public warning. His boss gave him a lashing in the press before posting him to Forbes as punishment. No lawman, at least none without a death wish, wanted to do any sort of policing in Forbes, the bushranger capital of Australia. Catch them and you were just doing your job. Fail to catch them and you were incompetent. The other scenario, of course, was being shot dead.

Colonial Secretary Charles Cowper wrote a stinging letter to Pottinger, slamming him for being in the 'fumes of tobacco' and in the company of 'the tag-end of society'.

'Your actions were highly discreditable,' Cowper wrote. 'And to be occupied in gambling and betting during the whole night must unfit those who indulge in such unseemly practices for the efficient performance of their duty.

'It occasions the Colonial Secretary considerable pain to be under the necessity of animadverting in such strong terms upon the conduct of an officer of whom he has entertained a high opinion and who has just been promoted. But, considering the state of the country more especially at the present crisis, from the large influx of diggers from the neighbouring colony and elsewhere, the officers whose particular duty it is to protect life and property, especially at the goldfields, cannot be too circumspect in their general behaviour and the Government will feel called upon to visit with the severest mark of their displeasure those who may be found acting at variance with this principal.'

* * *

Pottinger now knew his title would only get him so far. He was one fuck-up away from being a Sydney street beggar with a knighthood, or a bushranger's bullet away from being buried.

He didn't know which fate would be worse.

'And volunteers,' Pottinger said, the second baronet knowing he would need all the help he could get. 'Any man who can use a gun. We need as many as we can get.'

'I'll do my best, boss,' said the officer.

The finest force that the western New South Wales police force could muster was assembled by 11.30 pm. There were eleven troopers and two trackers. Zero volunteers.

They rode off into the darkness, every second gained on the road putting them closer to cuffing a crook.

Chapter 3

THE GETAWAY

Eugowra, 16 June 1862, 2 am

'What time is it?' asked Pottinger, the copper and his crew edging towards a pine-clad twist in the trail.

Dargin, who took the lead from another Aboriginal tracker known only as Charley, did not have a watch. 'Just past two,' said the tracker. 'Sun-up in four-and-a-half hours, boss.'

The crashed cart was soon in sight. The Ford & Co. was wrecked, all splintered wood and twisted steel.

And the gold was gone.

'Looks like they got it all, inspector,' said Sergeant Sanderson, second in charge to Pottinger. 'The only thing they left is some of the mail.'

Pottinger surveyed the scene. 'Search the place,' he demanded. 'Let's see if they left anything else behind.'

But all they found was blood and bullets.

'This way, boss,' said Dargin. The tracker was on his haunches, hands parting the wild grass. An officer illuminated the ground with a lamp. 'There are eight of them,' Dargin continued. 'They went up there. Into the mountains.'

'Can we follow them?' Pottinger asked. 'Can we find them?'

Dargin looked into the tightly packed scrub, stringy-barks and eucalyptus trees towering. 'Yes,' he said. 'I find 'em, boss. No worries.'

* * *

Nangar Range, 16 June 1862, 3 am

Bounty split, bellies full and evidence burnt, the bushrangers got on the booze.

'Pass me another bottle,' O'Meally said. 'This bushranging business is thirsty work.'

Hall looked at his hands, the light of the fire adding orange to the charcoal black and dirt brown. They shook again.

Is he dead? Did I kill him?

Hall had never shot another man. Kangaroos? Sure. Rabbits? Of course. He had even shot a horse, the stockman putting a bullet into the brain of his best mare after a splinter had rendered her lame.

But Hall had never shot a man. Today he had shot a police officer. And he'd hit him fair and square in the balls.

'We are soon to have company, men,' said Gilbert, who'd been out on night patrol. 'Time to go.'

'What do you mean?' asked Charters. 'Leave?'

Gardiner had been methodical in his planning and wasn't going to start taking chances now the job was done. The campsite was near a lookout, a cliff with a view back towards the scene of the crime.

'Lanterns,' said Gilbert. 'Lots of them. They are at the escort now. It can only be the traps.'

Charters, half pissed on the bush plonk, threw his hands into the air. 'Already?' he asked. 'They weren't supposed to be here yet. Frank, you said they wouldn't even leave Forbes until first light.'

'Well, we may have gotten away with a little more than I expected,' Gardiner said. 'They are going to come for us. Come at us with everything they've got.'

Charters stood up. 'Shit,' he said. 'What are we going to do? I can't go to gaol. I won't go to gaol.'

O'Meally walked over to Charters, grabbed him by the shoulders and shook him. 'You are going to pull yourself together,' O'Meally said menacingly. 'That's what you are going to do. And then we are going to get out of here.'

Hall stepped towards his mate. 'Don't worry about Dan,' Hall said. 'He will be right. I am more worried about Fordyce. Have a look at the old drunk. He looks like he is going to have a spew.'

The camp erupted in laughter.

'Okay, time to move,' Gardiner said. 'Just as we planned. Nothing has changed, we're just moving a bit earlier than expected.' He paused to study his men. 'Charters,' Gardiner said, looking at the weakest link, 'you stick with Hall. He will get you there. And Fordyce, don't fall off your bloody horse.'

There was more laughter as the men made for their horses, the tension eased.

'Righto, off to camp Wheogo,' said Gardiner. 'She'll be right. I have enough supplies there to last us a month.'

* * *

Eugowra, 16 June 1862, 4 am

'This way,' said Dargin. 'The tracks over there lead to the farm. These tracks over here … these belong to the fellas that took the gold.'

Dargin had only been tracking for the New South Wales police for a few months but he'd quickly established himself as one of the most skilled bushmen in the colony. Pottinger had already used Dargin to solve a number of crimes. Peter Dargin, a Bathurst squatter and landowner, had given Billy his surname after the Aboriginal man had become one of the most loyal and trusted workers on his farm. Billy was Wiradjuri, born on the Bogan River. He spoke in both English and his native tongue, a Wangaaypuwan dialect of the Ngiyampaa language.

There were fifty or so Aboriginal trackers employed by the combined police forces of the colony, with the aim to secure a tracker for each district. Used for their traditional knowledge of the bush and hunting, they were also one of the force's best weapons when it came to catching bushrangers.

'We have to go now, boss,' Dargin said. 'A storm is coming. The water will wash all the tracks away.'

Dargin led the eleven troopers into the scrub. Almost pitch black, the darkness before dawn, they were soon surrounded by thick bush. They moved in stealth, the only sound the dry foliage crunching under the horses' hooves.

The silence was suddenly shattered when a trooper screamed, 'What the hell?' and sent his lantern smashing into the ground. 'What in Christ's name was that?'

Dargin chuckled. 'It was a possum, boss,' he said. 'Your lantern gave it a fright. It was growling at you.'

'The lantern gave *it* a fright?' the trooper replied. 'That thing sounded like a demon.'

Dargin nodded. 'Yeah, but nothing to be afraid of,' he said. 'They will give you a good scratch but there are plenty of things out here that will do worse.'

The trooper continued without his lantern. Nervously.

Soon the sun was creeping through the foliage, some of the light making its way to the forest floor. The search party had outlasted the night, though the horses and men were weary. They had travelled more than three miles since leaving the robbed wagon.

Dargin had not said a word for an hour. The men had followed him compliantly, a train of mounted sheep.

'Here,' he said. 'They were here.'

Embers still flickered in the fire at the centre of the abandoned camp, empty bottles were strewn across the forest floor. A bush rat nuzzled at a spent can once containing meat. A bevy of bull ants marched through the middle of the mess, breadcrumbs on their backs.

Bottles, bush rats and bull ants, but not a bushranger in sight.

And there was nothing left behind that could tie either Gardiner or Hall to what would soon be called Australia's biggest crime. But Dargin had already found more tracks. The felons had made no attempt to hide their trail.

'They left in a hurry, boss,' said Dargin.

Pottinger smiled. 'We have them rattled,' he said. 'We will have them in chains before the day is out.'

And then it started to rain.

* * *

With no trail left to track, Pottinger had to theorise.

'Victoria, men,' he exclaimed. 'They will be heading to Victoria. That's the only place they could sell the gold without getting caught.'

Sergeant Sanderson raised a brow. 'Yes,' he said, 'but maybe they aren't going to sell it. Not just yet.'

Dargin continued his hopeless search for tracks in the mud, the tracker completely oblivious to the conversation between the coppers.

Pottinger folded his arms and nodded. 'Go on,' he said.

'I think they are more likely to bury it,' Sanderson said. 'Keep it in a hole until this all dies down. Then they will sell it off, bit by bit.'

Pottinger was now the one raising a brow. 'No,' he said. 'Gardiner has gone to Victoria before and that is where he is going now.'

'He might be,' Sanderson said, 'but how about the rest of them? How about Hall? He has a wife and a child.'

Pottinger was adamant he was right. But as much as he loved a punt, he wasn't going to gamble his career.

'We'll split up,' Pottinger said. 'Two groups. You take half the men and head to Mount Wheogo. Go to Hall's. Go to McGuire's. I'll take the rest and head south.'

* * *

Mount Wheogo, 16 June 1862, 5 pm

Gardiner stood at the entrance of the cave on Mount Wheogo. The group was drenched, the rain relentless.

'Here we go, men,' he said. 'Home sweet home. It's dry as a bone in there. And we have plenty of grog if you want to stay wet.'

The bushrangers had ridden all day. Through bogged fields, horses pulling hooves from mud, the men pushed the beasts as hard as they dared. Avoiding trails, they jumped fences and ploughed through scrub. The men dug in their heels and cracked their whips, especially for the final climb to the top of Mount Wheogo, more than three hundred yards above sea level.

And Gardiner was right: the cave was packed for a siege, with cans of meat stacked six high, bags full of bread and biscuit, and vegetables in baskets.

'How about some Weddin homemade?' Gardiner said.

They all wanted some – local moonshine to celebrate the money and mansions that loomed.

Again Hall started the fire. Job done, the roaring flames driving the wet from their lair, Hall at last got warm. He was also full, his stomach with food and his pockets with coin. But he felt empty. He stood and walked to the front of the cave and peered into the new night, looking across to where his home stood. He couldn't see it but he knew it was there. He also knew it was empty, nothing more than a shell. But still, it was his home, the only thing that linked him to his former life. It was there that he found both comfort and hope. He dreamed of filling it again with love. With Biddy. With Henry.

* * *

Orange, 16 June 1862, 3 pm

As the wagon proceeded along Orange's main street, Sergeant Haviland flicked through the newspaper. The robbery had apparently made the afternoon edition of every paper in the west. He hoped they didn't all run with headlines like this: 'Coward Coppers: Troopers Flee'.

The police were already being blamed for the robbery. Their security measures were slammed and so were their actions.

Haviland skimmed, and then studied, the front-page story of the *Lachlan Times*. He read slowly, the bumpy ride forcing him to focus.

The coach with its guards cooped up in a box, containing the precious treasures of the Lachlan, is to all intents and purposes a locomotive advertisement to the vile and criminal. The invitation

*to a splendid harvest is irresistible. And those few on board rested
in a state of inaction.*

He hoped the *Sydney Morning Herald* would be better. It wasn't.

*A very large amount of gold is accumulating in the homes of
the bushrangers of the Lachlan in consequence of the inefficiency
of the escort guard. The Government has wasted no time in
recommending steps be taken to provide a more efficient escort.
Better vehicles must be built for the colony with the purpose of
carrying these objects. It should also have a rear and forward guard.*

As he read on, the trap turned a bright shade of red. He had spent
the entire trip fearing he would be called a dastard. Now he was
sure of it. *I'm the only one that wasn't shot. They are going to go after me.
They will say I am coward. Maybe worse. A deserter? Will they hang me?*

Haviland had just arrived in Orange on the very same wagon
that had been robbed. It had been hastily repaired and sent back
into the fray. He'd bought the papers at a local store where the
men had stopped to relieve themselves.

Now Haviland was anything but relieved. *Coward or deserter?*

The cart continued towards town. Their destination, Dalton's
Inn – the hotel in Orange used as the main escort stop on trips
to Forbes – was only five minutes or so away.

Coward or deserter?

Haviland reached under his seat and pulled out a Colt
revolver, a standard police issue .36-calibre single shot, and put
it to his neck.

Bang!

The revolver report was heard all the way up and down the street. Two women rushed towards the wagon.

'My God!' one of the women screamed. 'A man has been shot!'

The other woman stuck the palm of her hand onto Haviland's throat. 'We need to stop the blood,' she yelled. 'Get a doctor. Someone get a doctor! This man needs help.'

There was no helping Haviland. The soon-to-be-disgraced – at least in his traumatised mind – officer had jammed the barrel of his handgun against the flesh of his throat, bent his head back and pulled the trigger. The blast blew out his brain; pieces of Haviland's spine were found on the back seat of the coach.

Some who knew Haviland said he was not the type of man to take his own life. They suggested it was an accident. But most thought the police officer blew out his brains with painful purpose.

The colonial secretary gave an update to parliament the following day. 'The men wounded on the escort are now in Orange,' he said. 'And one of them, Haviland, was shot just before the coach reached Orange. It is said that it was by his own hand. An inquest will be held this morning. I have men assisting in the pursuit. Sir Frederick Pottinger is on the tails with a party of thirty. The Government has offered a thousand-pound reward for the capture of any of the guilty parties. We have also put in motion every available policeman in pursuit of this desperate gang of bushrangers.'

The desperate bushrangers themselves thought that they had pulled off Australia's biggest heist without having to kill. A victimless crime.

They were wrong.

* * *

Mount Wheogo, 16 June 1862, 8 pm

Gardiner exploded. The mountain moonshine was notorious for inducing a temper tantrum.

'You are a fucking coward,' he screamed in a shower of spittle. 'You didn't fire? Not one shot?'

Banter had just turned into a blast after it was revealed that Fordyce had not fired his gun during the heist. An innocent remark by Manns, what he thought was a joke, sparked a tirade.

'You mean you hid behind a rock while the rest of us put our lives on the line?' Gardiner spat. He fast closed the gap between himself and Fordyce then grabbed him around the meat of the throat. He stared Fordyce down, eyes glazed by grog and filled with hate.

'I wasn't scared,' Fordyce protested. 'I was blind drunk. I couldn't shoot shit after you plied me with that gin. You said it would calm my nerves. It made me damn useless. I was as drunk as a skunk.'

Gardiner responded to the accusation by turning up the anger.

'That's it,' he said. 'You get nothing. You should get a bullet to the head, but instead you get nothing. You don't deserve your share. Your rations are cut.'

Hall calmly walked over and grabbed Gardiner by the shoulder. The young stockman was not drunk. He had been contemplating more than he had been drinking. *Biddy. Henry.*

Hall pulled at Gardiner, dragging him away from Fordyce and into the dark.

'Calm down,' Hall said. 'You are being a fool. What do you mean you will take away his share? What do you think he will do if you take his gold and coin? I'll tell you what he will do – he will dog us out. He'll go and tell Pottinger and collect the reward.'

Gardiner, still wide-eyed and breathing heavily, stood and listened.

'You only have two options here,' Hall said. 'You can change his luck and put that bullet in his brain. Or you can let him keep his share.'

Gardiner's continued silence suggested he was leaning towards the former.

'Oh don't be a fucking fool, Frank,' Hall said. 'There is enough money here to buy Queensland. Go over there right now and make out it was a joke. You know? You were giving him a bit of a scare for shits and giggles. That sort of thing.'

Gardiner's breathing had finally slowed, his hands were no longer clenched into fists. He shrugged his shoulders and turned back into the cave.

'So how about this fool thinking I was going to keep his share!'

* * *

Mount Wheogo, 17 June 1862, 6 am

All was forgotten by sunrise. Hall was packing his horse when Gardiner woke.

'Whatcha doing, Ben?' he asked groggily. 'You leaving?'

Hall nodded. 'I am not a bushranger,' he said. 'At least, not when it comes to the law. They aren't going to be looking for me.'

Gardiner shrugged. 'Fair enough,' he said. 'Where are you going to go?'

'Home,' Hall said. 'It is time to rebuild my life. This money will help me get things back on track. Help me with Biddy and the boy.'

Gardiner moved towards Hall and his horse. 'You can't take the money or the gold back there,' he said. 'You can't be caught with that.'

Hall winked. 'Ah, why do you think I wasn't blind drunk like the rest of you last night?' he asked. 'I was out taking care of things. I was making a bush safe. My share is somewhere out there, buried in a big ol' hole.'

Hall was gone when the morning sun broke through the clouds, turning the countryside a brilliant orange-pink. So too were Manns and O'Meally. The rest hunkered down. They would wait for the storm to clear, even though the clouds were heavy, the rain relentless.

Chapter 4

THE CHASE

Mount Wheogo, 19 June 1862, 9 am

Sergeant Sanderson and his party arrived in Wheogo four days after the escort was robbed. The officer had returned to Forbes after investigating the scene of the crime at Eugowra. He suspected the thieves would hide out in the bush before returning home.

'Let's head to Hall's house first,' the officer said. His men were unenthusiastic, most suspecting they were stabbing in the dark. 'He should be back by now. After that we will try O'Meally and then Gilbert. We might get lucky.'

And they did, after a search of Hall's house produced nothing.

'Boss, over there,' said Charley, the other Aboriginal tracker. 'Look!'

Sanderson peered into the distance. At the top of a ridge, not far from the home of Hall, a puff of dust had been kicked up into the air. 'Someone is in a hurry,' he said, the dirt cloud rising and heading quickly towards the scrub. 'And they don't like traps.'

They took off, heels slamming into horses, the almost fatally fatigued beasts obeying the command. They rushed towards the fast-fleeing speck at the top of the hill. Sanderson had no doubt he was chasing one of the men who had robbed the escort. He was equally sure he would be led to the rest.

'Go!' he yelled. 'Faster.'

The overworked horses were heaving, no match for the man on the quickly disappearing mount. They stopped at the edge of the scrub, right where he'd vanished from sight.

'This way,' said Charley, looking at the heavy tracks. 'We can follow.'

They lurched into the mountains, guns drawn and ready to fire. The rider had bolted, leaving them only broken branches and crushed foliage to follow.

The tracker led from the front.

'Push,' Sanderson bellowed. 'Harder. We will lose him.'

They ducked under branches as the horses steamed. Tracker Charley went as fast as his eyes could follow the freshly cut trail twisting and turning through the scrub.

'Stop!' shouted Charley. 'Pull up now.'

The posse broke, the horses kicking up dirt as they were reined in.

'What?' demanded Sanderson.

'They stop here, boss,' Charley said. 'The tracks. They gone. He gone across the stream.'

'Well get across to the other blooming side,' Sanderson yelled, 'and pick it up!'

They stepped through the shallow water and Charley found a new trail, finally stopping at a smoking pile. The fire had been kicked out, hastily and recently.

'Look,' a constable pointed, 'they left a horse.'

* * *

Gardiner was caught completely unaware by the police raid.

They had spent three days in camp without incident and he was sure any threat had passed. Gilbert and Fordyce had departed too, all burying their gold before going home, leaving just Bow and Charters with Gardiner.

He was planning his next move when Charters came back to camp in a fit.

'Traps!' Charters screamed. 'They are here. We have to go now. They are coming for us.'

Gardiner was furious. From their camp in the cave on a bluff at the northern end of the mountain they had a panoramic view of the surrounding country. They should have been able to see any approach. And they should have been able to make a quick getaway.

'You fool,' belted Gardiner. 'You've led them straight to us. Why did you run from them? Why did you lead them back here?'

Charters thought he had done the right thing. 'I came here to warn you,' he yelped.

The damage was done.

They threw what was left of their gold onto a packhorse, kicked out the fire and took off. They galloped away from the noise of the chasing squad: branches snapping, hooves pounding rock, men yelling this way and that.

'We'll have to split,' Gardiner screamed. 'Bow, you go south. Head for the waterhole. Charters, you head for O'Meally's place. I'll go deeper in. I'll take this horse with me and go and hide the rest of this gold.'

Gardiner had spots he could disappear into all through the mountain. With fresh rain pouring, their splitting trails to be washed away, he knew he wouldn't be caught.

'I'll find you when we are in the clear,' he said.

And they were off. Bow went like the wind, Charters vanished into the fog, and Gardiner climbed deeper into the mountain range.

Shit. They are gaining.

The police hunt had fully turned their attention to Gardiner, not noticing the split trails. And they were coming at speed. Gardiner was being slowed down by the packhorse, one of the old mules stolen from the escort during the robbery. He looked down the mountain and could now make out his pursuers through the trees, one of them a black man on a white horse.

'Blazes,' he said.

He pulled out his blade and sliced through the rope that joined the packhorse to his, sending it down the hill with a slap. Sent it packing, gold and all.

Free of his burden, Gardiner disappeared. The cops never stood a chance once nothing was slowing him down. He was hoping the police would not find the horse, planning on coming back for it once the coast was clear.

But tracker Charley found the horse. Sanderson found the gold. And the police celebrated.

'That has got to be half the loot!' Sanderson crowed. 'We are going to be the talk of the town. Good job, men.' He looked to Charley. 'Can we continue the pursuit?'

'No,' Charley said. 'They gone now, boss. And the trail stops at the stream. It will be washed away by the rain on the other side by the time we pick it up.'

Sanderson came down from the mountain, all gold and grin.

'We will send out another patrol once we get this gold back to Forbes,' he said.

The police had the gold, but not a lot else. None of the bushrangers had been identified. They suspected Gardiner, but that was all. Still, Sanderson was hailed a hero by the people of Forbes. They clapped and cheered when he returned.

'And where is Pottinger?' someone asked.

'Where is his gold? Who has he caught?' shouted another.

* * *

Hay, 30 June 1862

Sir Frederick Pottinger called it quits.

'We are chasing shadows,' he said. 'They are all in Forbes for all I know.'

Their search party was now just three, with Pottinger joined by Detective Patrick Lyons and volunteer Richard Mitchell. Pottinger had been on the road for two weeks. He was exhausted. He was also embarrassed.

'Sanderson is going to be quite the hero,' Pottinger said. 'He got gold. What did we get?'

Mitchell, a former detective and loyal friend to Pottinger, still held hope. 'But what about that lead?' he replied. 'We shouldn't give up.'

Only a day after hearing of Sanderson's success at Wheogo, Pottinger had questioned a band of travellers heading north who claimed to have been passed by Gardiner and his gang.

'You saw Frank Gardiner?' he asked. 'He went past you heading south?'

'See?' Pottinger had turned to Lyons. 'I told you. We are onto something here.'

'Definitely Frank Gardiner,' one of the travellers had said. 'I know what he looks like. You couldn't miss him. Looked like he was up to no good too. He had some rough types with him. I thought we were in some trouble.'

Pottinger had fronted the next traveller heading north.

'Have you come across anyone heading south?' he'd asked. 'A large group of men. Do you know what Frank Gardiner looks like?'

The traveller shook his head. 'Ain't seen no Frank Gardiner,' he'd said. 'And no groups of men like that.'

No one else had either. Pottinger had kept up the questioning with no further result. His hope had diminished a little every day. Now it was lost.

'They aren't here,' he said now to Mitchell. 'We got a bum steer.'

They had rarely slept in a bed since leaving Eugowra on the

night of the robbery. When the odd cattle station took them in, they ate, washed and slept, but mostly they slept under the stars, heads on saddles, backs on dirt. Their horses had been ridden to ruin.

'We would be useless if we stumbled across them anyway,' Pottinger said. 'These horses couldn't even catch a cold. No, we are done.'

'So what now?' Mitchell asked.

'We stop here,' Pottinger replied. 'And we leave for Forbes in the morning.'

* * *

Mount Wheogo, 4 July 1862

'We have to get out of here,' Gilbert said. Whisky in hand, he was looking sternly at Manns. 'It is getting too hot,' he continued. 'What good is having all this money if we can't spend it?'

They were in a sly grog shanty belonging to John O'Meally's father, Patrick – bushranger headquarters. Located on the west side of Tyagong Creek, at the foot of the Weddin Mountains, on Patrick's 26,000-acre Arramagong property, it had originally been built of bark in 1855 then reconstructed in brick by Patrick using a compensation payment he had received after scab killed half of his stock. Known as the Weddin Mount Inn, it encompassed a public house, stables and a water supply and was the only establishment of its kind in the region. Miners had flooded it first, bushrangers later.

Gilbert and Manns should have been celebrating their success. But instead of singing and sculling a drink, they were tucked away in a quiet corner discussing an escape plan.

Manns agreed. 'I've still got all my gold,' he said. 'Can't get rid of it. I'm terrified of getting sprung the moment I try to sell it.'

Gilbert had already managed to fence off his share – after getting others to sell it for him to multiple buyers. All his gold was gone. He had 2,500 pounds stashed in a freshly dug hole, and he would have had much more had he not sold his gold at a cut-price rate and handsomely rewarded those who sold it for him.

'Yeah,' he agreed, 'my gold is gone but my cash is useless too. I can't spend it without tipping off the traps. I am filthy rich but still dirt poor.'

It was a problem for everyone in Gardiner's gang. Hall had buried his cache under a tree, O'Meally had stashed his gold in a cave, and Gardiner had put his in wooden boxes in the ground. Manns, on the other hand, had all of his gold strapped to the side of his saddle.

'Do you trust them?' Manns asked, referring to the six other men who had taken part in the biggest robbery in the colony's history. 'All of them?'

Gilbert sighed. 'No,' he said. 'Most of them, yes. But all of them? No. Frank is the staunchest soldier I know. Hall would take a bullet for you. So would O'Meally. But Fordyce? He is a drunk. Who knows what he will say if they drag him in?'

Manns took a swig. 'It's Charters that worries me,' he said. 'He has a lot to lose. You know he inherited five cattle stations?'

Gilbert hit the bar-room table, the force knocking down bottles.

'Fuck this,' Gilbert said. 'I'm not getting caught. Let's hightail it out of here. I have money. You have gold. I say Victoria.'

Manns nodded. 'Too right,' he said. 'But what about your baby brother?'

'Charlie is coming with us,' Gilbert said.

Victoria. Settled. Manns, Gilbert and his brother Charles set out the very next day.

* * *

Narrandera, 7 July 1862

Rested, fed and resigned to failure, Sir Frederick Pottinger began the long trip home. Pottinger knew the questions would come.

Why on earth did you leave Forbes? What evidence took you to Victoria?

He would shrug.

A hunch?

They would laugh. And then they would demote him. And Sanderson would be there, smug-faced.

'Slow down,' he barked, looking at Mitchell. 'No need to hurry. Let's take it easy.'

The road was no place for a man with regrets. For much of the day it was just Pottinger and his thoughts. He tried to silence his head noise with conversation but the talk with his colleagues was only casual and short.

And then, after six hours, someone said something that was actually of interest.

'Have a look at these three,' said Lyons. 'Suits and stallions.'

Pottinger looked at the pacing posse ahead, rough men with good gear. They were all wearing suits, brown and bold, their horses fit for Flemington. Each man had a packhorse equally as good as the one they rode.

'What fine horses you have,' Pottinger said. 'Would you care to show me a receipt?'

Gilbert looked at Manns. They thought they were riding away from trouble; instead they had travelled three days to stumble across the very man who was hunting them down.

Gilbert turned back to Pottinger and pretended he did not know who the inspector was. 'And why should I show you a receipt?' Gilbert replied.

'Because I am Sir Frederick William Pottinger,' he spat. 'Inspector of police for the western New South Wales district, that's why. And who are you?'

'Oh,' Gilbert said. 'Me? I'm John Darcy.' He pointed towards Charles Gilbert. 'And that is my brother Charles Darcy,' he continued. 'We had no luck at Lambing so we are off to Victoria to see if we can find our fortune there.'

'So do you have a receipt for that horse?' Pottinger asked again.

Gilbert nodded. 'Sure,' he said. 'Let me get it for you.' Gilbert reached towards his saddle with his left hand. With his right he repositioned his horse, little taps, little pats. 'Just here somewhere,' he said. He continued to fumble, searching for a receipt he did not have, but really moving his horse. A gentle pull on the reins, a little nudge of his heel, he was making himself a clear path. 'Oh, here it is,' he said, winking at Manns and Charlie as he faked a reach.

Snap!

Like lightning, his hands reefed his horse's reins. Just as fast he kicked his spurs into his horse's hind and he was gone.

Gilbert looked over his shoulder, wind rushing through his hair, landscape reduced to a blur. He looked back, expecting to see his mate and his brother following.

They had guns at their heads.

Dash done, Gilbert shook his head, cursed and continued his charge.

Pottinger's finger was on the trigger. 'Move and I will shoot!' he screamed.

The barrel of his revolver was pressed against Manns' face. The other Gilbert was sobbing, Mitchell's shotgun jammed into the flesh of his throat.

Pottinger had not even attempted to chase the runner. The quality of the man's horse was what had sparked his suspicion, and that same quality meant he hadn't a hope in hell of catching him. Instead he had pulled his gun.

'So why did your mate run?' Pottinger asked. 'What is it you fellas are attempting to hide?'

'Nothing,' Manns lied.

'And what's your name?' Pottinger asked

Manns claimed to be Henry Turner.

'Well, Turner,' said Pottinger, 'let's have a look and see if you are hiding something.'

Pottinger stuck his hands into the pockets of the man who called himself Charles Darcy first. He pulled out a wallet containing two pounds, two shillings. He found nothing in the man's saddle.

Pottinger shook his head. *Here we go again …*

He turned to Manns then, first going through his pockets.

'What do we have here?' he asked as he opened Manns' wallet. 'That is a lot of money.' He was looking at 150 pounds.

Again, Pottinger shook his head. *Not indictable. Nothing that can't be explained.*

Now for the saddle. He stuck his hand into a pouch and pulled out a potato bag. And now he was nodding. Smiling, ear to ear.

'You are both under arrest,' Pottinger said. He looked towards Lyons. 'Quick,' he said, holding a fistful of gold, 'get the cuffs. Take a look what we have here.'

Pottinger had pulled a massive amount of gold from the packhorse's saddlebag, what would later be shown to be 215 ounces worth.

'Thought you said you had no luck in the Lachlan?' Pottinger commented. 'Care to explain this?'

Suddenly Pottinger was a new man, the road no longer lonely, the voices in his head full of praise. He was about to solve Australia's biggest crime. Go from demotion to promotion. And he knew there would be questions.

Why on earth did you leave Forbes? What evidence took you to Victoria?

He would shrug.

A hunch?

They would laugh. And then they would promote him. And Sanderson would be there, all sorry-faced.

* * *

Weddin Mountains, 7 July 1862

Gilbert was fuming. *Why didn't they follow? Idiots. That Pottinger would have never kept up.*

He was also in a hurry. *Gotta get the boys. Gotta get help and go back and get 'em. My brother. Can't leave my brother.*

Gilbert whacked on the reins, sending his horse hurtling into the fast-falling night. Nine hours later he was bursting through the door of O'Meally's shanty.

'Thank God,' he said looking around at Gardiner, Hall, Bow, Fordyce and O'Meally. 'You're here. They got Manns and Charlie. They got his gold too. They're going to get us next.'

Gardiner intervened. 'Slow down, lad,' he said. 'Take a breath. Who has got them and where?'

Gilbert composed himself. He grabbed a drink and told them the tale, blow by blow.

When he had finished Gardiner stood up and grabbed his shotgun. 'Well let's go and get them.'

* * *

Gardiner and his gang hit the road, riding through the night, on a rescue mission. Gilbert had ridden 130 miles by the time the sun rose, only stopping to get the others. The six men were closing in on a station known as Sprowle's, located on the route from Narrandera to Forbes.

'They will have to come past here,' Gardiner said. 'And we will be here to meet them.'

Guns drawn, scarves pulled up onto faces, they were soon knocking on the homestead's door.

'Don't move!' screamed Gardiner as he pointed the shotgun at a woman's head. 'Get on the ground and all will be well.'

Terrified, she obeyed.

'Who else is here? How many and where?'

There was only one other woman on the property, the men all out driving stock to town. Both were tied up and gagged. Later two travellers walked towards the house, and they too were tied up at gunpoint and shoved face-first into the floor.

'Load the guns,' Gardiner ordered.

* * *

Sprowle's Station, Temora, 8 July 1862

Sir Frederick Pottinger rode behind his prisoners, Mitchell by his side and Lyons out in front. Henry Manns and Charlie Gilbert were handcuffed, chains also tying their wrists to their saddles. Their horses had been coupled together too, and another rope latched to the packhorse. Pottinger was taking no chances. There were no warrants out for a Turner or a Darcy, as far as he could recall. But was that who they really were?

He would get to the bottom of it all when he returned to Forbes, triumphantly, with prisoners and gold.

Pottinger and his search party had travelled to Temora after making the arrests. He dispatched word to headquarters of the gold he had captured and the men he had caught. He had then eaten and slept, the best night's rest he'd had since the robbery. They'd set out for Forbes following a breakfast of eggs and bread.

They were approaching a station soon after setting off, mostly hidden behind trees and scrub, when the dreaded cry came.

'Bail up, you bastards!' someone yelled.

Three men sprung onto the path from the thick scrub, faces blackened, red scarves over their faces.

Bang!

There was no time to react to the shotgun exploding. One of the gunmen had opened fire, hitting Lyons' horse in the head. The detective was thrown from his mount as the horse reared before crashing to the ground. His revolver lost in the fall, Lyons pulled himself up from the dirt and bolted into the bush.

Pottinger raised his own gun and returned fire. He missed.

Three more men with blackened faces and red scarves came from nowhere.

Bang! Bang! Bang!

They all fired, one after another in rapid succession. Pottinger and Mitchell retreated on their mounts, attempting to reload their weapons while pushing back to find cover behind the trees.

'I know you,' screamed one of the attackers. 'I know you, you bloody bastard Pottinger. I'll put a pill through you, you bastard!'

Bang! He shot at Pottinger again. Mitchell returned fire. So did Pottinger. They bravely went shot for shot with the attackers. But they were hopelessly outmatched. The bushrangers had a cache of weapons. After emptying a gun they would simply throw it down and grab another. Five minutes later, Pottinger had two charges left in his revolver, Mitchell one.

'Should we charge at them?' Mitchell asked. 'Try to take them to the ground?'

'No,' Pottinger replied. 'We have the gold.'

So they rode off, leaving both prisoners and attackers behind.

* * *

Gardiner found Detective Lyons hiding behind a bush.

'The keys,' Gardiner said. 'The keys to the cuffs or your life.'

The trap nodded before reaching to his belt.

'Where is my gold?' Manns shouted after his chains hit the turf.

Lyons trembled as a gun was pointed at his head. 'Sir Frederick has it,' he said. 'He packed it into the saddle of his horse.'

Manns looked at Gardiner. 'Let's go get it,' Manns said. 'It's all I have. It's for my new life.'

Gardiner shook his head. 'They're gone. They will already be calling for backup. We have to let that go.'

Pottinger had indeed called for help. He soon was surrounded by cops, ten of them escorting him back to Forbes with his gold. He might not have had the crooks, but he had the treasure.

Chapter 5

THE ARRESTS

Forbes, 25 July 1862

Sir Frederick Pottinger was not welcomed back to Forbes as a hero.

What do you mean you let your prisoners escape? The only lead you had in Australia's biggest robbery ever and you lost it?

They called him incompetent. They called him arrogant. Worst of all, they called him a coward.

'Do they know I stood toe to toe with them in a shoot-out?' Pottinger asked the officer who had gamely told him the word on the street. 'Outnumbered three to one. It is a miracle that I am alive. And they call me a coward?'

Nothing could convince them otherwise. Pottinger was slandered in the press. 'Some men are born to luck, while others have generally to contend with unfavourable circumstances and unforeseen accidents,' the *Burrangong Courier* wrote. 'We fear that Sir Frederick is one of the latter class.' 'A very good farce might be made of the details of Pottinger's pursuit of the bandits,' said the *Albury Border Post*. They even wrote poetry.

While Sir Frederick Pott,
Shut his eyes for a shot,
And miss'd – in his usual way.

Pottinger did his best to ignore everything that was being said. Everything that was being written. Few were brave enough to confront him to his face, and for now he would avoid the press. He'd got straight back into the investigation when he'd arrived home, knocking on doors and stopping men in the street.

Two weeks had gone by and he was still without a fresh lead. A man called Charles Darcy had been arrested at Murrumburrah a few days after the ambush, but he did not match the description of any of the men. The poor bugger just happened to have the same name as the one given to the police by one of the escapees.

Pottinger was running out of ideas. Gardiner was the only name he had for the robbery, and the 'Darkie' was a ghost. Probably in China by now.

Pottinger was flicking through some papers on his cluttered desk when an officer addressed him.

'Sir,' he said. 'Someone is here. I think you should come and see him. He is asking about the reward.'

Pottinger jumped up, sending papers flying. In the foyer stood a man with a reward poster in his hand. 'Have you come here to collect that?' Pottinger asked, nodding at the flyer.

Thomas Richards, lemonade seller from Forbes, nodded.

'I know who robbed the escort,' Richards said. 'But I want a hundred pounds per name like this notice here says.'

'Oh, you will get your money if I get my thieves,' Pottinger said. 'Let's go and have a chat.'

Pottinger sat down and took Richards' statement. And indeed he gave him names. Richards claimed he was at John McGuire's a few days before the robbery to collect a ten-pound debt. He said that Frank Gardiner was there with his gang, men he recognised as Ben Hall, Johnny Gilbert and John Bow.

'And then I was sent to bed,' he said. 'Another six came in after that. I could hear them from the bedroom. I don't know who they were.'

Pottinger asked him if he had heard what was said.

'No, but I reckon they were talking about stealing that gold,' Richards said.

Pottinger pressed. 'And why do you think they were talking about the gold?' Pottinger asked.

Richards said he was back at McGuire's after the robbery. 'McGuire told me that the escort had been robbed,' he said. 'A bloke called Dan Charters was riding away and he pointed at him saying that they had the gold a few miles away in the bush.'

Now Pottinger wanted to hear the whole story. Word for word.

'Let's start back at the beginning,' Pottinger said after showing Richards to his office and sitting down pen in hand, paper back on his desk.

The inspector ended up taking two statements. They were signed and put into a safe.

'I am going to arrest you tomorrow,' Pottinger said. 'That way they won't think you were the one who turned them in. You won't be charged, of course.'

Finally Pottinger had his names; they would call him a coward no more.

'We are heading to Mount Wheogo,' he smiled at a junior officer. 'Let's round up a crew.'

* * *

Mount Wheogo, 27 July 1862

Sir Frederick Pottinger arrived at Mount Wheogo at first light, flanked by a small army of police. Guns drawn, they burst through the door of John Brown's house, looking for Gardiner.

Catherine 'Kitty' Brown – John's unfaithful wife – answered the door.

'Is Frank Gardiner here?' he screamed. 'We have a warrant for his arrest.'

Pottinger had been told of Gardiner and Kitty's not-so-secret affair and knew the lovestruck pair had been taking full advantage of John Brown's long and frequent trips away to buy and sell cattle.

'Where is Gardiner?' Pottinger yelled. But Gardiner was not there. 'Where is his hideout?'

Kitty played dumb.

Pottinger ordered his men to tip up the house. One found gold.

'It is John McGuire's,' Kitty lied. 'He gave it to me to hold. He brought it back from Pinnacle Reef.'

Bullshit. But McGuire? He is involved in all of this.

Pottinger left some men to watch Brown's house.

'Shoot Gardiner if he comes here,' Pottinger ordered. 'But only if he tries to run. We are going to McGuire's.'

* * *

McGuire was in his yard, holding a blade in his blood-covered hands.

'You lads looking for a feed?' McGuire asked. 'Plenty here.' He pointed down to the freshly killed cow.

Pottinger was all business, the officer pulling the nugget of gold from his waistcoat and shoving it in McGuire's face.

'I have a nugget of gold here. Have you ever seen it before?' Pottinger asked.

'No,' McGuire replied. 'I have never seen it before.'

'Did you get it at Pinnacle Reef?' Pottinger continued.

'No, Sir Frederick,' McGuire said. 'If you are a judge of gold at all you will see that it is not reef gold, but alluvial and water-worn.'

Pottinger continued. 'So you know nothing about it then?' he asked. He turned tack. 'Now, you know a lot about the escort robbery,' he said. 'And I want you to tell me all about it. If you do then I will not interfere with you.'

'I know nothing about it, Sir Frederick,' McGuire said. 'I know it was robbed but I know nothing of the identities of the men that robbed it.'

Pottinger pressed. 'Tell me now or I will arrest you,' he said. 'I have enough against you to make sure you are hanged.'

'Do you want me to swear a lie?' asked McGuire.

Pottinger turned to his officers, patience exhausted. 'Put the cuffs on him,' he ordered. 'We are taking him in.'

'Can I wash my hands first?' McGuire asked. 'They are covered in blood.'

Pottinger agreed to the request, then cuffed McGuire and threw him on the dining room floor. He ordered two sentries to stand watch.

'I'm going to bring in Ben Hall,' Pottinger said.

* * *

Hall was mustering cattle with his brother William. Daniel Charters had come to lend a hand.

'How many head will it take to get all this going again?' he asked Charters. 'William here is going to come and work for me full-time.'

Gold hidden in the hills, guns gone, Hall had begun his mission to win back his wife and son. He was not cut out for a life of crime. He was determined to go straight. First things first: he needed to get his station going again.

Suddenly William shouted, 'Look. Over there. It's a bloody army. And it's coming our way.'

Hall soon had a shotgun in his face, and Pottinger was making declarations, no questions this time.

'You are under arrest for cattle thieving,' he shouted. 'And for robbing the gold escort in Eugowra.'

Hall laughed, but it was all a front. 'What evidence do you have?' Hall asked. 'Where is your warrant? You remember how it went down last time you arrested me?'

Pottinger remembered – he wouldn't forget. He couldn't forget.

'I have enough evidence to see all three of you hang,' Pottinger said as he put Hall in irons.

As Pottinger led his catch towards Hall's hut, Hall started wondering. *What could he have? Has someone given us up? Fordyce?*

An officer kicked the flimsy wooden door of Hall's hut in; hinges shattered and splinters flew.

'Get on the floor while we search this hut,' Pottinger shouted. 'Let's have a look–see. Maybe we can find a little more.'

Hall knew he wouldn't, with his gold buried beside the billabong, cash in the hollow of a tree.

The officers searched the house: drawers were pulled out and thrown on the floor, cabinets tipped over, beds upturned. They didn't find a thing. Pottinger turned his attention to the prisoners. Ben and Charters were clean, but he pulled a fifty-pound note from William's pocket.

'That's a lot of money for a young squatter,' Pottinger said.

'It's mine,' William yelled. 'And I earned it fair and square.'

'We will see,' Pottinger said. 'I am taking you all in.'

Horses tired, men needing a feed, Pottinger didn't fancy his chances in a chase should they be ambushed on the way back to Forbes.

'Get a horse each for this lot,' Pottinger said. 'We are going to take them to McGuire's. We will spend the night there before taking them to Forbes in the morning.'

They also arrested John Brown, Kitty's unloved husband. Pottinger suspected he would be well informed. He also suspected he may want to throw Frank Gardiner under a cart.

* * *

Forbes, 28 July 1862

The bolt snapped shut, an officer named Kennedy sending it thudding into a metal recess anchored in the wall. *Clack!*

The oversized padlock was now latched, the equally oversized key about to be turned.

'Don't bother getting comfortable,' he hissed. 'You will be swinging from a rope before you know it.'

The officer turned and walked away.

Ben Hall, William Hall, Dan Charters, John McGuire and John Brown had been paraded through the streets of Forbes. More than five thousand people had turned out to see the show, the prisoners brought in on horseback, hands chained, heads slumped. Some of the crowd cheered and others booed. Now the five men were in an eight-by-ten-foot cell in the lock-up known as The Logs. Built from pine logs, it was reinforced with iron, a cage in its centre.

Hall waited until the trap called Kennedy was back out on the street. He turned to Charters, McGuire and his brother William.

'A word,' he said, waving them towards the corner of the cage. 'They haven't found anything on us,' Hall continued 'And they can do nothing to us. Don't say anything.'

McGuire nodded. 'I don't know a thing,' he said.

'Okay,' Hall said. 'Stick tight. We will be out by morning.' Hall then looked at Brown. 'And don't you go telling any tales,' Hall said. 'Whatever you have heard, we haven't done a thing. Don't go giving any false statements. They will put things to you and threaten you if you don't agree. But it is all wind. The only threats you have to worry about will come from me. And don't think this is your chance to get back at Gardiner. Mention his name and you are done.'

The five went quiet. They sat on the floor, waiting for whatever it was that was coming next.

Hall suspected this was nothing more than a witch-hunt, Pottinger's last play. Hit and hope. But deep down he wondered.

Has someone dogged us? Given us up?

Hall had seen the size of the reward. More importantly, he had seen the offer of a pardon for the first person that turned.

Manns. What if they have recaptured Henry?

Only a member of the gang could give him up, and none of them would. But Manns was young. He had been dragged in for the job and was hardly involved. He was also stupid.

Manns. They have already seen him. They already have his gold. Would he put us in to save himself?

Time would tell.

Charters began to sob. Hunched over, head in hands, he sniffed and snuffled.

Hall launched his elbow into Charters' ribs. 'Pull yourself together!' he commanded.

'But Ben, what if they find—'

Hall cut his sentence short. 'They might be listening, you fool,' he whispered. 'This is what they want. They are trying to rattle us. Get into our heads. Not another word.'

Charters nodded morosely and Hall slapped him over the head.

'This is serious,' Hall said. 'Got me? I have a lawyer coming. He will sort it out.'

* * *

The court was a one-room weatherboard shack.

'What are the charges?' asked the magistrate.

Pottinger stood, straightened his coat and looked directly at the Hall brothers, Charters, McGuire and Brown. 'These prisoners, your honour, have all been charged with suspicion of stopping and robbing Her Majesty's mail and gold escort on Sunday, the fifteenth of June 1862,' Pottinger said. 'I would like to request a remand of seven days to produce an important witness to identify notes found in the possession of one of the prisoners during the arrest.'

Hall glanced quickly at Charters beside him. *Witness? Damn. Who?*

'And what evidence do you produce now to detain them?' the magistrate continued.

'We have in possession a fifty-pound note connected to the escort robbery.'

Solicitor Redman, acting on behalf of Hall, intervened. 'There are no grounds to hold my client,' he said. 'And I don't believe there were even grounds to arrest him. I call on the prosecution to produce a copy of the warrant under which my client was arrested.'

'Sir Frederick?' the magistrate responded.

Pottinger looked askance. 'Yes, I can produce the warrant tomorrow.'

Redman requested immediate bail for Hall.

'That request should be denied,' Pottinger said. 'These men are likely to flee should they be taken out of custody. Should I remind you of Frank Gardiner? Gardiner, the man at the centre of this disgrace, was in custody recently in Lambing. He was given bail and has not been seen since. He would not have masterminded this crime if he had been denied bail and would not still be on the run. Bail should be denied for William and Ben Hall, John McGuire and John Brown. I request them to be remanded for at least seven days while further evidence is gathered.'

'And what of Charters?' the magistrate asked.

Pottinger said nothing. Hall looked at his mate, an eyebrow raised.

The magistrate denied bail for the Halls, McGuire and Brown.

'They will be remanded until the next hearing on the fifth of August,' the magistrate said. He set bail for Charters at five hundred pounds.

'I will be making an application to the Supreme Court of New South Wales regarding the proceedings taken by the police,' Redman said.

His declaration was met by silence. All five men were marched from the court.

* * *

The bolt was snapped back into place. The oversized key clicked into the oversized padlock.

'Bail?' Hall said to Charters. 'Why were you offered bail?'

* * *

Pottinger's deputy was asking the very same thing.

'Ah, he is the weak link,' Pottinger replied, feet on his desk. 'He has been white as a ghost since he was arrested. And did you see him in court? He was shaking.'

'But why give him bail?' the officer asked. 'We need to keep him in a cell. Keep him scared.'

Pottinger smiled. 'What do you think is going on in that cell right now?' he asked. 'I'll tell you what. Right now the other four are pointing their fingers at Charters. They are asking why we didn't oppose his bail. And in their heads, maybe even out loud, they are accusing him of giving them up. And if they are not doing it yet, they soon will be.'

Pottinger sat back and folded his arms. 'Go over to The Logs now,' he said. 'Pull prisoner Charters out and tell him he has a visitor. Take him from the cell and go for a walk.'

'What shall I say to him?' the officer asked.

'Nothing,' Pottinger said. 'Sit him down for twenty minutes and then take him back.'

The officer nodded.

'And then prepare the troops for a little trip tomorrow,' he said. 'We are going back out to Wheogo to bring in the O'Meallys.'

Pottinger smiled, case coming together. The lemonade seller's testimony wouldn't be enough to convict any of the men, but along with the bank note taken from William Hall, and his plan to turn Charters, he thought he could make his case. Pottinger was waiting on the three banks involved in the robbery to check the note. A serial number would help sink them.

* * *

Forbes, 5 August 1862

John O'Meally and his father, Patrick, joined the five prisoners in court. Arrested at their shanty, they had been collared, cuffed and thrown into what was already a crowded cell. Now they stood next to William and Ben Hall, Charters, McGuire and Brown, awaiting their fate.

Again the prosecution offered very little. Again they asked for seven days. Again they opposed bail.

'And what of Mr Charters?' asked the magistrate. 'I understand he has been able to raise the surety against his release. Do you have any new evidence to make an application for that bail to be denied?'

'I do not,' Pottinger said. 'But I would ask the court to keep the others in remand for another seven days when we will be able to produce an expert witness crucial to this case.'

The magistrate agreed and all the prisoners except one were sent back to their cell.

'How did Charters come up with that sort of cash?' O'Meally asked.

'His brother-in-law paid it,' Hall said. 'James Newland. Didn't you see him there?'

McGuire nodded.

'Yeah, but where did he get five hundred pounds?' O'Meally asked. 'That is more money than he will see in his life.'

Hall shrugged.

'I'll tell you where he got it from,' said Patrick O'Meally. 'The goddamn police.'

* * *

Weddin Mountains, 9 August 1862
Dank, dirt-covered and longing for his lover, Frank Gardiner pulled himself from his hole.

Coast clear? Surely.

He was desperate to see her. Gardiner knew of the arrests, his bush telegraph always crystal clear. He was tired, hungry and most of all alone. He could see Kitty's place from his hilltop hideout, her light on, lover home.

No one will see me. I'll only be out in the open for a moment.

And he would be covered by the dark, now falling fast. Gardiner could already smell her perfume, feel her touch.

Speaking of smells … Gardiner stuck his hands in his bucket, cupped a handful of rainwater and slapped it on his face. He did his best to wipe away the filth, two weeks of grime and gunk. And then he jumped on his horse. *Here I come* …

The sun had already set, and the crickets and cicadas were in full song. Gardiner followed the falling fog. Soon the trees thinned, holes in the canopy allowing the moonlight to touch the forest floor. He edged towards an opening, the scrub giving way to a field. He was almost there.

Are you an idiot? His head noise returned. He reminded himself of the risk he faced, traps everywhere, reward on his head. Gardiner had avoided capture because he was methodical, meticulous and completely careful. His calculation and cunning had stopped him from being caught.

But so close …

Wishing he had his fortune-telling book, Gardiner gently pushed his white mare, both his favourite and fastest horse, into the unfiltered lunar light and onto the field. Instinct told him to bolt, to cover the distance as fast as he could, like a kid running to his mother after imagining a ghost. But sense told him to go slow. To look and lurk. So he did, one hoof at time, peering left and right, forward and back. Soon he could smell the kerosene, a lamp on the porch burning, seemingly put out for him.

But then came a cry: 'Stop in the name of Her Majesty!'

Gardiner went for his gun.

Bang! He heard the shot but felt no pain. He looked to his left and saw a carbine aimed at his head. Smoke spewed from the barrel. He put his hand to his face. His head should have been hanging off.

'No!' Pottinger screamed. 'Shoot! Shoot! Shoot!'

But Gardiner was already on his way. He had turned, pulled reins and driven his spurs into his horse's hind.

Bang! Bang! Bang! The traps shot. They missed.

Again Gardiner checked his head, wiping his face with his hand before looking at his palm. *No blood. Not dead.* It was a miracle. Pottinger had put a gun to his head and pulled the trigger. He should be dead. He shook his head, still very much on his shoulders, and rode on.

A misfire. A blooming misfire!

As he entered the scrub, forest thickening, moonlight thinning, he reinforced his vow. *I'm done. That's it. I'm going straight. I'm getting Kitty and leaving.*

Frank Gardiner was dead. The bullet had misfired but it had killed him all the same. Frank Gardiner, King of the Road, Prince of Thieves, never came out of that forest. But a man called Francis Christie did, resurrected, reborn and, even more astoundingly, reformed.

* * *

Forbes, 10 August 1862

There was no way of avoiding it. No way of spinning it. It was a fucking disaster. So Sir Frederick Pottinger sat his arse in a chair and he wrote. He dug his fountain tip into the page, the force ripping parchment and spilling ink, the black pigment pooling on the page like blood. Fitting. This report was more painful than the deepest cut.

'Being aware that Frank Gardiner, the bushranger, was enamoured of Mrs Brown, and believing that he would take advantage of her husband's absence to tender his addresses, I proceeded on Saturday with eight men to the premises,' Pottinger wrote.

I arrived at 12 pm, and leaving four of the men in charge I went with Senior Sergeant Sanderson and Trooper Holster to watch the place; I subsequently sent Sub-Inspector Norton and Trooper Holster to guard the front while Senior Sergeant Sanderson and I hid ourselves in the bush. We discovered the house dark and silent as though he was asleep.

After about half an hour we saw a light struck and in a few minutes a woman made her appearance and commenced to collect wood for the purpose of making a fire, but neither Sergeant Sanderson nor I could identify the woman, as we were concealed at a distance of 150 yards from where she was standing, in a thick pine-tree scrub. It might have been 20 or 25 minutes after my seeing the woman that I observed a man mounted on a white horse approaching Brown's house at quite a pace.

I called upon Sanderson to fall back, and we did so to our original position; suddenly the noise of horse's hoofs sounded nearer and nearer when I saw Gardiner cantering leisurely along. I waited until he came within five yards of me and levelled my carbine at him across his horse's shoulder (the weapon, I swear, being about three yards from his body).

I called upon him to stand; I cannot be mistaken, and on my oath I declare that the man was Frank Gardiner. Deeming it not advisable to lose a chance I prepared to shoot him, but the cap of my piece missed fire. Gardiner's horse then began to rear and plunge, and before I had time to adjust my gun, he had bolted into the bush.

As Gardiner was riding away on the back of the frightened animal, Sergeant Sanderson fired at him, as also did Holster; I called out to those who could hear me to 'shoot the wretch'.

Gardiner, however, made his escape.
Sir Frederick Pottinger

Ink spilled, page torn, he put his pen down. 'Damn you to hell, Gardiner,' Pottinger growled to the room.

The anonymous, unlikely tip-off that Gardiner was lurking around Kitty Brown's place had been good. Pottinger knew about the affair, but he didn't think Gardiner was stupid enough to remain anywhere near Forbes. But he'd had to check it out. This was Gardiner, his great white whale, and suddenly he was Ahab, spear in hand, beast breaching. And he had missed.

More failure was to come.

* * *

Forbes, 14 August 1862

Sir Frederick Pottinger slammed his hand onto his desk, palm first and with fearsome force.

'What do you mean none of the serial numbers were recorded?' he screamed.

Pottinger's case had just fallen over.

'All three of the banks?' he barked. 'All three failed to make records of the notes?'

Whack!

Both his palms belted the desk this time, sending a stack of papers into the air.

'Well, we have got nothing,' he said. 'No Gardiner, no notes, just some secondhand hearsay from a bloody lemonade seller. And a blooming lemonade seller with a criminal record, at that.'

Pottinger had recently learned that his star witness was facing numerous charges in Victoria, one of them rape. His palms hit the desk again then he took a breath. 'Time to bring in Charters,' he said.

Sir Frederick Pottinger was down to his last roll of the dice. He needed Daniel Charters to give up his mates.

* * *

Charters, the colour of chalk and shaking, stood in front of Pottinger.

'So have you thought about my offer some more?' Pottinger asked.

Charters had. In fact, that was all he had been thinking about. Pottinger had been working him over from day one, a poke here and a jab there.

'You know your mates think you put them in?'

'Be careful in there. They might do you in.'

'What do you reckon they are thinking now?'

'Better sleep with one eye open.'

Pottinger's end game had been revealed when Charters had been released, bail mysteriously met.

'Give us names and you won't go back in,' Pottinger had said. 'They will kill you if they see you again. We have told them you are our informer. We will give you some time to think it over.'

That time was now up.

Pottinger held a pair of cuffs in his hands and shook the chains. 'So what will it be?' he asked. 'We going to put you back in that cell?'

Charters stayed silent.

'You can be the only man who doesn't hang,' Pottinger said. 'We have matched the notes, we have witnesses, and we have the gold. I'm offering you your life. One man will get immunity. If it is not you, it will be someone else. Do you think you are the only one we are talking to?'

Charters shrugged.

'Well, I would like the man that goes free to be you,' Pottinger continued. 'I know you were dragged into this. I know this is your first crime. But make no mistake, you will be put to death if you do not accept what I am offering right now. So what will it be?'

Charters nodded, slowly but surely. 'I'll give you the names,' he said.

And he did – at least some.

'It was Frank Gardiner,' Charters said. 'Gardiner forced me to do it.'

'And who else?' Pottinger pressed. 'John Gilbert? Henry Manns?' He swung the cuffs, the chains taking a chunk out of his desk.

Charters nodded. 'Manns,' he said. 'Yes. Gilbert too.'

'And who else, goddamn it?' Pottinger bellowed.

'A guy called Billy,' Charters lied. 'Another called Charlie. I don't know their last names. I had never seen them before.'

Pottinger was losing his patience. He knew Gardiner was involved. Everyone knew he was involved. But Gardiner couldn't be found. And Gilbert and Manns? He had already arrested them, caught them red-handed with the gold, and now they too were on the run.

'What about Hall?' he shouted. 'I want Hall. I know that bastard was there.'

Charters looked like he was going to vomit. 'No,' he said. 'Hall wasn't there.'

Time to go for the throat.

'So you have admitted guilt?' he continued. 'You just told me then that you were involved. And you have given us nobody we didn't already know. So right now you are the only person we have. The governor is demanding a scapegoat: this is the biggest robbery in the history of the colony. Do you want to be the only man that hangs? Should we go let your mates out now? Send you off to the gallows?'

Pottinger got another name.

'John Bow,' Charters said. 'John Bow was involved.'

And then he got another.

'Alexander Fordyce,' Charters said. 'The barman. The drunk.'

But that was all. Charters refused to give up his best mate, Hall. And he refused to dob in O'Meally, the madman, because retribution from his equally violent family was assured.

Pottinger pushed and prodded. Made threats and false promises. He was desperate to get Ben Hall. But Charters would not yield, and without Charters he had nothing and no one. Just further failure, ridicule and ruin.

'Very well,' Pottinger said.

He produced a piece of paper, soon to be signed and secured in his safe. As for Hall, well, Pottinger would get him sooner or later, legally or not. Gardiner too.

* * *

Forbes, 23 August 1862

Sir Frederick Pottinger removed the padlock himself. He swung back the heavy iron door and looked into the cage.

'Ben Hall,' he said. 'William Hall, John Brown, Patrick O'Meally. Step forward.'

They did so.

'You are being released,' he said. 'Charges against you have been dropped.'

Pottinger said it matter-of-factly, his face devoid of emotion. But he was furious. He knew he was letting at least one guilty man walk free. He had spent the last nine days searching for some new evidence that would keep Hall behind bars. Again he had knocked on doors and bailed up men on the street. He'd gone back to Sandy Creek and searched Hall's house. He'd found nothing. In a fit of rage he'd considered burning Hall's hut to the ground. *He might go free but I could make sure he has nothing to come home to.*

But he'd resisted. Pottinger had also gone back to Charters. He had pressed as hard as he could, but this Judas would not give up his Jesus.

'What about me?' asked John O'Meally.

Pottinger smiled. 'Not you,' he said. 'You are still facing charges.'

Pottinger had next to nothing on O'Meally, but by the grace of God he had convinced the court to continue his remand.

'See you soon, Ben,' O'Meally said, giving him a nod. He shook his father's hand. 'Keep a drink on the bar for me, Dad,' he said.

O'Meally grunted at Pottinger, turned and walked to the back of the cell.

McGuire looked stunned that his name was also left out of those released. And Pottinger didn't wait for him to ask.

'Oh, we have something on you too, McGuire,' he said. 'I told you that you were going to swing. You should have talked when you had the chance.'

Chains clattered outside the hut.

'Bring 'em in,' Pottinger said.

An officer opened the outer door to The Logs and pushed in two men, their hands cuffed, their faces blank.

'Bow?' said O'Meally. 'Fordyce? What are you doing here?'

'Shut up, John,' Hall barked. 'Don't say a thing.'

This time Pottinger showed some emotion. He smiled. After his latest chat with the turncoat Charters he had gone to Wheogo earlier that day and arrested these two men. He pushed them into the cage.

'You know these fellas, lads?' Pottinger said to Bow and Fordyce while looking at O'Meally. 'Fancy that.'

But Pottinger wasn't smiling when he was forced to give William Hall back the cash he was sure had come from the robbery. He growled before handing over the fifty-pound note that would have hanged them all had the bank just done its job and recorded the serial numbers.

Pottinger at least had the men to go with the names Charters had given up. He would get his conviction, case solved and job well done. Maybe they would never love him, but they would respect him. Surely.

* * *

Murrumburrah, 2 December 1862

Henry Manns should have been in China. He wasn't. No, this man who was wanted for the biggest heist in Australian history was still in New South Wales. In fact, he was in Murrumburrah, less than a hundred miles away from where he committed the colony's most famous crime.

Manns knew he was one of the most wanted men in the colony. He also knew there was a thousand-pound reward for any information that would lead to his arrest. Yet still he walked down the main street of Murrumburrah after working a full day in the mines.

Manns saw a police officer up ahead on the street and instinctively turned and made off in the opposite direction. He made for the bush, a man suddenly in a hurry.

'What are you doing?' shouted the officer, Constable Moore. 'Stand!'

Manns gave up his attempt to escape and emerged from the bush.

'Name's Henry Turner,' Manns said. 'I was just going for a piss.'

Moore continued with his questions about where he had come from and where he was going, but Manns hesitated and couldn't give the trap a straight answer. So Moore arrested him.

'What for?' Manns cried.

'For being a suspicious person,' the copper said flatly.

Manns was taken to Lambing Flat and locked up to face further questions.

* * *

Pottinger could not believe his luck when he chanced upon the prisoner in the lock-up.

'Well, I'll be …' he said. 'If it isn't Henry Turner. Do you think I would forget your face? I have been seeing it every night since you escaped. And I know who you really are.'

Pottinger had been called a coward because of this man. Ridiculed and almost ruined.

'Henry Manns,' he said in a low voice, 'you are under arrest for robbing the Eugowra escort. And you are going to hang.'

Manns was soon one step closer to his fate when he and his fellow prisoners were escorted to Bathurst Gaol. Fearful of an escape attempt, the authorities had decided to move the four men – Pottinger had reluctantly released O'Meally after failing to find enough evidence to charge him – to this much more secure and daunting prison, 100-odd miles closer to Sydney, where they would eventually face trial in the colony's highest court.

* * *

Bathurst, 22 January 1863

A metallic noise rang out as the guard knocked his baton against the bars.

'McGuire,' the prisoner officer said, 'you and your mates are being transferred tomorrow. Prepare yourself.'

McGuire had been waiting for this moment ever since he had been locked up in a solitary cell. The place was a nightmare: stinking of shit, hot in the day and freezing at night, and full of flies, rats and riffraff.

It had been lonely too, with Manns, Fordyce and Bow locked away in other wings of the sprawling gaol. Each of the accused had been placed in solitary confinement, the Crown taking away any chance for them to conspire.

McGuire didn't think Sydney would be much better – Darlinghurst Gaol was also notoriously bad – but at least he would be a step closer to being freed. McGuire had no doubt he would walk. He hadn't been part of the robbery, after all.

So McGuire got out of bed, a smile on his face. That smile was soon wiped away, though, when the officer put him in cuffs and chains before locking him back in his cell.

'How am I supposed to sleep in these?' McGuire asked.

'You'll figure it out,' came the reply.

McGuire, Manns, Fordyce and Bow were all placed in restraints on the day before they were due to be transferred to Sydney to face trial. All four prisoners complained of a lack of sleep, cuts and bruising when they were collected at six o'clock the next morning.

'I didn't get a wink,' said McGuire when he was reunited with Fordyce, Manns and Bow in the prison eatery for breakfast. 'Bloody things rattled and woke me every time I moved.'

After they'd been fed bacon, eggs and pancakes, the quartet were marched out of the goal, just as the clock struck 8 am.

'Well what have we got here?' McGuire inquired, as he was confronted by a crowd, half the town turning out to get a glimpse of the alleged bushrangers. 'Bloody famous we are.'

The onlookers cheered as McGuire waved and smiled, the stockman every inch the celebrity. He thought he was another step closer to his freedom. The others, well, they weren't in such a good mood.

Newcomer Manns — still calling himself Turner — was still loudly professing his innocence. 'You have the wrong guy,' he said as he marched past a procession of armed troopers and towards the four-horse cart that would take them to Penrith. 'I haven't done a thing. I shouldn't be here.'

McGuire smiled at the young fool. Alexander Fordyce remained expressionless as he was pushed into the box, wooden walls reinforced with iron. He took up little room, being all skin and bone, half starved and sick. He sat next to John Bow, who was heavier but equally as glum.

The prisoners were guarded by sixteen armed police officers for the trip from Bathurst to Penrith, where they would be transferred onto a train. The escort stopped after forty gruelling miles, the road rugged, the horses tired.

'This isn't Penrith,' McGuire said. 'What's going on?'

An officer replied as he unlocked the box that had kept McGuire and the others safe and secure. 'We are at Hartley, lad,' he said. 'We've had enough for the day. We'll stop here tonight and have you on the train in the morning.'

McGuire was hoping for a good night's sleep after his night in chains. 'Another bloody cell,' he said, as he was led into a police station lock-up. He'd been expecting a hotel.

Things got worse. A local church minister was let into the cell. He preached for thirty minutes.

'That'll do,' McGuire shouted after the minister declared him a scoundrel who deserved the punishment that was sure to come his way. 'Get the fuck out of here or you will get some punishment of your own.'

The prisoners fared better the next day. The coach stopped at a pub eighteen miles from Penrith.

'You find another preacher?' McGuire asked, as he was released from the box.

The copper shook his head.

'Nah, just an innkeeper,' the officer said. 'Thought we would make up for the preacher with some booze.'

McGuire, Fordyce, Manns and Bow sat in the morning sun and drank a freshly poured beer delivered roadside by the publican. 'Best of luck lads,' he said. 'We're all rooting for you.'

Soon the men were at Penrith, where they were locked aboard a specially fortified and heavily guarded carriage. Next stop Sydney.

Chapter 6

THE TRIAL: DAY ONE

Darlinghurst, 24 January 1863

Sydney had come to a standstill. People lined the streets, wagons stalled, horses stopped. Police blew whistles and waved batons.

'Move,' they shouted. 'Clear the road. They can't get through.'

Soon a horse-drawn cart – fifteen feet long, blacked-out windows reinforced with iron – turned onto the street. Inside were Australia's four most notorious prisoners.

Henry Manns, John McGuire, Alexander Fordyce and John Bow were chained, cuffed and on their way to the Central Criminal Court to be tried for a capital crime. Australia's biggest ever criminal trial would begin in ten days.

'Let 'em through,' screamed the trap.

More whistles blew, more people were pushed off the street.

The pandemonium had begun at sunrise, news of the bushrangers' arrival sending the city into a spin. A human flood swamped Central Station as thousands pushed, pulled and elbowed their way onto the platforms. Finally the Penrith train arrived.

'Have a squiz at this,' McGuire said. 'Must be all of Sydney here to get a look at us desperate men.'

Sixty mounted troopers kept the heaving mass at bay. McGuire hadn't been far wrong in his estimate of the size of the crowd surrounding the celebrity prisoners. Another eight officers, immaculately dressed in their show uniforms, white gloves and polished boots pushed McGuire and the other prisoners into a coach that had been backed up against the platform. People in the throng booed, as they'd barely got a glimpse of the infamous men.

'Kings we are,' McGuire chirped. 'It's a royal equipage. We just need us a queen.' He winked at Fordyce. 'Or have we got one?'

Whistles and waving arms dispersed the crowd, and the 'black maria' prison car rattled and rolled its way through the freshly cleared street. Next stop Darlinghurst Gaol ...

Opened in 1841 after twenty years of on-again, off-again construction, Darlinghurst Gaol was a Gothic Revival nightmare. Made from sandstone cut by convicts, whipped as they lugged every brick, it was built by pain and, more so, built to punish. The gaol was linked by an underground passage to the central court so that the prisoners could be tried, convicted and killed on the same block. Twenty-seven people had been executed in the prison by the time the escort robbers arrived, Robert Hudson the first to be thrown from the gallows twenty-two years before in 1841 in a double execution with George Stroud. It was a house of the damned.

The thrill of seeing Sydney streets lined for him left Manns as soon as his cell door was slammed shut.

'You have a room with a view,' said the prison guard as he locked him in. 'Take a look-see through your door.'

Manns did and his heart sank. He was looking death in the face: a wooden platform raised twenty feet from the ground with no railing, a trapdoor and a one-way set of stairs.

Manns had been locked up in E wing: the home of the hangman, last stop for the damned. He cried himself to sleep.

* * *

Darlinghurst, 3 February 1863

'Stand,' said the officer. 'It's time.'

Manns was ready. Showered, suited up, he had been sitting in the holding cell with the rest of the accused for an hour. He didn't speak to any of them.

'Out,' the officer continued, pointing to the concrete corridor.

Manns followed McGuire.

Ouch! He was hit with a barrel in the back.

'Give me a reason to use it,' said the officer.

Eight armed officers escorted the four prisoners to the court through the underground concrete passages, up a flight of stairs and into the dock of the Central Criminal Court. The court was crowded, but for this arrival there were no cheers. The silence was eerie. Reporters sat with pens and pads. Lawyers with piles of papers. The four men took their place in the dock. They sat and soon they were asked to rise.

'Alexander Fordyce, John Bow, John McGuire and Henry Turner,' the court clerk said moments after Justice Edward Wise took his seat, adjusted his glasses and gave the clerk a nod, 'you are charged that you, in company with other persons to the attorney general unknown, did on the fifteenth June in the year 1862, near Eugowra in the colony of New South Wales, assault James Condell, Henry Moran, William Haviland and John Fegan, did put them in bodily fear and danger of their lives, and did steal from them four boxes and ten bags, 2,719 ounces of gold, the property of Her Majesty the Queen, and 3,700 pounds in cash, and that you did steal two firearms, to wit Terry rifles, and a cloak, the property of Her Majesty the Queen, from the persons of the said Condell, Moran, Haviland and Fegan, and that immediately before the said robbery, you did feloniously wound Condell.'

The clerk addressed Fordyce.

'Alexander Fordyce, how say you? Are you guilty or not guilty?' the clerk asked.

'Not guilty!' Fordyce shouted.

The declaration brought a cheer.

'Silence!' the judge ordered.

And they obeyed.

'John Bow, how say you?' the clerk continued.

'I'm not guilty!' Bow said.

More applause.

The judge again called for calm.

'John McGuire, how say you?' the clerk asked.

'Not guilty!' he beamed.

The court hissed and howled.

'Silence,' the magistrate said. 'This is not a carnival. Order!'

The clerk turned his attention to the final prisoner. 'Henry Turner, how say you?'

And all of a sudden Henry Turner became Henry Manns.

'I am not Henry Turner,' he said. 'And I have never been known by the name of Henry Turner. My name is Henry Manns.'

No cheers now, just silence. Defence counsel Mr Robert McIntosh Isaacs rushed to the dock.

'What are you doing?' he asked Manns. 'This is stupidity.'

The lawyer was dumbfounded. No one would believe a word that came from his client's mouth after this.

'I'm coming clean,' Manns said. 'I don't want to die.'

The lawyer urged his client not to change his name. But Manns was adamant he was now Manns.

'Please delete the name Turner from the record,' said Isaacs, 'and replace the name with Manns.'

The judge agreed and the clerk addressed Henry Manns. 'And how so do you plead?' he asked.

'Not guilty,' said Manns.

The court erupted.

'Silence,' the judge said, 'or I will adjourn proceedings.'

Isaacs then pleaded for Manns' trial to be postponed, arguing that he had had no way of communicating with his client until this point.

'I will not at present decide whether this prisoner should be tried at this sitting or not,' the judge said, 'but I will merely say that he will not be tried today. I will postpone his trial until further order, but I might mention to the prisoner that if he can ascertain anything in respect of his witnesses, he had better do so and lay such information before the court. Should nothing further transpire the prisoner will most probably be tried this sitting, though not today.'

Henry Manns was escorted from the court.

It took ten minutes for the court to civilise, the courtroom having become more a colosseum than a house of tort.

'I will be representing the remaining prisoners,' James Martin QC said. 'McGuire, Fordyce and Bow. I will prove they are all not guilty of the crime alleged.'

And finally the trial began. Attorney General John Fletcher Hargrave rose for the prosecution. Educated in Cambridge and trained in London, Hargrave was a formidable force. The court seemed to hold its breath while waiting for him to begin.

'I need not ask the jury, in dealing with the merits of this case, to dismiss from your minds the technicalities with which the information appears to surround it,' Hargrave started.

'As lengthy as that document is, the facts of the case lay only in a few words. It contains three counts, all setting out the same offence but charging the infliction of the wound at different times. This is because an Act of parliament requires that it should be stated whether the wound was inflicted before, after or at the time of the robbery, so that in all cases it should be shown the robbery and the wounding were immediately connected with each other and therefore a capital offence. This is the cause of repetition of facts in the case.'

He took a moment's silence, looking at the crowded court and then towards the dock. All three prisoners sat without expression.

'The substantial offence for which the prisoners are charged is wounding and robbery,' Hargrave said. 'The indictment names all the articles which were stolen. I need scarcely tell you to dismiss as much as possible from your minds about what you have read or heard in the print in relation to the robbery and fix your attention on only the facts that will come before you in sworn testimony.

Hargrave took another pause.

'The facts are these,' Hargrave said. 'On the fifteenth of June last year, the gold escort, proceeding in the mail with the regular driver and escorted by three police constables, some of whom will give evidence today, started from Forbes and was stopped at a place known as Eugowra Rocks. Arriving at that spot the escort found their way impeded by drays and bullock teams drawn across the road, which compelled them to leave their usual track and travel closer to rocks that bordered the road.

'They were at once, when close to the rocks, fired upon by a number of persons concealed behind those rocks. Luckily, despite the large number of shots and the short distance, no loss of life followed, though two troopers were wounded and the coach riddled with bullets. Now, a more atrocious breach of the peace than this can scarcely be conceived.'

He stared directly at the dock after making the poignant declaration.

'Her Majesty's mail was deliberately stopped by a number of persons who had banded themselves together to make war, as it were, upon the government, to stop the escort and to deliberately shoot the troopers,' Hargrave continued. 'When that had been done the robbers showed themselves in numbers doubling that of the escort and after ransacking the mail took possession of the gold that was being carried down to Sydney, seized the rifles and cloaks of the police, and took two horses.

'Now can you possibly conceive a crime more hostile to the peace and well-being of society at large than this, the more especially as the escort was at the time coming down with property to the amount of over ten thousand pounds?'

Hargrave looked directly at the jury, twelve men seemingly cut from the same cloth.

'In regards to the crime itself,' Hargrave said, 'there can be no doubt it was committed, nor will my learned friends who conduct the defence deny it. I need not, therefore, labour this point, although the law requires that the robbery should be proved by evidence.

'Now, the first general observation that strikes the mind on hearing of an offence of this kind is that it is one that was not likely to have been taken up by a number of men who were strangers to the district in which it was to be carried out. It is utterly impossible that a number of persons coming together accidentally and meeting in a part of the country unknown to them could have concocted such an outrage as this, and consequently the conclusion is naturally arrived at that the whole affair must have been got up by persons well acquainted with the district and with the movements of the escort, who were fully aware of the hour at which it passed different points and of the spot at which it might be most easily attacked.'

Fordyce was already sweating, the courtroom fast becoming a February furnace.

'This impression is still further corroborated by the fact that the men concerned in the outrage were all closely disguised with red scarves and crimson shirts as though they feared to be recognised, a fear they would not have entertained had they been strangers in the district,' Hargrave said.

'Persons who enter upon lawless undertakings of this kind are guided by the same spirit of self-protection as others who are engaged in good purpose, and therefore it was that precautions were taken against being recognised and that so much care was afterwards taken to remove all possible traces of their complicity in this nefarious transaction.

'The robbery then will be proved to have unmistakably taken place and the wounds will be certified to by the parties who received them and from the evidence of these persons there will be no doubt as to their having occurred at the time of the robbery and to their having been inflicted by the persons committing the robbery.

'The whole transaction will be shown to be one of one single, undivided character, so there will not be the slightest necessity for proving the particular individual who fired the shots that inflicted the wounds, since all parties to the felonious act of robbing would be aiders and abettors in the wounding, if not its perpetrators.'

Hargrave, in his groove, audience completely his, again looked to the dock.

'The most important part of the evidence, as affecting the prisoners at the bar, will be that which relates to their identification as forming part of the robbers,' Hargrave said. 'From the care with which the robbery was concocted and the skill displayed in doing away with all traces of guilt, you cannot expect to have that clear and explicit evidence of identification that might be expected in other cases.

'But you will have laid before you a number of minute points which fit into each other, and which in the aggregate form such a connected link that I think when you come to look into it, you will see such a chain of events as will convince you that the prisoners are three of the men connected with the robbery.'

And then the attorney general rolled his gun, a cannon in the case called Charters.

'Further to assist you, you will have, what is often obtained in these cases in which so many parties are participators, the evidence of one of the parties in the transactions,' Hargrave said, chest now puffed like a peacock. 'The informer, Daniel Charters, will be prepared on oath to detail all the facts of the case in so far as he knows them. This person was a resident in the neighbourhood and, under a compulsion that he found impossible to resist, was compelled to join them.

'In all such enterprises it was absolutely essential that the men should be under the leadership and guidance of some person who was well acquainted with this country, all the ranges and gullies and with the best mode of retreat in order to make good their escape after the outrage had been committed.'

Pausing for effect, he looked around the courtroom.

'Such a person to whom was confided this task will be placed before you,' Hargrave said. 'He will detail to you the way in which he guided the robbers to the spot, all that occurred beforehand and all that was done in regard to the placing of these men in the ambush. He was not present during the actual conflict, for he was sent to the rear with instructions to hold the horses, but he will tell you how he heard the firing and how after it ceased these persons, whose names he will give, came towards him with the gold, how they mounted their horses, how he guided them to different parts of the country, and how at last they divided themselves into parties of three and scattered in different parts of the country, he himself going with two others who were afterwards chased by the police so closely that they had to leave the packhorse with the gold behind them.'

McGuire squirmed, Fordyce frowned, the dock suddenly more uncomfortable than ever.

'Of the conscientiousness and truth of this witness, it will be for you, the jury, to judge and you will be able to come to a pretty correct conclusion after hearing the searching cross-examination to which he will be sure to be subjected to by my learned friends,' Hargrave continued.

'After this, you will give the evidence such weight as you consider it entitled but also receive in its support such circumstances as may be given in evidence by other witnesses and which, coming out independently and without the possibility of collusion, will be safely accepted in confirmation of this witness.'

Once again Hargrave looked at the jurors, some also showing the effects of the summer heat.

'I would never be one to suggest to a jury that they should press evidence against a prisoner,' Hargrave said. 'Or even that they should weigh it too strictly against him where they cannot completely satisfy their minds that it is sufficient, but at the same time I ask you to take this into consideration that eight violent men have deliberately set the law at defiance and have endeavoured, from a place of shelter and concealment, most basely to strike down three policemen who were in the execution of their duty to the Queen and to the colony and who were entirely unprotected, that they by these means possessed themselves of the large sum of over ten thousand pounds and they had then most carefully destroyed every trace of their crime.

'The evidence will be sufficient to convince you that these prisoners have all been parties to the crime. I should also mention that parties to a deed of this kind are not expected to meet at the point where the crime is to be committed and there concoct all the details at the moment. On the contrary, much deliberation and preparation is required and accessories before the fact are wanted, at whose houses the meetings are held and under whose counsel the proceedings are taken.'

Attorney General Hargrave now looked directly at John McGuire.

'Such a person as this is now before you in the prisoner McGuire,' Hargrave said. 'He was not present when the crime was committed, nor had he gone with them, but the robbers met at his house before proceeding to the spot where the outrage was committed and it was to his house that they had been sent after the robbery had been consummated, in order to procure rations.

'This will be clearly proved and thus more complete evidence to show McGuire to have been an accessory before the fact can scarcely be expected.'

Hargrave walked to the centre of the room, making sure all eyes were on him, a showman steeled for a spectacular send-off.

'I shall now bring the evidence before you,' Hargrave said. 'But prior to doing so I will make this remark: the extreme solemnity and importance of your duty in a case which involves a capital punishment I fully recognise, and whilst I am sure that every reasonable doubt of the prisoners' guilt will receive due weight at your hands, I would yet point out to you that you must come to a conclusion upon the evidence alone, and without any regard to what may follow your verdict. You, as well as myself, gentlemen, may have a painful duty to perform but it is an imperative one and in doing it we must place out of view any consequences that may follow to the prisoners.

'With those consequences we have nothing to do. The law has divided our duties so as to divide the responsibility. I, in my capacity of public prosecutor, place before you the evidence that tells against the prisoners and I do so unhesitatingly, despite the consequences. Did I allow myself to think of the consequences to these prisoners? I can assure you, gentlemen, that I ... that I ...'

Now the show had really started, Hargrave stopping, with tears in his eyes as he looked at the men he would be doing his best to damn.

'At any rate, gentlemen,' Hargrave said, composed again, 'I am sure you will do justice in the case and I shall now lay the evidence before you.'

Hargrave walked from the floor and looked to where Sir Frederick Pottinger sat, giving him a nod.

'Call Sir Frederick Pottinger!' the clerk barked.

The baronet police inspector entered the witness box and rested his right hand on a Bible. 'I swear that this evidence will be the truth and the whole truth and nothing but the truth,' Pottinger said. 'So help me God!'

And then he began, well rehearsed and ready.

'I am an inspector of police,' Pottinger said. 'I arrested the prisoner, McGuire, on the twenty-seventh of July 1862. I also arrested Bow on the twenty-third of August and was present when the other prisoner was taken. I arrested McGuire at his own place at Wheogo. I apprehended McGuire and four others at the same time.'

He looked towards McGuire; the prisoner was staring daggers.

'Some banknotes were found on McGuire,' Pottinger continued.

'Objection,' came the cry as James Martin jumped to his feet. 'I object to this evidence concerning notes,' he shouted. 'Such evidence cannot be given unless the notes referred to are produced in this court.'

The judge agreed and consulted Pottinger before directing him to continue.

'Some papers were found on him,' Pottinger corrected. 'They had the appearance of having been wet and were given back to McGuire. I had no conversation about the escort robbery with him. He was present, I think, when a conversation took place about a nugget of gold. I also know a person named Turner, or Manns, who was arraigned today. I apprehended him at Mirrool with another man, named Darcy, who was afterwards rescued.'

Pottinger turned to look for Manns, momentarily forgetting he was no longer there.

'I found on Manns 215 ounces of gold in an escort bag,' Pottinger said. 'It was enclosed in a sack and attached to the saddle of the horse he was riding on. Some banknotes were taken from his person but I observed nothing more on him. I now produce the bag.'

Pottinger pulled out a sack and handed it to the clerk of the court.

'It is similar to the bags used by the escorts,' Pottinger said. 'But I did not notice any seal on it when I found it on the prisoner.'

Pottinger took a moment before he got to the part he wanted to forget, not speak about it now with all the eyes and ears of the colony watching and listening.

'On the ninth of July 1862, Manns was rescued and the notes were lost by the horse on which they were carried getting away,' Pottinger said. 'I was in search of the robbers from the fifteenth of June to the tenth of July.'

Now Pottinger waited for the questions. Hargrave stood and addressed his witness.

'Were you present during the evidence of Baldwin and Charters at Bathurst Court?' Hargrave asked.

'I was present when Mr Baldwin, the storekeeper, was examined,' Pottinger replied. 'When Charters was examined at Bathurst I am not sure I was present, but Charters has given me information—'

'Objection!' Martin stole the floor. 'We know nothing of Charters in connection with this case,' he shouted. 'Let him be produced and examined!'

He was overruled.

'It was about a fortnight after his arrest that Charters gave me some information,' Pottinger continued.

There were no further questions.

Sir Frederick Pottinger left the witness box, the court filled with murmuring.

'Call Inspector Sanderson!' the clerk shouted.

The police officer who chased the bandits into Mount Wheogo took the stand. He looked every inch the hero.

'I am a sub-inspector of police,' Sanderson said. 'I remember the escort robbery. When I went in search of the robbers I started from Lachlan at nine pm on the eighteenth of June and reached Wheogo on the Thursday morning. I was just about leaving the house of a man named Hall, whose place I had been searching, when we saw a horseman coming from the mountain. He bolted on seeing us.

'We followed and by the aid of a black tracker came upon a camp where there were bottles, some straps of leather, a bone of meat, some tea and other indications of men having very recently camped.'

Sanderson turned to the judge.

'We lost the track in some broken ground but afterwards again came upon it,' Sanderson said. 'I saw at least the tracks of five horses and they all seemed fresh made. We followed the tracks through a dense scrub till about four in the afternoon, till we came upon a packhorse. I dismounted and seized the horse and found on it 1,250 ounces of gold, two rifles and a police cloak. I knew by the stamp that they were government rifles. I believe but cannot swear that Sergeant Condell saw the rifles. I produce the cloak found on the horse. It is a police uniform cloak.'

Mr Hargrave smiled as the second piece of evidence was handed to the court clerk.

'When the gold was found it was made up in three loose bags similar to the one now on the bench,' Sanderson continued. 'The bags were strapped on the horse's saddle in a leather valise and fastened with some reins. I produce the three bags. They are enclosed now in new bags for protection. I do not remember anything else in particular that was found.'

Hargrave sat still. No questions. No queries. Sanderson was dismissed.

'Call Sergeant Condell!' the clerk said, the court now in full swing.

The officer shot and wounded in the robbery walked to the stand, ready to tell the story of Australia's biggest heist.

'I am a sergeant of police,' Condell said. 'I was stationed at Forbes. I took charge of the escort at Forbes on the fifteenth of June with Moran, Haviland and the driver. There were four gold boxes and we had the usual arms with us. Mr Sanderson gave us the gold boxes and I saw them put in the carriage. We left Forbes at about twelve o'clock.'

He spoke without expression.

'We proceeded about thirty miles and on reaching Eugowra, where there are some high rocks over the road, we saw some bullock teams,' Condell said. 'The bullocks were lying on the road and caused us to cross the road at an angle, and turning that angle we heard some shots.'

He paused, collecting himself before continuing his self-convenient version of the truth.

'The turning off the road took us closer to where the shots came,' Condell said. 'I was struck in the left side. There was continuous firing. The horses took fright and started off but the coach came to some stones and was capsized. On coming to, I saw Haviland assisting Moran, who was wounded.'

He turned towards the prisoners, his eyes suddenly finding fire.

'Afterwards I saw two men,' Condell resumed, 'and they said, "There's the bloody wretches, shoot them!" Two other shots were then fired. I saw the men rushing down to where the coach lay. I was hurt in the fall and crept into the bush. Afterwards I heard shouts from the direction of the coach.'

The gripping account had the spectators in the gallery on the edge of their seats.

'I saw the coach afterwards at Clements' station,' Condell said. 'Three balls were in it, the gold was gone. Clements' station is about a quarter of a mile from where the coach was attacked. I never saw the gold boxes afterwards. The coach was brought in with two horses; it left Forbes with four. I never saw the other horses afterwards.'

Condell looked down, his eyes examining his torso.

'The wound I received bled,' Condell said, 'and there were six other shot marks in my clothes. There was continuous firing. They fired till I fell from the coach and fired two shots afterwards.'

Hargrave rose and fired his own shot, a question for his witness.

'Did you fire on the attackers?' the attorney general asked.

'I fired in return after the first volley,' Condell said proudly.

'That is all,' said Hargrave.

James Martin declined to cross-examine the witness. His notebook, however, was fast filling.

The prosecution called for its next witness.

'Call Senior Constable Moran!' the clerk cried.

Moran took the stand.

'I left Forbes with the escort,' he said. 'I saw the gold boxes put into the coach. At the Eugowra Rocks we noticed the road was blocked up with two bullock teams and some horse teams. I heard someone say, "Fire!" I looked up and saw five or six men looking down from the rocks, their faces were blackened.

'There were four men in front and two behind and they were all dressed alike in red shirts. They fired at the word "fire" and I was wounded at the first discharge in the groin and the wound bled.'

The courtroom groaned as one.

'Haviland and I were on the back seat and returned fire,' Moran said, twisting the truth to save face. 'When the coach got to the rocks I was thrown off and I heard the men say, "Shoot the wretches!" Then, thrown off, I got close to Clements' fence. Haviland helped me down the road. There was firing after I fell.'

Moran was dismissed.

'Call John Fegan!' the clerk said.

The driver of the coach was soon recalling the shoot-out at Eugowra Rocks.

'I was mail driver of the escort on the fifteenth of June last year,' Fegan said, 'and had four horses in my coach. I lost some of the horses in the attack. They were the property of Ford and Co., and Phillip Mylecharane was also one of the owners.'

Fegan looked uncomfortable, he was very much a driver and not a public speaker.

'I was in the coach when it was attacked,' Fegan continued. 'I then lost all four horses but next morning saw two of them at Clements' where they went after getting away.

'About a week later I saw a black horse, one of the leaders, and afterwards at the Forbes camp the other. This was a dark brown horse with a switch tail. I was asked to identify the horses as the property of Ford and Co. and I did. I received that horse from Sanderson.'

Hargrave rose and asked the driver if he had been shot in the attack.

'I was not wounded but a ball went through my hat and another through my coat,' Fegan said. 'There were eight or ten bullets in the coach. The gold boxes were gone when we came back to the coach, the mailbags were opened and the contents scattered about.'

And that's when the prosecution dropped their bomb.

'Call Daniel Charters!' said the clerk.

The court erupted, people jumping to their feet, twisting and turning towards the back of the room, all agape.

'Silence! shouted the judge, his court out of control.

Daniel Charters walked slowly, eyes to the floor. He refused to look at the men who he was likely to condemn to death.

'Judas,' said McGuire, under his breath.

Silence was again called for as the clerk produced the Bible.

'The evidence you are about to give to the court and the jury sworn and between our sovereign Lady the Queen and the accused will be the truth, the whole truth and nothing but the truth so help me God,' the clerk said. 'Please say, "So help me God".'

'So help me God,' whispered Charters, his declaration just audible.

'What is your name?' asked Hargrave.

'Daniel Charters,' the witness replied.

'Where do you live?' Hargrave asked next.

'The Lachlan,' Charters said. 'I live at Humbug Creek.'

'Will you tell the court about the incidents in which you took part in June of last year?'

Charters hesitated. 'In the beginning,' he started and then stopped. 'In the beginning of June last, I was within twenty-five miles of Forbes – it was on the fifteenth of June.' That was all he could get out.

'Do you know the prisoners?' Hargrave asked, taking a more direct approach.

'I know the prisoners,' Charters said, daring to take his first glance towards the dock. 'I saw John Bow and Fordyce on the twelfth of June when they were within a quarter of a mile off Mrs Pheeley's station. I was driving some horses and met Frank Gardiner – Gardiner is a bushranger – John Gilbert and the two prisoners, Bow and Fordyce. They were coming towards me.'

'Continue,' urged the attorney general.

'Gardiner rode up to me about fifteen yards in advance of the others,' Charters said.

'He asked me where I was going to. I said to my sister's. He then said he wanted me to go with him for a few days. I said that I could not for if I was seen with him I should be thought of as bad as him. He said I must go with him as he wanted me to show him the road to some place that he did not name.

'Gardiner was armed. He had a double-barrelled gun slung to his horse and two revolvers on his person. Gilbert was armed and Fordyce was also armed.'

Martin shook his head, the defence counsel unimpressed as Charters painted himself the victim.

'When I declined going with him Gardiner put his hand on his revolver and told me I must come,' Charters said. 'We went towards John Reeve's place. When we got there Gardiner went with Gilbert to fetch oats. They went and came back after a few hours.

'On the next morning Gardiner said we had to go in the direction of Forbes. On the Friday we got within six miles of Forbes and camped there. We were within a mile-and-a-half of the police camp at Forbes.'

Martin's pen went into overdrive.

'We camped again and Gilbert went into Forbes,' Charters said. 'I heard Gardiner tell him to fetch six double-barrelled guns, some rations, an American tomahawk, some blacking, some scarves and some caps and also a flask of powder.'

Charters was now speaking confidently for a man telling pork pies.

'The men were at this time camped at a fire,' Charters continued. 'They were lying down. Gilbert returned about one or two in the morning. He had some other men with him, one of them named Charlie.'

The prisoners raised their eyes. *Charlie? Who is Charlie? Fucking liar.*

'When the men came they had six guns and the other articles they were sent for. They also had some rations and we consumed part of them. I heard Gilbert say that he had great trouble in getting the guns and the axe as there was only one store where he could buy them.'

Charters moved on, the courtroom fully engrossed in this first-hand account from one of the men involved in Australia's most famous robbery.

'On the Saturday morning Gardiner said we would go on to the Eugowra Mountain,' Charters said. 'We cantered across a piece of clear ground towards the river and, in doing so, Gilbert lost his revolver. Gardiner rode mostly behind the others. I asked him where we were going and he said he would tell me by and by. We camped on Saturday night near Eugowra.'

The spectators again sat on the edge of their seats, faces forward, utterly engrossed.

'On the Sunday Gardiner rose early,' Charters continued, 'and loaded the arms. I asked what he was going to do and he said, "You'll see – if I'm lucky today I mean to stick up the escort." I saw Gardiner load the pieces. He put seven or eight balls in each gun barrel. We then had some lobsters and sardines for breakfast that were bought by Gilbert. The blacking was used in disguising the faces on the Sunday morning.'

Now to the crime.

'On Sunday morning we went to the mountain,' Charters said. 'We tied our horses up at the direction of Gardiner and were each given a gun. We then went to the large rocks overlooking the road. Gardiner went down to the road, stepped the distance, returned and said, "That will do."'

Charters looked to the jury before continuing.

'I then suggested that someone should go back and look to the horses that we had left tied up,' Charters said. 'Gardiner studied me for a while then said, "Very well, you go. You're bloody frightened for your life and you're the best to go." I said I had never done anything of this kind and did not like firing on men who never did me any harm.'

Bow and Fordyce could not believe what was being said. Their looks were thunderous.

'I then went away leaving seven men at the rocks of whom Fordyce and Bow were two,' Charters said. 'Fordyce was under the influence of drink and two or three times Gardiner had said, "If you don't wake up and look sharp, I'll cut your rations bloody short." I went and found the horses alright and while away I heard firing of several discharges.'

Hargrave gestured for Charters to continue. He was outwardly pleased with his witness. *So far so good ...*

'The men returned with some gold boxes, some rifles and a cloak,' Charters said. 'The gold was placed on the horses. Gardiner made the remark that it was a very narrow escape. When the men came back I asked Gardiner if anyone was shot. He said, "No and I am bloody glad of it, but if there has been it was their own fault. I told them to stand and they fired upon me." Gardiner then ordered us to move off to the place where we made camp the previous night.'

Now Charters would reveal how the score was divided and how they escaped.

'We came on a piece of clear ground,' Charters said, 'about a mile-and-a-half on, and near a creek. Gardiner said, "We'll stop and open these boxes and lighten the loads on the horses." The boxes were opened with a tomahawk and we all had a hand in the opening. I saw the gold bags and money taken out of the boxes. We left the boxes there and we burnt some of the red scarves, which had been used in the attack for disguise. We packed the gold afresh on one of the escort horses and on Gardiner's own horse. This occurred on the piece of clear ground near the fence.'

Charters took a deep breath before continuing. 'We then went on and soon Gardiner said to me, "Go on as direct as possible to where we camped Saturday night." We went on till we reached Clements' fence. I knew it and we turned and went along it. I was leading the way and also leading Gardiner's packhorse. We were all together and we came to and crossed an awkward deep creek. After crossing it we again came to a fence. Gilbert got off and cut down the fence. We then travelled towards the Lachlan Road. After that we camped on the bank and made a small fire at the foot of a gum tree.'

Charters looked towards Fordyce. Maybe he could do him some good.

'Fordyce's gun was found to be loaded but the caps were off,' Charters said. 'Gardiner swore at him and said, "You were afraid to fire. I'll stop your bloody rations." We camped only a short time there. It was about nine miles from the place where we opened the boxes to where we camped that night. The place where the boxes were opened was about two miles from the scene of the attack.

'When daylight arrived, Gardiner said we would go on to Wheogo Mountain. We reached the top of that mountain, where we would camp, about two pm on the Monday. This place was about sixty miles from where the robbery was done.'

Martin continued with his notes, his pen frantic, his paper full.

'On Tuesday night it rained,' Charters said. 'We weighed the gold, rigging up three sticks to support the scales. Gardiner told us there was about twenty-two pounds weight for each man. He shared out the gold and notes and everyone packed it up.'

The informant pointed at McGuire.

'Gilbert went away in the direction of McGuire's house,' Charters said. 'He was absent for about two hours. He returned with some rations in a large dish and he had a tin can with tea.

'We remained at the camp till the Wednesday morning. On Thursday we got up to start. Gardiner asked Gilbert to go and see if McGuire had any saddlebags. He went away but returned very shortly after in a fright, saying that as he came near McGuire's he saw a lot of police coming from the direction of Hall's towards McGuire's.'

McGuire clenched his teeth and shook his head.

'After that we got ready to start,' Charters continued. 'And after we got ready we could hear the tramp of the police horses coming up the mountain. We left the bottles and several other things. We had no time to shift them. We were then myself, Gardiner, Gilbert, Fordyce and Bow. We five in number travelled through some thick scrub and Gardiner had got off his horse to take a drink of spirits and water when I heard the police horses behind us.

'I looked back and I saw what I thought was a blackfellow on a white horse about four hundred yards behind us. I could see him through the scrub. I pointed him out to Gardiner and he said, "Oh Christ." We split up. Gilbert went in one direction, Fordyce in another. Gardiner was prodding his packhorse with the end of his gun to urge the horse along but he could not get the horse going. So he left him in a very scrubby place.

'Gardiner galloped after me and said, "Pull up! I've lost the gold, it's a bad job."'

Hargrave stood, nodding. He was happy with what he had heard. Still, he had points to hammer home. He fired questions, rapid-fire and on target, and Charters gave his answers succinctly.

The questioning continued, Hargrave now targeting McGuire.

'Have you often seen Gardiner at the home of the accused McGuire?' he asked.

There was an objection. It was dismissed.

'I have frequently seen Gardiner and McGuire together before the event took place,' Charters said. 'And after the event too. I saw Gardiner playing cards at McGuire's a month before the robbery took place.'

More objections. More dismissals. McGuire struggled to contain his fury. He wanted to run across the room and punch Charters in the face.

'That is all from the Crown,' Hargrave said.

Charters sighed.

Done. Not so bad.

He was about to stand down.

'Is it the intention of the counsel for the defence to proceed at once to cross-examination?' the judge asked.

Charters started to shake.

'I would prefer to go on with the cross-examination tomorrow morning as the trial cannot finish tonight,' Martin said.

Charters took a gulp of air.

'I will consult the jury,' said the judge. 'I am quite prepared to go on but I think the jury must be suffering from the extreme heat and would prefer if the court would adjourn.'

The jury agreed.

'Members of the jury, you cannot be permitted to separate as this is a capital case,' the judge said. 'You will be detained for the night and arrangements will be made to render you as comfortable as possible.' The gavel came down. 'This court is adjourned until nine o'clock in the morning of tomorrow.'

This first day of the trial ended at 5.50 pm. Charters stepped down from the witness box. He knew he would not sleep that night.

Chapter 7

THE TRIAL: DAY TWO

Darlinghurst, 4 February 1863

Daniel Charters was back in the witness box at 9 am, dreading what would come next. Defence lawyer James Martin was standing on the floor, anticipation lighting his face.

Martin's colleague Robert Isaacs had won the fight to have Manns' trial postponed. The judge had ruled he would be trialled at a later date. Same man. New name. Same charge.

So Martin went to work, just three lives on the line for now.

'Were you born in this colony?' Martin asked, kicking off his cross-examination of the Crown's star witness.

'I am not a native of the colony,' Charters replied.

'How long have you lived on the Lachlan?' Martin asked.

'I have resided on the Lachlan for about eighteen years.'

'When did you meet the accused?' Martin continued.

'I became acquainted with Bow two years ago while residing at my cattle station in Burroway. I became acquainted with Fordyce at Nowlans.'

Martin took a sip of water. Charters took a breath. And then the questioning continued.

'How long have you known Frank Gardiner,' Martin asked, 'and how well do you know him?'

'I have known Frank Gardiner for about thirteen years,' Charters said. 'But I have not known him to speak to him until the last eighteen months. He used to be a well-known horse racer in the district. I did not know him as a bushranger until lately.'

Martin jabbed away, Charters growing comfortable, the questions not tough.

'When did you see him next?' Martin asked.

'I saw him next at The Pinnacle,' Charters said. 'He had been sticking up some people all along the road and came in there for something to drink with another man. He was at that time pursued closely by the police and he had to escape round by the fence of the house. He presented a pistol and told me to fetch him a horse that was near. I did as I was told and brought the horse to him. He got away on that occasion.'

'And after that?' Martin asked. 'When did you see him next?'

'I saw him afterwards at Wheogo,' Charters answered. 'I have seen Gardiner at McGuire's more than at any other place. He came in when I was there on two occasions.'

McGuire clenched his fist. He wanted to throttle the traitor.

Martin decided it was time to turn up the heat. He moved on to the robbery.

'So when did you decide to take part in the robbery?' Martin asked.

Charters thought about his response. 'I was pressed into this affair by Gardiner,' Charters said. 'He compelled me to go with him.'

'Gardiner made you do it?' Martin continued. 'You mean you were a hostage? He was guarding you the entire time?'

Charters began squirming in his seat and looking about the room. His discomfort was obvious.

'I met Gardiner first on the Thursday, at sundown, and remained with him till he gave me the money and the nugget and let me go away,' Charters said. 'The robbery was committed on Sunday about three o'clock. I was never allowed out of Gardiner's company the whole of the time I have mentioned. I made no effort to escape. I asked Gardiner to let me go and he said he would not.'

Martin saw an opening and took it, the QC throwing his first punch.

'Were you not right near a police station the night before the robbery?' he asked. 'Didn't you say you were one-and-a-half miles away from the police barracks on the Saturday night? Why didn't you simply walk over and inform them of the affair?'

Charters took his time. 'I was within one-and-a-half miles of the police station on the Saturday night,' he said, turning parrot, 'but I am quite certain that I was not out of Gardiner's company from the time he first obliged me to go with him until he let me go away, after the gold was retaken.'

Martin looked down at his papers in mock confusion. 'But earlier you said Gardiner left camp,' he said. 'To get oats, I believe? Would you like me to check my notes?'

Charters hesitated. This was getting tricky. He was having trouble remembering what he had said and what he hadn't said.

'I forgot Gardiner was away, for not more than a quarter of an hour,' Charters said. 'He went away for some oats to Reeve's place. I was left with the other men.'

Now Martin did indeed go to his notes. He left the witness sweating bullets while he frantically flicked through paper.

'You said he was away for a few hours yesterday,' Martin said. 'Now it is a short time. Should we ask the court for your transcript to be sure?'

Charters had tripped. He attempted to turn it into a mere stumble.

'Sorry, it was a few hours. If I said not more than a quarter of an hour, it was a sad mistake,' Charters said.

Martin continued the attack. He questioned him about the guns, about the firing and then he got to the loading.

'In your first statement, the one you gave to the police, you said the guns were loaded on the Friday night,' he said. 'And in the same statement you said they were not shot until Sunday. But yesterday you said they were loaded on the Sunday. You said, clearly and specifically, that you saw Gardiner loading the guns.' He looked at his notes again. 'Putting seven or eight pieces in each gun,' Martin said. 'That is very specific. So you can remember how many pieces he put in the gun but not the day he did it?'

Charters was rattled. He couldn't answer.

Martin turned his attention to Charters' claim of being a hostage. He asked him if he'd been alone when he went off to mind the horses before the robbery.

'You had all the horses, correct?' Martin asked. 'How would they catch you? You could have easily escaped.'

'I was afraid of Gardiner,' Charters fired, 'and thought I should be safer if I stayed where I was. I might easily have warned the persons in the escort, but if Gardiner had got away from the police he would have come and shot me. He was better acquainted with that part of the country than I was and had more friends there, too.'

Bingo. *Better acquainted with the country?* Martin didn't even need his notes for this one.

'In your evidence in this court yesterday you stated that Gardiner wanted you to show him the road,' he said. 'That he recruited you because you were in fact better acquainted with that part of the country than him. That is what you said? I can consult my notes if you like.'

Charters attempted to change the subject. 'I asked Gardiner to let me go away but he refused,' Charters said. 'I did not leave Gardiner when the police were close upon us because he galloped after me and I stopped when he told me to stop. After I had received fifty pounds and the nugget from Gardiner, I did not see him again. I went to look after my cattle and was taken about two months afterwards.'

'So what made you finally go to the police?' Martin asked. 'You say you were terrified of Gardiner. Were you no longer worried Gardiner would shoot you? He was never in custody. Aren't you still afraid he will shoot you? I put it to you that you did it for the reward.'

'I saw that a hundred pounds was offered for each of the guilty parties apprehended and free pardon would be offered to an accomplice,' Charters said. 'But I understood an accomplice was not entitled to the reward. I was out of custody for ten days or a fortnight before I gave any information about Gardiner and these men. I went and spoke to Sir Frederick Pottinger. He made me no promises. I went to get a free pardon, under the proclamation, as an accomplice.'

Martin then went through statements he made to police. They were very different to the deposition he had given in court.

'At first you said there were only three shares of gold and that you didn't receive any,' he said. 'But you received your share of both money and gold. You took it willingly?'

Charters nodded.

'That will be all,' Martin said.

He turned his back on Charters and looked towards his clients. They all looked pleased.

Daniel Charters did not. He sighed as he slumped out of the witness box, a man defeated as he walked through the court, eyes firmly set on the floor. The courtroom buzzed, the prosecution's star witness had been ripped to shreds.

'Silence in the court!' called the clerk as the informer continued his walk.

But the prosecution was not done. The next witness was called.

'Call Thomas Richards!' the clerk barked.

An odd-looking fellow, small with spectacles, waltzed into the room. He took his place in the witness box.

'I am a lemonade seller in George Street, Forbes,' Richards said after he was sworn in. 'I was at Wheogo on the fifteenth of June last. I know John McGuire and John Bow by sight. On the eleventh of June I started from Forbes to go to John McGuire's place. This might have been about five o'clock in the evening.

'Men I know to be Gilbert and Gardiner arrived sometime after I got there. John Bow came in soon after and shook hands with Gardiner. Bow, Gardiner and McGuire went out together after a few minutes. This was on the Tuesday or Wednesday. I cannot say which. Before they went out we had some gin together.

'They came in again shortly, that is Gardiner and McGuire, and shortly afterwards Gilbert. Bow did not return. Gardiner was reading a fortune-telling book. We had some gin and then Gardiner told Gilbert to get some more gin. A man named Hall came in. I saw no arms but those of Gardiner. There was more gin drunk and then Gilbert and McGuire went out again and after a time McGuire told me that I had better go to bed. He told me several times. Ultimately I went to bed.'

The defence team was bemused.

Is that it? What is this all about?

The prisoners were equally miffed.

He was in another room. He is making all of this up.

Richards continued with his evidence.

'I slept in a room off the sitting room where McGuire and Gardiner were,' Richards said. 'I did not see O'Meally. I heard a lot more men come in after I had gone to bed, five or six it must have been. They went into the room that I had left. I heard them go away and I afterwards heard McGuire go to bed. I slept there that night and on the following morning breakfasted at the same place with McGuire and his wife.'

McGuire was staring daggers. *Yes. My wife made you breakfast. I took you in. And this is how you repay me?*

Richards continued, job far from done, reward not yet in his pocket.

'There was another person who took breakfast with us. I think his name was Walsh,' Richards said. 'The next morning I went out to tail cattle and I asked McGuire if I should go round to the paddock. He told me not to go there as there were some persons camping there who did not wish to be seen. I did not go down to the paddock. I went in a different direction and came back to McGuire's in the evening. I stayed a few nights.'

Richards paused, thinking about what he would say next. And then he went on.

'On the Monday night I had a conversation with McGuire,' Richards said. 'He told me that the only one who was well armed was Johnny O'Meally and that he was nearly as well armed as Gardiner.'

Again he paused.

That's it?

Richards remembered what he wanted to say. 'McGuire told me about a month before, at my door in George Street, Forbes, that he would like to stick the escort up,' Richards said. 'He said this to me on a Sunday morning about eleven or twelve o'clock. The escort was just starting at the time. I said it would be much better to stick up the escort than to stick up drays. He did not reply.'

John McGuire squirmed as the lemonade seller continued his damning testimony.

And I am the only bloke here who did not rob anyone!

'I was also at McGuire's on Monday after the robbery,' Richards said. 'I saw Charters riding away from the house of McGuire. He was about fifty yards from it. McGuire said to me, "The gold escort has been robbed and they have got the gold only a few miles away from here in the bush." I was outside McGuire's door when he said this about the robbery of the escort. I said something about Charters. McGuire then said, "About this time they are pretty busy." He did not say whom he meant by "they". We were walking outside together at the time and McGuire said, "They are pretty busy now. It will do them good for they are poor." I answered, "It is better to be poor than be mixed up in that sort of thing, for it is sure to be found out." He then passed a remark about the Melbourne escort being robbed and the affair not being found out.'

That was the end of the deposition. Martin was invited to cross-examine the witness.

'I'd like to confer with my client first, your honour,' he said.

McGuire struggled to contain himself when Martin arrived at the dock.

'Shhh,' Martin said. 'Keep it down. Be calm and speak softly.'

McGuire checked himself. He spoke quietly but had plenty to say. With his ear next to McGuire's mouth, Martin scribbled furiously into his notepad as McGuire talked. Martin stood tall before turning to face the bench.

'I am ready, your honour,' Martin said.

The cross–examination began.

'What occupations have you been following?' Martin asked.

'I was living at Forbes making lemonade and soda water,' Richards said. 'Before that I was butchering at Tipperary Gully, Lambing Flat, for five or six months. Before that I was at Stoney Creek for five or six months. Before I was at the Fish River, doing nothing in particular.'

Martin was not satisfied. 'Have you been to Victoria?' Martin asked.

Richards' lip twitched.

'I have been in the colony of Victoria,' he answered, short and sharp.

Martin went for the throat.

'Were you tried in Victoria between the years 1850 and 1860 for rape?' Martin fired.

Richards lost some of his composure.

'I was never tried there in 1850 and I decline saying whether I have been tried or whether I have been sentenced on a charge of rape.'

Richards looked ready to jump from the box and attack the defence counsel. Martin continued to provoke.

'Have you ever been on trial anywhere for rape?' Martin continued.

'I was never tried in Victoria on a charge of rape,' Richards said.

'But you have been on trial?' Martin quickly snapped.

Richards calmed himself. He didn't want to trip up. 'I decline saying whether I have been tried or sentenced for any offence,' Richards said.

Martin then asked Richards about brothels and illegal gambling. The witness declined to answer. Martin changed course.

'Why did you go to the home of the accused McGuire?' Martin asked.

'I went out to McGuire's to get ten pounds that he owed me. I had no other business with him except to get money that was owed to me.'

Now it was Martin who was gathering his thoughts. He looked at his notepad before resuming the attack.

'This accusation that McGuire told you he was going to rob the escort,' Martin said. 'At Forbes, in front of your shop. Why was this never put in any of your statements to police?'

The witness shrugged. 'They didn't ask me of it,' Richards replied.

Martin turned pit bull.

'Are you aware that you would be classified as an accessory to the robbery if you knew of that attack before it occurred and failed to tell police?' Martin asked. 'Maybe you should be sitting there with your friend McGuire.'

Richards backtracked. 'I do not remember swearing to the police officer that McGuire told me the escort was going to be robbed,' he said. 'I do not think he ever told me that. I am almost sure he did not. In fact, no one did.'

McGuire finally cracked a smile. His counsel continued.

'Why did you continue to stay at the accused's home if you suspected him of being involved in the robbery?' Martin asked. 'Of being involved in Australia's greatest crime?'

'I remained tailing cattle,' Richards said. 'I stopped to do this because business was slack.'

Martin decided to go for a knockout blow.

'You were involved in the whole affair,' Martin barked. 'You wanted some of the spoils. That is why you stayed.'

Richards was taken aback by the outburst. He considered his response.

'When I saw these men gathering I remained for a time,' Richards said after a moment. 'Not to get a share in the booty but because I was afraid that if I left I might find trouble.'

Martin accused Richards of mixing fiction and fact in a calculated and cunning bid to claim the reward. And then he asked a final question.

'Were you convicted of rape in Adelaide?' Martin asked.

'I decline to answer,' said Richards.

'That is all,' Martin said.

And with that Richards left the witness box, his head held low, his face now red. No amount of money in the world would spare him from the disgrace of the entire country suspecting him of being a rapist. He was ruined.

The prosecution case continued. A procession of bankers took the stand to state how much money was on board the escort and how much gold. A grazier spoke of stolen oats, a squatter of missing sardines. The defence team sat still. Only one witness of consequence remained.

'Call William Baldwin!' the clerk said.

Martin picked up his pen as the final witness was sworn in.

'I recollect the thirteenth of June last year,' Baldwin started. 'I kept a store at Forbes, nearly opposite the Harp of Erin Hotel. Two unknown persons came to my place on the evening of the thirteenth and asked if I had some double-barrelled guns for sale –'

Martin dropped his pen and jumped to his feet.

'Objection!' he bellowed. 'How can the purchase of any guns be linked to this crime?' he asked. 'Did the Crown recover any of the guns that were used in the crime that can be presented to this witness for a match? No. This man's testimony cannot be admitted.'

Now the attorney general was on his feet, his witness about to be snuffed out.

'The question is proper as it is going to support a link in the evidence as to the crime,' Hargrave said, 'though it might not immediately affect the identity of the particular prisoners before the court.'

Overruled. Continue.

'On that occasion I sold two double-barrelled guns and an American axe or tomahawk to two men,' Baldwin resumed. 'This was about six or eight in the evening. One was about five feet and nine inches high, square built and about twenty-five years old. The other was a younger-looking man, but I did not pay particular notice to him.

'The two came there together. I was not in when they paid for the things but I saw them going away with the guns and the tomahawk. I don't know if they bought any ammunition.'

James Martin was again on his feet, witness deposed.

'Do you know the prisoners?' Martin asked.

The shopkeeper nodded. 'I have seen the prisoners before at Forbes,' Baldwin said, 'but I don't know them personally.'

'What time was it when the persons you spoke of were at your store?' Martin asked.

'It was about dark when the two men left the shop,' Baldwin replied.

'Dark,' Martin said. 'As in, visibility poor. I have no more questions, your honour.'

Attorney General Hargave stood and addressed the court. 'This closes the case for the Crown, your honour,' he said.

'The court is adjourned until nine am in the morning of tomorrow,' Justice Wise pronounced.

His gavel came down.

Chapter 8

THE TRIAL: DAY THREE

Darlinghurst, 5 February 1863

Martin was given the floor as day three began. Witnesses done, cases put forward, the final round of the fight began.

'Members of the jury,' Martin began, 'in opening this case, my learned friend the attorney general said there was something peculiar and important in the circumstances which distinguished this case from most other criminal cases.' He paused. 'And I quite agree with the remark,' Martin resumed.

'Yes, I agree with the prosecution. At least, that is, I say I concur in the observation that in the description of the circumstances said to have attended the perpetration of the outrage charged, a peculiar atrocity was displayed. But though this is the case, a reference to the character of the offence is not the province of the jury.

'The nature of the circumstances attending the offence is important only in two points of view. If the jury finds the prisoners guilty, it is important that the judge should have regard to the circumstances under which the crime was committed and that he should take those circumstances into consideration when passing sentence.

'This is one sense in which the case assumes an aspect of importance as remarked by the attorney general. But before the proceedings arrive at that stage, you have a duty to discharge, a duty which you will discharge honestly, impartially and cautiously: you have first to say that the prisoners are guilty.

'You will have to weigh, carefully, all the facts laid before you and give to the prisoners the benefit of any doubt that may impress itself upon your minds. You will have to decide whether these prisoners are the persons who committed the outrage which has been so forcibly described.

'This duty you will enter upon with the utmost caution. You will enter upon it with caution in any case but more especially so in a capital case where the lives of the persons before you are at stake and depending on your verdict. The necessity of caution in such cases of this nature entrusted with the defence of the prisoners in my own opinion is that declamation is not to be indulged in.

'It seems to me that in all criminal cases, counsel's duty is simply to bring the leading facts before the jury and to explain as clearly and as ably as I can the law as it bears upon.' Martin stopped to study the twelve jurors. 'Having said this much,' he resumed, 'I will invite the attention of the jury to the charge preferred against the prisoners. These men are indicted under a clause of the Act, where the offence charged is made capital. It is in fact one of the few crimes, in addition to murder, that is still made punishable with death. The indictment contains several counts and charges of wounding as well as robbery. You, the jury, will see, therefore, that it is necessary for the Crown that either at, before or after robbery that someone was wounded.'

Now time to attack Charters. Again.

'Members of the jury,' Martin said. 'It is clear, I submit, that there must be a confirmation not only as to the circumstances of the offence but also as to the identity of the prisoners. His honour will tell you that you may, if you choose, convict on Daniel Charters' testimony alone, but he will tell you also that it is not safe to do so unless you find that he is confirmed in regard to the identity of the prisoners.

'In fact, you are bound to receive the evidence of the accomplice with the greatest caution. If you find that he has told one story at one time and another at another, it is for you to say how far the two accounts tally with each other and how far they are supported by the testimony of other witnesses.

'If you find that he is a man of bad character, that his statements conflict, that he contradicted himself in material points, you, the jury, will be perfectly justified in throwing overboard his evidence altogether. I will be prepared to show that from the thorough worthlessness of his character, from the fact that he was an active accomplice and from his repeated contradictions, the testimony of this man, Charters, is not to be relied upon.'

He studied the jury again for a moment before continuing his attack on the witness.

'The jury will have observed that Charters gave his account so worded that it would be inferred he was dragged forcibly into connection with the robbery,' Martin said. 'If this were really the case he would not be an accomplice any more than captured sailors on board a vessel would be held responsible for acts committed while they were forcibly kept on board by pirates. However, he would have you believe that he was an unwilling actor in the business and that he was forced by Gardiner into the position of unwilling guide.'

Now he looked at the gallery before again turning his attention to the jury, the twelve men now beginning to sweat as the morning heat crept into the courtroom.

'The thing is ridiculous,' he shouted. 'Do the jury suppose that Gardiner — a highwayman, a man of strong resolution, a man who has successfully eluded justice for two or three years — did not know the country quite as well as Mr Charters? Do you suppose that he required a guide when his achievements prove that he must know every nook and crook, every mountain, every river and every stream in that part of the country? Do you, or could you, believe a word of it?'

The jury remained silent; the gallery did not, gasping and groaning.

'For those reasons I submit that Charters was an accomplice, an active and willing accomplice,' the defence counsel continued. 'If Mr Charters was an unwilling participant, how was it that he made no attempt to escape? He replied that he did not because Gardiner was always with him, whereas he had otherwise said that he was separated for an hour or more.

'The whole thing is preposterous. His testimony being false in one respect, you, the jury, are entitled to discredit it altogether.'

And then he turned his attention to Thomas Richards, claiming the witness's testimony as nothing but hearsay and make-believe, a bold attempt to collect the reward despite not having a shred of evidence, except for the mere claim he saw the accused meet.

'Can you imagine if such a robbery was being planned,' Martin said, 'that Gardiner and his companions would allow a stranger to come amongst them? To go quietly on his way afterwards, and without even collecting the ten pounds he said he was there to get in the first place? And then to come back and be given more information about the robbery?

'I contend that the man's whole story is fictitious. It is an insult to you to suppose you will give the slightest bit of credence to what he has said.'

Martin now launched into his finale, no punches pulled, looking to land a knockout.

'There is not, in fact, anything proved against the prisoners in the prosecution's entire case,' Martin said. 'Has anyone proved they were seen on the line of road taken by the robbers? Has anyone shown that they were in possession of large quantities of gold? That they had been seen sporting their cash at public houses or elsewhere immediately after this robbery? No. This hasn't been proved by anyone. Nothing of the kind is shown.

'Cut away the testimony of Charters and there remains not a scrap of evidence to show that the prisoners were in any way connected with the crime. What was the use of showing that tracks were found, that lobsters were eaten, that guns were purchased, that shares were made of the gold – what was the use of all this unless the prisoners are shown to have been connected with it?'

He now walked over and stood face to face with the twelve men who would decide whether three men would live or die.

'Gentlemen of the jury,' he said, 'your object is to arrive at the truth. That is the object of the trial. Prosecutions, I would remind you, are not instituted for the mere sake of vengeance. The law does not strike a criminal for the sake of punishment alone. It does nothing vindictively. It rather compassionates prisoners when they fall under its powers and it punishes them solely in order to deter others from the commission of crime. In every case, where a doubt exists as to the guilt of the person accused, the law mercifully provides that the prisoner shall have the full benefit of that doubt. That he shall be deemed innocent until he is clearly shown by the evidence to be guilty.

'It is highly important that you, the jury, must bear this in mind, for if from any cause you give a verdict that is not clearly borne out by indisputable evidence, you do not assist but you frustrate the ends of justice. Impressing this, then, upon your minds, I leave the fate of the prisoners confidently in your hands, satisfied that you will give the most careful attention to all the facts adduced and return a verdict on the evidence which will not alone vindicate your own judgment but which will also meet with the conscientious approval of every honest, intelligent man in the community.'

Martin slowly made his way back to his seat. He gave the prisoners a nod before handing the floor to the prosecution.

Hargrave wasted no time, making his way straight to the jury.

'I remind members of the jury not to be swayed by the consequences of your verdict,' Hargrave said. 'The punishment should not have any bearing on the decision you make. If such a principle is admitted, there will be an end at once to the utility of criminal trials and the proper administration of justice.'

He took a breath.

'I maintain that the case against all the prisoners is as convincing as it can possibly be,' Hargrave declared. 'I maintain the evidence is quite sufficient to uphold the charges against all the men. Gentlemen, the evidence, on the whole, is clear and convincing against all of the prisoners.'

And with that the prosecution was done. The gallery, the jury and the prisoners turned and looked towards the judge. He sat scribbling, pen in hand, paper fast filling. Eventually he spoke.

'The case is one of extreme aggravation in so far as the crime itself is concerned,' Justice Wise said. 'And it is sufficient to fill anyone with regret and alarm for the future of this colony. I am frightened to even think a crime like this could take place, that such a large number of persons would willingly band together and be prepared to take the lives of innocent people. Such a state of things is absolutely alarming.

'This is a crime that is unparalleled in the history of the colony and long may it remain so.'

Justice Wise turned to face the jury.

'What is your duty?' he asked. 'It is to determine the guilt or innocence of the persons accused by the evidence laid before you at this time, instructed by the information received from the addresses of the learned counsel, either for or against the accused. Having weighed all these, you can come to a decision with your conscientious convictions as to the guilt or innocence of the prisoners. You cannot be influenced by any suspicions you may have of their criminality, or be moved in their favour by sympathy. You must rely solely on the evidence that has been provided in this court.'

Justice Wise was now fully focused on the jury, the long and hot trial beginning to take a toll on some of the twelve, obviously agitated and uncomfortable.

'With these observations you will retire to consider your verdict,' Justice Wise said. 'I press on you to weigh well all the circumstances given in evidence and come to your verdict irrespective of the enormity of the crime or of any suspicion that may have been attached to the prisoners from outside this court. If on the evidence you have any fair and reasonable doubt, the prisoners are entitled to it.'

At 4.35 pm, the clerk led the twelve men of the jury out of the courtroom. They returned at 10 pm.

'Members of the jury,' the judge asked, 'have you agreed to a verdict?'

'No, your honour,' the foreman of the jury replied.

The court erupted.

'Silence!' Justice Wise demanded. 'Silence in the court.'

Soon the court was tomb-like.

'Do any of the jurors wish me to read any portion of the evidence or explain any point in order that you may come to a decision?' Justice Wise asked.

The foreman shrugged before looking at his colleagues, staring at one in particular.

'I do not think any of the jurors require such assistance, your honour,' he said. 'I think there is very little probability of the jury reaching a verdict.'

The courtroom again became a circus, the judge unimpressed.

'Silence,' he demanded.

And again the carnival returned to a courtroom.

'Under such circumstances I cannot discharge you,' Justice Wise said. 'I must therefore lock you in for the night. You may have the room in which you have been deliberating in this court. I will give instruction to have tea, coffee, lemonade and anything of the sort. I will meet you in this court at half past nine in the morning.'

The gavel fell, and the court erupted. They would all return the following day.

Chapter 9

THE TRIAL ENDS

Darlinghurst, 6 February 1863

More than a thousand people waited at the steps of the court, the mass of them flooding back onto the street and down the road. The curious, the voyeuristic and those with nothing better to do were all hoping to get a front-row seat for the most important verdict in the colony's history. Most would be disappointed, the courtroom soon full.

Those who did make it inside watched as the prisoners filed into the dock, whispering their predictions.

They will hang. Guilty for sure.

That Charters is a liar. They will get off.

The jury filed in, the twelve members dishevelled, weary and worn. Evidently it had been a long night for the men who had been locked in the courthouse.

The clerk addressed the jury at 9.30 am on the dot.

'Gentlemen of the jury,' he said. 'Have you reached your verdict?'

The appointed spokesman rose.

'We have not agreed on a verdict,' the foreman replied. 'And there is not the slightest possibility of members being likely to agree.'

The public gallery groaned with shock, disappointment and disbelief. The judge was not, however, so surprised.

'I have already considered what I would do in the event of this being the case,' Justice Wise said. 'The possibility of locking you, the jury, up for another twenty-four hours will leave matters the same as they are now. It also may be that by locking you up again unanimity may be secured and that a verdict, placing the lives of the prisoners in peril, may be obtained. But in such a case it would be a verdict arrived at by the torture of one or more of you whose physical powers are not capable of such endurance as those of your fellows. On the other hand, it would be an injustice to society if the prisoners were acquitted for the same reasons.'

The judge paused to look around his courtroom, his eyes stopping on Hargrave.

'The Crown can place the prisoners on trial again,' Justice Wise said. 'And it will be for another jury to hear and decide the case upon evidence. I have now decided the course I intend to take and the grounds on which I intend to take it. The gentlemen of the jury are now discharged.'

The court erupted, both boos and cheers in equal measure. The prisoners smiled.

'Silence,' demanded the judge.

Three armed police officers marched into the courtroom.

'I have been informed that earlier this morning a number of stones and missiles were found in this courtroom,' Justice Wise said. 'For what purpose they were put there remains unknown. Suffice to say these constables have now been brought into the court to prevent any type of mischief.'

Police had earlier been told that the projectiles were to be thrown at Charters, Richards and the jury should a verdict of 'guilty' be delivered.

And with that the trial ended in sensation, with the prisoners sent back to their cells, the jury discharged, the public stunned.

* * *

Sydney, 7 February 1863

Sir Frederick Pottinger stepped onto the footpath outside the police headquarters on Phillip Street and began the long, lonely walk back to his hotel. It was now midnight and the streets of Sydney were deserted. Or at least he thought they were.

Click. Clack.

He heard the sound of boots hitting the pavement. He turned and glanced behind but saw nothing, only shadows and restless rats. He resumed his walk, a little faster now.

Click. Clack. Click. Clack.

He turned again, this time with purpose, and he saw them. Three men about forty yards away, though he couldn't make out faces in the dark. He told himself it was nothing out of the ordinary, just some men leaving the pub, another night out in Sydney town.

He turned and resumed his walk, even faster now.

Click. Clack. Click. Clack. Click. Clack.

The three men had picked up their pace too. They were closing ...

Whack!

His knees buckled and his world went black.

* * *

Pottinger came to a few minutes later. He was lying face-first on the footpath, his head resting in mud. He pulled his face from the slush, mud mixed with manure, and wiped at the muck. He then looked at his hand, brown filth and blood.

He hadn't seen the blow coming. He hadn't seen who'd hit him, or what they had hit him with. The blood on his hands and the cut on his head suggested it was more than a fist.

Now sitting, he looked down the street. He saw a group of men gathering outside a shop, the commotion bringing them out. He waited for them to come to his aid. But they didn't. They just stood, pointed and laughed.

'There's that poor fool Pottinger,' one said. 'Looks like someone has given him a bit of his own back.'

Pottinger pulled himself from the ground, found his feet and stumbled away. This day couldn't get any worse. He had been embarrassed at the trial when the jury did not convict his prisoners, berated by his boss for his failed prosecution and now beaten on the street.

The thugs had obviously been waiting for him to leave police headquarters, where he had been locked in a three–hour crisis conference with Inspector General McLerie.

'This is a disgrace,' the police boss had screamed. 'You promised me a conviction.'

Pottinger had kept calm. 'And we will get one,' he said. 'It was just one juror. The rest would have had them all hang. We will make sure of the jury for the next trial.'

'We are still a laughing stock,' McLerie said. 'The whole case was about Frank Gardiner. It was all Gardiner this and Gardiner that. But where is Gardiner? Where is the leader? The man who planned it all?'

Pottinger had looked straight ahead.

'I will tell you where he fucking is,' said McLerie. 'Out there counting his cash. He is laughing at us. They are all laughing at us.'

McLerie had slapped a document in front of Pottinger, which he'd scanned quickly.

£1,000 REWARD for the apprehension of
FRANCIS GARDINER alias CLARKE, and JOHN
alias JOHNNY GILBERT.
Whereas the above named Francis Gardiner alias Clarke, and
John alias Johnny Gilbert, are charged with the commission
of numerous and serious offences, and have hitherto eluded
the efforts to apprehend them, principally by their being
harboured, assisted and concealed by parties resident in
the districts they frequent. It is therefore notified that the

Government will pay a Reward of Five Hundred Pounds for such information as will lead to the apprehension of either of them, and should such information be given by any person charged with the commission of any offence, his case will receive the favourable consideration of the Crown. All parties are also hereby cautioned against concealing, harbouring, assisting or maintaining the above named offenders, as by so doing they render themselves liable to be dealt with by law, as accessories to the crimes of which the offenders so assisted may be found guilty.
CHARLES COWPER

DESCRIPTION OF FRANCIS GARDINER, ALIAS CLARKE
Native of Goulburn, New South Wales, 32 years of age, 5 feet 8 inches high, a labourer, dark sallow complexion, black hair, brown eyes, small raised scar in left eyebrow, small scar on right chin, scar on knuckle of right forefinger, round scar on left elbow joint, two slight scars on the back of left thumb, short round scar on cap of right knee, hairy legs, mark on temple from wound by pistol ball or whip.

DESCRIPTION OF JOHN, ALIAS JOHNNY GILBERT
Between 22 and 24 years of age, boyish appearance, 5 feet 7 or 8 inches high, between 9 and 10 stone weight, slight, light brown straight hair, worn long in native fashion, beardless and whiskerless; has the appearance and manner of a bushman

or stockman, and is particularly flippant in his address and appearance.

'Cowper wants Gardiner,' McLerie yelled. 'Gilbert too. Put word out of the new reward. Now get out of here. I don't want to see you until you have them in chains.'

So the beating was just another blow in a succession that day, and probably the least hurtful; it certainly would not end his career. Pottinger was in two minds whether or not to report the assault, fearing further ridicule. He reluctantly reported the matter the next morning. No arrests were ever made, but he was right about one thing: he was indeed ridiculed some more. The only way out was to find Frank Gardiner.

Chapter 10

THE WANTED

Apis Creek, Queensland, 8 February 1863

Gardiner grabbed one end of the freshly cut log, ripped and sawed that morning, now ready to become a beam.

'Lift,' said the foreman, a local man Gardiner had hired. 'Let's get it up there.'

So Gardiner heaved, all triceps, elbows and shoulders, sweat and strain, and got his end to the top of the post.

'She is going to be a beauty, Mrs Christie,' said the foreman, turning to the woman in the white dress, her equally white umbrella shielding her from the blistering tropical sun. 'It will be the best general store from here to Rockhampton.'

The woman twirled her umbrella. 'What do you think, Mr Christie?' asked Kitty, blushing as she looked at Gardiner.

'Depends how much gold I have left in my pocket,' said Gardiner, red like Kitty but from exhaustion, not the thrill of a shared secret.

He gave 'Mrs Christie' a wink. Now he was blushing just like her.

* * *

Gardiner had convinced Kitty Brown that they could start again in Queensland. His lover came to his Weddin Mountain hideout a few days after he survived his shoot-out with the police.

'I should be dead,' Gardiner had said. 'But I am not. I don't know why, or how, but I am here. And all I have been able to think about is you. I am here because of you. It is meant to be.'

Gardiner was still shaken up by his last run-in with the law. Pottinger had held a shotgun to his head and fired at point-blank range. His head should have been taken off. He was not a religious man, but the misfire that had saved his life had him thinking of miracles.

Superstitious to the point that he had planned the escort robbery with guidance from his fortune-telling book, Gardiner believed in fate. And fate was telling him it was time to go straight, to leave New South Wales with the love of his life and start again. No guns, caves or bloody traps aiming shotguns at his head.

Kitty had kissed his cheek. 'Of course it is,' she said. 'So what next?'

Gardiner had grimaced. 'A new life,' he said.

Kitty nodded. 'Where?' she asked. 'And how?'

Gardiner had winked. 'Fret not,' he said. 'All will be revealed. Make your preparations.'

Kitty Brown had soon received word. One day she answered a knock at the door.

'Frank is ready,' said the young man standing on her verandah. 'Pack your things and I'll come and collect you tomorrow.'

Kitty had packed her bag: scissors, bleach, a tweed suit, perfume and her Sunday dress, flowing and floral. How she loved that thing. She went to the basin with long hair, raven black, and left with a short blonde bob. She hardly recognised herself.

She woke early the next morning, ready and waiting for her escort. Soon she was would be with Frank.

'So where to, Frank?' she had asked as she dismounted her horse. 'China?'

Gardiner had grinned. 'And who are you?' he asked, wolf-whistling. 'If I wasn't taken I would …'

'Oh stop it, Frank,' Kitty interrupted. 'You are a fool. Tell me where we are going. Will we be eating Chinese food soon?'

'No,' he had chuckled. 'Why would I go where they are already saying I am?' He laughed some more. 'Ever heard of Rockhampton?' he had asked.

Kitty shook her freshly blonde head.

'Yeah, I hadn't either,' he said. 'And then I heard it was the next Forbes. It's in Queensland. North, beyond Brisbane another four hundred miles. They have struck gold there.'

Rockhampton had been founded in 1853, after Charles and William Archer had explored the Fitzroy River. In 1859, the first North Australian gold find had turned the nothing town into Queensland's second biggest port. Now gold prospectors were abandoning the established mines in New South Wales and Victoria and heading there.

'Booming,' Gardiner had said. 'And it is not just the gold. The land is fertile. The farmers will come and they will be there for good. This is a city in the making. We will start a store. We will sell everything from pickaxes to grog.'

Kitty was sold. Rockhampton or Russia, she didn't care. Mrs Brown was already gone, her hair dyed and her life his.

'And Frank Gardiner is dead,' Gardiner said. 'He was killed in a goddamn awful shoot-out.' He looked at his love. 'And Kitty Brown?' he asked. 'Well, whatever happened to her? Maybe there is a future for me and this strange blonde that stands before me now.'

Kitty punched Gardiner in the arm. He played hurt, then turned serious. 'We are married now. My name is Frank Christie and you, my dear, are my wife. How does Mrs Christie sound?'

She raised a brow. 'Mrs Christie it is,' she laughed.

Then Kitty pulled the suit, the scissors and the bleach from her bag.

'Well, let's meet this Mr Christie then,' she said. 'He sounds like a gentleman.'

Kitty first trimmed Gardiner's bushy beard back to stubble and his long, wild hair short and neat. With her bottle of bleach he went from jet black to a blond red. Gardiner put on the suit, a tan wool tweed bought by Kitty the day before. And with that a famous bushranger Frank Gardiner was gone and Frank Christie was born. Or, as a matter of fact, resurrected.

'Well, Mrs Christie,' Gardiner said, 'shall we begin?'

They mounted and rode off into the unknown. Despite his new name and look, Gardiner was on edge. He was Australia's most wanted man. There were pictures of him everywhere. And soon they would be looking for a woman and a man. They wouldn't be hard to spot.

* * *

Gardiner and Kitty had been cautious. They had stuck to the road less travelled, trails away from the main road. At night they camped in cover, thick scrub hiding them from other travellers, a bucket of water ready to douse their fire. Gardiner also always picked a spot with a view and a getaway. He'd spend most of the night looking out over the land, bucket nearby and ready to go. Gardiner wanted to see them before they saw him.

They slowly made their way north.

One evening, the sun had begun to set and another night of lookouts and little sleep loomed.

'Let's find a place to camp,' said Gardiner. He stopped and pointed. 'Up there,' he said. 'Let's head up that hill.'

They headed into the scrub as dark fell fast. Gardiner stopped suddenly, his horse pulling up with a jerk.

'Smell that?' he asked.

Kitty had nodded. 'Fire,' she said.

Gardiner pointed. 'There,' he said. He could just see the flickering of flames through the trees.

'Shhh,' Kitty said. 'Listen.'

And Gardiner did. 'Singing?' he'd asked.

'Not just singing,' Kitty replied. 'Beautiful singing. I have never heard anything of its kind.'

Gardiner sighed, his tight shoulders suddenly relaxed. 'They ain't no traps,' he said, 'that's for sure. No trap I have ever met can sing like that. Let's go have a look. It could be our lucky night.'

They tied up their horses and pushed forward, slowly and one step at a time. The singing became louder, the voices even more beautiful.

'They are singing in Italian,' Kitty said. 'It's heavenly.'

The singers were soon visible. A woman, forty or so, two young women and six men of all shapes and sizes. They sat around a blazing fire. Eight horses rested in front of a wagon, a fully equipped Cobb & Co.

Gardiner stepped into the light of the fire. 'Fellow travellers,' he said, 'what voices you have. We couldn't help ourselves. We had to come over and get a front-row seat.'

The group stopped singing abruptly, startled.

'You scare us,' said the older woman in a thick foreign accent. 'I thought we was going to be a robbed. We hear of these banditos called bushrangers.'

Gardiner laughed. He would have robbed them a year ago. Sitting ducks.

The woman continued. 'Per favore,' she said, 'come and sit. We have fire, food and song.'

She had introduced Mr and Mrs Christie to the members of the Purantini Concert and Opera Company.

'I am Madame Purantini,' said the woman. 'This fantastico baritone is Mr Irwin, the tenor is Mr Melchior and the basso is

Signor Perdi.' She pointed to a man holding a violin. 'And this is Mr Rozelle,' she said. 'A maestro of anything with strings. We are most of us *italiano*.'

Gardiner and Kitty accepted their invitation to join the troupe around their fire. They ate, sang and drank. Eventually they slept.

'Can we travel with you?' Kitty asked the next morning. 'We are a little afraid to be out here on our own. We have also heard there are bushrangers.'

Madame Purantini looked Kitty up and down, seeing only sweetness.

'Can your *uomo* drive the coach?' she asked. 'Our driver left us in Sydney and Mr Melchior has been driving since. He is not used to it and could use a rest.'

And so it was settled: Mr and Mrs Christie became honorary members of the Purantini Concert and Opera Company.

'We are go to Brisbane,' Madame Purantini said. 'We do some shows then head to a place called Rockhampton. Where do you go?'

'Rockhampton would be perfect,' Kitty said.

They hit the road.

* * *

Five days later Gardiner was on top of the coach. He looked every bit the driver, holding the reins firmly in his hand and chatting to the man riding beside him. Madame Purantini and Kitty were safely and comfortably secured in the coach.

Is that …? Yep.

He squinted as he looked ahead, into the rising sun. Two riders were approaching.

Travellers?

His pulse began to rise.

Traps?

He could feel his heart beating against his chest. The conversation he was having with the opera singer beside him suddenly stopped.

'Frank,' Irwin said. 'Are you okay? What is it? Banditi?'

Ha. Much worse.

Gardiner remained silent, adjusting his hat as low as he dared, the brim now covering his eyes.

'Just *polizia*,' Irwin said. 'Don't worry.'

Frank was not just worried. He was shitting bricks. Soon the traps would be upon them, immaculately dressed in their military-style uniforms of white gloves, gold buttons and high hats.

'Pull down the blinds,' Gardiner called down to the carriage. 'Traps.'

Irwin glanced at him, startled. 'What's the problem?'

Gardiner gave him a look. 'These traps are the biggest crooks in the colony,' he said. 'They will rob us worse than any bushranger.'

The two troopers were closing in.

Pass. Nod and pass. Don't stop us. Please. Just nod and keep going.

'Stop,' barked one of the troopers.

And with that Gardiner thought he was done. He looked down towards the ground, his face completely hidden by the

A photographic portrait of Ben Hall, taken in 1863, at Freeman Brothers in Sydney *(State Library of New South Wales, P1/693)*

The *Dream Book* owned by Frank Gardiner *(courtesy of Mark Matthews)*

A wood engraving depicting 'Frank Gardiner, the bushranger', published in *The Australian* in 1864 *(State Library of Victoria)*

Prospectors panning for gold on the River Turon, in central New South Wales, in 1853 *(Alamy)*

A typical police gold escort, as depicted by artist S.T. Gill *(State Library of Victoria)*

Bailed Up, painted by artist Tom Roberts in 1895, famously depicts a bushranger hold-up in northern New South Wales. *(Alamy)*

Eugowra Rocks near the site of the heist. The rugged terrain helped the experienced riders make their getaway. *(Wikimedia Commons)*

The hold-up at Eugowra Rocks, as depicted by artist Patrick William Marony in 1894
(National Library of Australia, nla.obj-138420908)

A Richard Hollis & Sons' .66-calibre
single-shot percussion pistol probably
used by Frank Gardiner *(photo by George
Serras, National Museum of Australia)*

A Colt Navy revolver, 1851 model,
believed to have been used by Ben Hall's
gang *(photo by Jason McCarthy, National Museum
of Australia)*

Sir Frederick Pottinger in the 1860s
(State Library of New South Wales, P1/1372)

Darlinghurst Gaol in Sydney, where Frank Gardiner was imprisoned. This image was painted by inmate Henry Louis Bertrand, who was jailed for twenty-eight years in 1865 for murdering his wife's lover. *(State Library of New South Wales, SV1/Gao/Darh/2)*

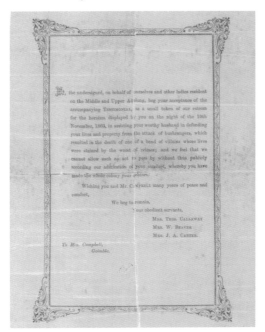

Gifts given by grateful locals to the Campbell family after they fought off Ben Hall's gang at Goimbla in 1863. At left is a silk cloth bearing a message of thanks and admiration, at right a coffee urn, also inscribed. *(both National Museum of Australia)*

A rather romanticised rendering of the killing of Ben Hall, painted in 1894 by Patrick William Marony *(Alamy)*

Ben Hall's well-tended grave today, in Forbes cemetery *(Alamy)*

The grave of Johnny Gilbert, in Binalong, New South Wales *(photo by Peter Phelps)*

A contemporary illustration of the capture of Frank Gardiner at Apis Creek, west of Rockhampton, Queensland, in 1864 *(Alamy)*

This engraving showing the trial of Frank Gardiner at the Supreme Court in Sydney appeared in *The Illustrated Melbourne Post* in June 1864. *(State Library of Victoria)*

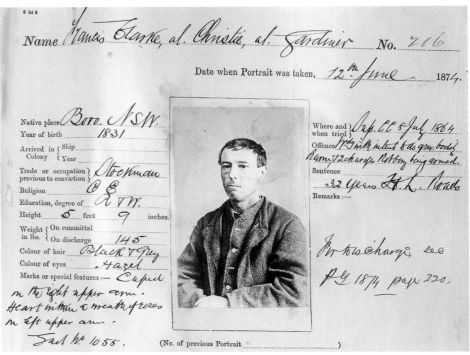

Prisoner record of Francis Clarke, alias Francis Christie (alias Frank Gardiner), from Darlinghurst Gaol, 1874 *(photo courtesy of Cowan's Auctions Inc., Cincinnati, USA)*

San Francisco in the late nineteenth century, around the time Frank Gardiner arrived there. An estimated 11,000 Australians moved from Sydney to San Francisco between 1848 and 1850. *(Alamy)*

brim of his hat, and then pulled the reins. The four horses stopped and the wagon rolled itself still.

Madame Purantini swung the door open. 'What is this? Why are you stopping us? We have a show to get to.'

The eldest officer blushed when confronted by the large, loud and clearly foreign lady. 'Oh,' he said. 'Sorry. No bother here. Just checking in. You carnival folk?'

The madame became a madwoman. 'Carnies? No! We are an opera troupe. The world-famous Purantini Concert and Opera Company.'

The trap tipped his hat. 'Right. We best be on our way. Good luck with the show.'

Gardiner grabbed the reins and went to slap them against the horse.

'Wait,' said the trap. 'That's a mighty fine horse.'

He was pointing at Pedro, Gardiner's stallion. A former racehorse, he had stolen it from a meet at Lambing eighteen months before.

Before Gardiner could formulate an answer, Madame Purantini had swung her door back open.

'Do you wish to buy it?' she asked. 'It eats a more than it pulls. Name your price!'

The trap baulked. 'Nah,' he said. 'We will be on our way.'

Gardiner slapped the reins and sent the wagon forward.

'And why were you trying to sell my horse?' Gardiner called down to the coach, traps gone.

'I thought he was going to steal it,' Madame Purantini explained sheepishly.

Gardiner cut Pedro free the very next day, giving him a kick in the bum and a goodbye. He couldn't risk attracting further attention, one bullet already dodged.

'Anyone seen my horse?' he asked later that evening. 'I think he's done the bolt.'

Three days later Gardiner officially became part of the Purantini Concert and Opera Company.

'I will pay you to look after the lockbox,' Madame Purantini said as they arrived in Brisbane for a string of shows. 'Guard the horses and money while we perform.'

Gardiner nodded. He would guard what he once thieved.

And he did his job. He played the role of a security guard as the troupe performed their Brisbane shows. No one suspected a thing. The lockbox was still safe and full when they arrived in Rockhampton. Kitty was saddened when the tour closed, at least for her and Frank.

'Goodbye,' Kitty said as she hugged Madame Purantini. 'You will never know what you all mean to me.'

Gardiner shook each man's hand and then kissed Madame Purantini and her daughters on the cheek.

'Until we meet again,' he said.

* * *

Six months later and their general store was built, about a hundred miles from Rockhampton, near the Peak Downs goldfields. It became known for its fair prices, good quality products and friendly service. The success prompted an extension, the Christies building a hotel next door. It became a favourite stop for travelling prospectors, the grog good, the beds soft and the owners welcoming.

Mrs Christie was always smiling. Now twenty, pretty and petite, she was with the man she loved and wanted for nothing. It was a far cry from her former life, marrying a man she could barely tolerate when she was sixteen and all but confined to a shabbily built hut at the bottom of a hill. Now she was happy, in love and running a booming business. Sometimes she was overheard singing in Italian.

Chapter 11

THE SECOND TRIAL

Darlinghurst, 23 February 1863

'Righto,' said the officer. 'It's time.'

Manns was ready: showered, suited up and sitting in the holding cell. There would be no surprises this time, no name changes or trial-evading adjournments. Having declared himself to be Henry Manns and not Henry Turner, he had been ordered to stand trial again with John McGuire, John Bow and Alexander Fordyce.

'Out,' the officer continued, pointing to the concrete corridor.

Manns followed McGuire.

The prisoners were once again escorted through the concrete corridor and into the Central Criminal Court. Seventeen days had passed since the juror bombshell that had delayed their fate.

'You will hang now,' said one of the eight armed officers escorting them to the court. 'They will have more on you fellas this time round.'

The prosecution had indeed spent the previous two weeks attempting to uncover the smoking gun that would condemn all of the accused escort robbers to death. But so far they hadn't. The second trial would almost be a replay of the first.

'We will die in this shit–hole regardless,' McGuire said, referring to an outbreak of typhoid that had claimed the lives of four prisoners the week before. Inadequate sewerage, overcrowding – as many as five to a cell with a total prison population of five hundred – had sparked a contagion called 'prison fever'. 'You keep us like pigs,' he said to the officer.

Whack! McGuire copped a baton to the ribs. He had nothing more to say about the open cesspools that were killing the inmates.

Sydney had again come to a standstill. People lined the streets, wagons stalled, horses stopped. Police blew whistles and waved batons. The unexpected finish to the last trial had created even more anticipation for trial number two. The streets were flooded with onlookers and the courtroom was full as the four men took their place on the dock.

The court clerk looked over to the new judge, Chief Justice Sir Alfred Stephen. He nodded and the clerk began.

'Alexander Fordyce, John Bow, John McGuire and Henry Manns,' the court clerk stated. 'You are charged that you, in company with other persons to the attorney general unknown, did on the fifteenth of June, in the year 1862, near Eugowra in the colony of New South Wales, assault James Condell, Henry Moran, William Haviland and John Fegan, did put them in bodily fear and danger of their lives, and did steal from them four boxes and ten bags, 2,719 ounces of gold, the property of Her Majesty the Queen, and 3,700 pounds in cash; and that you did steal two firearms, to wit Terry rifles, and a cloak, the property of Her Majesty the Queen, from the persons of the said Condell, Moran, Haviland and Fegan; and that immediately before the said robbery, you did feloniously wound Condell.'

The clerk addressed Fordyce.

'Alexander Fordyce, how say you? Are you guilty or not guilty?' the clerk asked.

'Not guilty!' Fordyce shouted.

The declaration brought a familiar cheer.

'Silence,' the judge ordered.

'John Bow, how say you?' the clerk continued.

'I'm not guilty!' Bow said.

More applause.

'John McGuire, how say you?' the clerk asked.

'Not guilty!' he beamed.

The court clapped and cheered.

'Silence,' the chief justice barked.

The clerk looked at Manns. 'Henry Manns, how say you?'

'Guilty,' Manns said.

The court erupted again, loudly and hysterically, all shocked by Manns' decision to suddenly change his plea. He'd made the stunning decision after his first-trial reprieve. Sitting alone in his cell, peering out through the rusted iron bars on the door, he could see the gallows. It was then he decided he didn't want to die, and he had been crippled by nightmares ever since: dreams of ropes, hoods and a horse-drawn hearse.

'Silence,' the judge said. 'The pleas have been recorded.'

'I would like to apply for a postponement,' said solicitor for the defence, Mr Foster. 'I have just been appointed this case and we have not obtained counsel. I know nothing of this case except for what I have read in the newspapers and I can't say what course I will take until counsel is engaged.' The prisoners had run out of money and had not been able to convince Robert Isaacs to defend them for free.

'I will adjourn this court for one hour,' Chief Justice Stephen agreed. 'But then this case will begin. There will be no more delay.'

A desperate plea to Isaacs was answered in the break, the QC agreeing to take on the case, the lives of the prisoners put in his hands.

'Mr Isaacs has been retained as counsel,' said Foster when the court resumed. 'But he won't be able to attend until tomorrow as he has a prior engagement.'

Foster then asked for another adjournment. He was denied.

'We will hear the prosecution's case today,' the judge said.

Attorney General John Hargrave took to the familiar floor, the prosecutor already battle-hardened and ready for war.

'Gentlemen of the jury,' Hargrave said, 'I am quite sure you all feel the importance of the position in which you are placed and recognise the duty before you is as arduous as a jury has ever faced. You will have to decide on the evidence brought before you and then determine the guilt or innocence of the prisoners at the bar. This is a capital offence in which they have been charged and I am sure you feel the extreme importance and responsibility of your duty.

'There are two things you have to bear in mind – first the consideration of your duty towards the prisoners by calmly weighing the evidence and the duty towards society and its protection which has been put in your hands. The consequences that follow the verdict have nothing to do with you. The prisoners have brought any consequences on themselves by breaking the law.

'I will now outline the case as it will be presented to you in evidence.'

And Hargrave did, an almost perfect replica of the case he put forward in the first trial. He called his witnesses: Inspector Sanderson first, Sergeant Condell, Senior Constable Moran and then Inspector Pottinger.

And then Chief Justice Stephen addressed the court.

'As the next witness for the court will be Dan Charters,' he said, 'I propose to adjourn the court in order that his evidence will be taken in when the counsel for the prisoners is present.'

The court became a circus.

'Quiet!' the clerk of the court shouted. 'Silence. Stand up please. All persons having any further business with this court depart hence and give your attendance at ten o'clock tomorrow forenoon, Tuesday. God save the Queen.'

The jury were led out at 5.05 pm and locked up for their first night.

* * *

Darlinghurst, 24 February 1863

Robert Isaacs QC was in court on day two, defending the four men charged with Australia's greatest crime. His appointment was both sudden and charitable.

'Thank you,' said John McGuire from the dock. 'I will repay you when I can.'

Isaacs nodded before heading to his seat. He did not expect to be paid.

'Call Daniel Charters!' said the clerk, the announcement sparking pandemonium in the spectators.

'Silence in the court,' the clerk ordered. His plea fell on deaf ears. 'Silence please!' the clerk yelled again, louder this time.

The roar was reduced to a growl, and then finally a whisper. All was quiet when Charters was sworn in. Charters spoke for the next twenty minutes, his deposition as mechanical as it was clinical, giving the same evidence as the first trial. Charters was then grilled by the defence – the questions the same, as too the answers.

Why didn't you escape? Because I was afraid Gardiner would shoot me. *But you weren't with Gardiner the whole time?* No, but I thought he would find me later and shoot me. *You only gave information to save yourself, didn't you?* No, I did it because it was the right thing to do. *You have made up this entire story, haven't you?* No.

And so it went on. He spent the entire day on the stand.

* * *

Darlinghurst, 25 February 1863

Charters thought his agony was over. He was wrong. The witness was called back to the stand, and unlike the previous day – all replica and rigmarole – Isaacs had found a new angle.

'Have you discussed the robbery with Benjamin Hall or John O'Meally?' Isaacs fired. 'Will you swear that these two people who you have not named were not with you at the robbery?'

Charters was stunned by the question; it was both unexpected and seemingly an afterthought. It wasn't. Armed with more information from the accused, the defence was again looking to discredit the witness, maybe even catch him out lying under oath.

'Neither indirectly or directly have I had discussions with Benjamin Hall or John O'Meally relative to this matter,' said Charters, choosing his words carefully.

Isaacs turned up the heat.

'You were given money to leave the names of Benjamin Hall and John O'Meally out of the information you gave to police,' bellowed Isaacs.

Charters began fidgeting nervously, wondering what he should say next. 'I will swear I have not been offered a sum of money to leave their names out,' said Charters. 'I gave all the information I had in regard to this robbery.'

Isaacs then laid bare the friendship of Hall and Charters. He had documents that showed Hall had helped him beat a horse-stealing charge by giving evidence in his favour during a trial. And, as James Martin had done in the first trial, Isaacs pressed Charters on his motivations to betray his mates by becoming a police witness.

'I have no expectation in regard to myself in connection with these trials,' Charters said. 'If the prisoners are found guilty I do not know whether I shall be pardoned or not. I do not expect to be pardoned, for I have no right to expect it. I am not well enough acquainted with the law to say whether I shall or shall not be trialled for my part in the robbery in the event of the prisoners being found guilty. I do not know whether I will be set free. I do not expect it. I may most likely be detained until all the others are taken. I have had no promises of release made to me. I have admitted my guilt, fully, and it will depend upon the authorities as to whether I will be sentenced or not. I expect I shall be tried.'

'Has not some government authority said that it would be better for you to give evidence?' Isaacs asked.

'No,' Charters replied.

'Was it not said to you that if you did not give the information then somebody else might, and that even Hall's name had been mentioned as that of a person likely to do so?'

'No,' Charters repeated. 'Nothing of the kind was ever said to me.'

'But you knew you would be pardoned for the robbery should you turn informer, correct?' Isaacs asked.

'I saw it printed on bills that were stuck up that one of the offenders who gave evidence for the Crown would be pardoned.'

The attack was over, Charters admitting he knew he would be pardoned. The case rolled on with lemonade seller Thomas Richards taking the stand. Again, all replica and rigmarole.

The prosecution, for the second time in that month, concluded its case against Australia's most famous prisoners. The court was adjourned, the jury locked up, and the prisoners taken back to their cells to ponder their fates.

More than a thousand people would turn out the following day. Would there be a hanging or another hung jury?

* * *

John McGuire, John Bow, Alexander Fordyce and Henry Manns watched as the twelve jurors stood up and walked out of the room after Chief Justice Stephen, in his white wig and red robes, had given his final address. The prisoners' lives were now in the hands of these ordinary men.

The prisoners also left the room and were offered a meal as they waited to learn if they would live or die. None of them ate.

At 9.45 pm they were summonsed. Soon the clerk was addressing the jury. Fordyce said a prayer, as did Bow; McGuire crossed his fingers and Manns stood, sweating and shaking.

'Foreman of the jury, please stand,' the court clerk said. 'Gentlemen of the jury, have you agreed upon your verdict?'

'We have,' replied the juror.

The court didn't erupt. Not this time. The spectators were stunned and silent. All was still. The clerk continued.

'How say you?' he asked. 'Is the accused John McGuire guilty or not guilty?'

'We find him not guilty.'

This time the people in the court cheered. McGuire said nothing. He stood silent and still. Bow looked at McGuire.

'Good one, mate,' he said. 'I am happy for you.'

McGuire gave him a nervous smile.

'John McGuire,' said the clerk.

McGuire turned and the clerk was waving him down from the box. The judge stopped him.

'Is there any other charge against McGuire?' the judge asked, looking towards the prosecution.

'No,' said a police officer. 'But there is a bail bond of forty pounds that has not been paid, your honour.'

McGuire looked up to the judge. 'Thank God that is not a hanging offence,' he said.

The court erupted into laughter as he was taken from the court. He would be free to leave after paying his bail.

'Gentlemen of the jury, how say you: is the accused John Bow guilty or not guilty?' the clerk asked.

'We find him guilty,' said the juror matter-of-factly.

Bow's head went down.

'Gentlemen of the jury, how say you: is the accused Alexander Fordyce guilty or not guilty?' the clerk asked.

'We find him guilty,' said the juror.

Fordyce remained unmoved.

The judge now took over, his honour looking to the three men, faces white, sullen and full of shock. He reminded the court that Manns had already pleaded guilty before continuing.

'John Bow,' he said, 'the court has found you guilty. Have you anything to say why the court should not pass sentence upon you according to law?'

Bow struggled to contain his emotion. He took a moment to compose himself, the gravity of the situation still sinking in. He squeezed the rail of the dock, his knuckles turning the colour of his face.

'The jury have found a verdict of guilty against an innocent man,' Bow said. He loosened his grip after getting it out.

The judge went down the line. 'Alexander Fordyce,' he said, 'have you anything to say why the court should not pass sentence on you according to law?'

Fordyce spat it straight out. 'I am not guilty,' he said.

The judge turned to Manns, next and last in line.

'Henry Manns,' he said, 'you have pleaded guilty to the charges. Have you anything to say why the court should not pass sentence on you according to the law?'

'I have nothing to say,' said Manns.

The courtroom, however, could no longer be contained. With the verdicts delivered and the fate of the men soon to be sealed with a sentence, the spectators jeered and booed.

'Silence!' screamed the judge. 'Order in the court.'

The furore continued.

'Silence,' he barked again. 'All persons are commanded to keep strict and profound silence under the pain of imprisonment while I pronounce the awful sentence of the law.'

And then there was silence.

'It now becomes my painful duty to pass the sentence of death upon the prisoners,' Chief Justice Stephen said, his voice flat, his head raised. 'In the case of prisoner Manns, who expressed a wish to plead guilty, it is most distressing to me to have to say anything that can add to poignancy of your feelings at this moment. But it is impossible for me to avoid saying that, by the document I hold in my hand, you stand convicted of perjury – of wilful perjury. In an affidavit, sworn to by the prisoner, he applied for and obtained a postponement of his trial on the ground that if he were allowed he could produce witnesses to prove he was not the person who was arrested.

'This he swore but following the postponement granted he now desires to plead guilty. Here is a man swearing to an affidavit of facts in the hope, and no doubt with the expectation, he would be able to procure witnesses to perjure themselves on his behalf. How are judges supposed to protect themselves from proceedings like this?

'As to the offences which Manns and the other two prisoners stand convicted, the jury has expressed the opinion in which I entertain. Their guilt is confirmed by the testimony of numerous witnesses. There is ample evidence to convict them of this crime. I think the jury are quite right in the conclusion at which they arrived.'

He turned to face the damned.

'I can feel for the prisoners as men,' the chief justice continued. 'But I can tell you candidly that if the sacrifice of your lives by means of, in any degree, checking the present lawlessness that prevails, the cause of society, the cause of mercy and humanity, will be served by your deaths. The interests of society are paramount, and it is imperative that crimes of this cruel, reckless and ferocious nature must be effectively punished and repressed.'

The chief justice paused. He studied the prisoners. Then he ordered them to be put to death.

'John Bow, Alexander Fordyce and Henry Manns,' he said, 'the sentence of this court on you is that you may be taken back to the place whence you came and thence on such a day as may be appointed by the executive, to the place of execution and that you be then and there hanged by the neck until you are dead. God have mercy on your souls.'

The trial ended at 10.20 pm, with three men sentenced to hang. They left the courtroom in silence, even the louts in the gallery stunned and still. The newspapermen headed back to their offices to type their reports, including this one printed in *The Empire*:

All the prisoners appeared to fully feel their awful situation. Fordyce, who is a man of puny and emaciated frame, had previously been leaning with his head on his right hand, rose up with a start, and then supported his head against the iron railing of the dock – in fact, he became completely subdued. His nerves were at once prostrate. Bow, who presented a marked contrast to Fordyce, being both strong and athletic, and of very healthy appearance, gave a deep sigh, and changed colour immediately, wiping his face with a handkerchief. He seemed to have been quite unprepared for the result. He is twenty-five years of age, and has a numerous circle of relatives in the Weddin Mountains to deplore his untimely fate. His prospects were good, so far as a nice farm, well stocked, could afford.

Manns looked quite dogged, and was the beautiful ideal of a young Australian stockman. He held his head down in a sullen manner and one would suppose that he made his mind up not to stir a muscle even if put to the torture of the rack.

But yet a close observer could not fail to perceive that with all this apparent determination he felt his position acutely. In fact, his legs at last trembled, and he was obliged to support himself by his breast and arms against the dock.

The court was densely crowded during the trial, and the greatest propriety characterised the conduct of the spectators throughout the entire proceedings.

* * *

Sydney, 2 March 1863

The cell door swung open.

'Prisoner Fordyce,' yelled the guard. 'Out. You have a visitor.'

Fordyce did not move.

'Out,' the guard said again. 'Now!'

The inmate dragged himself from the bed that he had not left since being sentenced to hang. He hadn't eaten, had barely slept, and now looked like the walking dead.

'Come on,' said the guard, pushing him along the corridor towards the room where visits took place.

Fordyce had been wasting away ever since his arrest. The eldest of the escort robbers at forty-two, he seemed to be losing both mind and body bit by bit. The happy-go-lucky barman no longer told jokes. In fact, he hardly spoke. And as a withdrawing alcoholic, he shook and he spewed, desperate for just one drink.

Maybe they will give me one before they drop me?

Fordyce was a sorry sight, his life seemingly already taken. A solicitor was waiting for him in the visiting room. He didn't have any beer.

'What now?' Fordyce asked. 'More charges? I am already going to hang.'

'No,' said the solicitor. 'I have good news. Your death sentence has been commuted to life in prison. The Executive Council met earlier today and decided to show leniency. Your life has been spared.'

Fordyce smiled for the first time in 191 days, for the first time since Pottinger had stormed into O'Meally's shanty and arrested him while he worked. Dobbed in by Charters. Locked up in Forbes, Bathurst and finally Sydney. Trialled, convicted and sentenced to die. And now a reprieve? Thank God.

'And the others?' Fordyce asked. 'Have they been spared too?'

The solicitor shook his head. 'No, Alexander,' he said. 'Only you.'

It took Fordyce a while to speak again. 'But why?' he finally asked. 'Why me?'

'Because you didn't fire a shot,' the solicitor replied. 'And they did.'

Fordyce was smacked in the spine by the coldest shiver he had ever had.

He had been spared from death because he had been so drunk on the morning of the robbery that he could not fire a shot. The cartridge Frank Gardiner found in the end of the gun had saved his life.

That same mercy was not extended to Bow or Manns. They were scheduled to hang on 16 March.

* * *

Sydney, 9 March 1863

Governor Sir John Young took his seat at the table when the Executive Council met seven days later.

'Gentlemen, we have a very important decision to make,' he said, addressing the other six members. 'I am sure you are all aware of the hysterics in the colony regarding the scheduled execution of prisoners John Bow and Henry Manns. What you might not be aware of is this.'

Sir John put a stack of papers on the magnificent rich mahogany table.

'There are more than fourteen thousand signatures on this petition,' he said. 'Read what it says.' He handed the uppermost paper to the man on his left.

We, the undersigned, humbly pray that your Excellency will be graciously pleased to exercise the Royal prerogative of mercy in

the case of John Bow and Henry Manns, lying under sentence of
death in Darlinghurst Gaol.

Each of the men took only a moment to read the few lines
before passing it on. Sir John studied their faces both before and
after they took their turn.

'And those signatures,' Sir John said, 'were all collected in
just eighteen hours.'

He produced another document, a letter.

'This one has been signed by six thousand,' he said. 'It
has been written by the mother of Henry Manns, evidently a
highly religious and respected woman from Campbelltown.
It has been endorsed by four ministers of the Church of
England.'

To his Excellency Sir John Young, KCB, Governor in Chief of
the colony of New South Wales.
May it please your Excellency,

We, the undersigned, desire to call your Excellency's
attention to the following mitigatory circumstances in the case
of the condemned criminals John Bow and Henry Manns, now
lying under sentence of death in the gaol at Darlinghurst.

That Bow is a youth on the verge of manhood, being only
twenty years old, and Manns not yet twenty-four years old.
That both are without even elementary education, neither being
able to read or write. That this is their first conviction of crime.
That heinous as we consider the offence of the culprits to be, it
yet falls short of actual murder. That the accomplice Fordyce, to

whom the clemency of the Crown has been extended, is equally guilty with them.

Your memorialists, therefore, pray that your Excellency may be pleased to review the decision arrived at by the Executive Council, and that taking the above circumstances into consideration, your Excellency may see that in this case justice to society may be tempered with mercy to the culprits, and that their lives may be spared as in the case of Fordyce.

A councillor threw the letter down in disgust.

'And what of this?' he asked. 'Of course a mother will plead for the life of her son. And who would refuse to sign a petition to save a life once it was shoved in your face? How about the rest of the colony? Those who want to see the law upheld? Those who want to send a message to the bushrangers that their time has come to an end?'

Sir John nodded. 'That is the other side of this difficult argument,' he said.

He produced a stack of newspapers and handed one to each man.

'This is the most scathing of the editorials calling for their death,' he said.

THE CONDEMNED ESCORT ROBBERS

And so the dread vengeance of the law is about to be carried into effect. Society triumphs and the ruffian falls. Without sympathy, without friends who dare show their grief, or without one good man to shed a tear, those escort robbers Bow and Manns will undergo the last penalty of the law, and be launched the end of the murdering robber. The verdict was one that did credit to the jury, and, dreadful as it is, must meet the entire approval of every man in the colony except Gardiner and his ruffianly. It shows clearly that those scoundrels cannot rob murder with impunity under the impression that if one of their number turn approver his testimony will not be. The evidence of Daniel Charters, there is no doubt whatever, is the evidence of truth. They were a band of wretches who secreted themselves like cowards, and assassins (as they undoubtedly are in their hearts) and tried to shoot down a number of men without giving them time to defend themselves, or one moment to prepare for eternity. Out and out monsters! These were men who sheltered themselves behind rocks and shot down their victims in cold blood.

Men like this, at any costs, must be rooted out of the district, and then the reign of Gardiner and his gang of murderers would be very short. The country would have a nightmare lifted from its bosom by knowing that this were done and that Gardiner was dangling from a gallows. This must be his fate if he is not shot in the meantime. We cannot leave the subject without remarking on the growing practice of these men, when the law overtakes them, to set up an alibi. Manns was prepared in this way. He filed an affidavit that he could bring witnesses to prove that he was at Gundagai at the time of his arrest. There is little doubt but he could have brought men to swear anything. But the most terrible part of the matter is that shortly after, unable to endure the pangs of conscience, he desired to plead guilty. Such, then, being the state of moral degradation into which the country

*is sinking, it behoves every man to render the law and its officers
every assistance in his power to use every legal means to cause
the gang of murderers that infest the neighbourhood to be taken,
and those who harbour them to be rooted out; and then, and not
till then, will peace and safety be restored.*

'And I agree,' said a councillor.

'And me too,' said another.

On it went. All six members, barring the governor, declaring
both men should be executed. And they would have been had
the governor not used his executive power to intervene.

'No,' he said. 'As I have said before, the Queen's prerogative
is to show mercy. So we will commute the sentence of John
Bow.'

The men hissed and hit at the table.

'Quiet,' Sir John said. 'Your prerogative is to see the law
upheld and the sentence carried out in full. And that it will be
for Henry Manns. That will send the message that both you and
the colony desire to these bushrangers and the lawlessness that
prevails. We will show both mercy and none.'

Sir John decided to save one life and end another, his right
hand soft and his left hand firm.

'John Bow's sentence is hereby commuted to life. He will
spend the first three years of his sentence in irons. Henry Manns
will be executed by way of hanging on the twenty-sixth of
March.'

Chapter 12

THE HANGING

Darlinghurst, 21 March 1863

Manns had not slept a second. Head on the pillow, finally about to drift …

Whack!

He snapped straight up, jumped from his bed and ran to the cell door. He looked through the bars into the dark.

Who? Why did they do it in the middle of the night?

Manns was sure he had been awoken by an unscheduled execution, the sound of a neck breaking, a slack rope ripped taut. But he could see no one. Nothing. Only dark.

He looked harder, expecting to see someone swinging, a last kick, the final death throes. But there were no priests, no guards and no hangmen. Only darkness looked upon by a man facing his fate. Manns went back to his bed and put his head on the pillow.

Whack!

He snapped straight up, jumped from his bed, but this time he didn't get to his cell door.

'You're keen,' said the guard, key in lock, on a wake-up call.

Manns wobbled on the spot.

Must have slept after all …

He saw the morning light creeping into his cell and looked past the guard towards the gallows. The trapdoor was firmly shut. There were no priests, no hangmen and no blood-splattered hoods.

'You coming?' the guard asked. 'Or staying in again?'

Manns replied by way of walking back to his bed.

'Suit yourself,' the guard said. 'I'll bring your breakfast. And then come and take it away untouched again.'

Manns put his head down. There was no pillow, just a mattress, hard, dirty and damp. He closed his eyes. Soon he was drifting back to sleep.

Whack!

He was upright again, shaking and sweating.

'Visitor,' the guard said after banging on his cell door.

Manns looked up and squinted, the light now pouring into his cell. 'Who?' he asked.

'Your mother,' the guard replied.

And with that Manns broke down. He fell back onto his mattress and started to sob. He pulled his knees into his chest and rolled around the bed like he was seasick, on a small boat battling a big swell.

No. What will she think? I can't let her see me like this.

'Settle,' the guard said. 'It's your mother. Pull it together.'

Manns took a deep breath,

I have to. For her. So she can say goodbye.

He let go of his legs and set them straight. Soon the shakes stopped, then the sobs.

'Come on, mate,' the officer said.

Manns obliged, swinging his stick-like legs onto the floor and pushing his skinny arms into the bed.

'I got ya, mate,' said the guard, helping the skeleton from his bed. 'Here you go.' The guard frowned. 'Sorry, but we have to put these on,' the guard continued, shaking the irons. The restraints were snapped shut and locked tight, the guard almost expecting the weight of the chains to send the inmate crashing to the ground. 'Let's get moving then,' he said.

Manns began shaking again as the door to the visiting room neared.

The guard was helping him towards the door. 'Come on,' he said again, 'I got ya.'

Manns took a deep breath, drawing the stale and putrid air deep into his lungs.

Get yourself together. You owe her a goodbye.

He pulled his shoulders back, lifted his head, and walked into the room standing tall. And with just one look he was reduced once more to a blubbering mess.

'Ma,' he said looking at the woman sitting at the table, empty chair by her side waiting for him. 'I'm … I'm …'

Mary Manns rushed to her son. 'It's alright, Henry,' she said, putting her arms around him. 'It will be alright.' She pulled her son into a tight embrace.

'No it won't be, Ma,' he said. 'I will be dead in a week.'

Mary Manns helped her son sit.

'That is why I am here,' she said. 'I have good news. Our member of parliament has helped me write a petition. I am presenting it to the governor this morning.' She pulled a neatly folded piece of paper from her purse. 'It has been endorsed by another seven members,' she said, opening the note, 'and also by four ministers of the church. And we have more than five thousand signatures. They can't ignore this one.'

Manns' ma read to her illiterate son.

To His Excellency the Right Honourable Sir John Young,
The humble Petition of the undersigned humbly approach
your Excellency, and with all due respect, desire to draw your
attention to the following reasons why the life of Henry Manns
be spared:

1. That the prisoner is a young man who has passed
his life in the interior, away from all moral and religious
influences.

2. That hitherto he has borne the character of honest and
industrious persons, this being the first crime with which he
has been charged and into which he may have been drawn
(as Charters the approver has sworn to the Crown) from fear
of the notorious Frank Gardiner, or by force of other such
circumstances.

3. That no person in this colony has ever suffered the
extreme penalty of the law for any crime which has not resulted
in someone else's death.

4. That the majesty of the law will be sufficiently upheld by
penal servitude for life.

*5. That your Excellency having been pleased to spare the
life of John Bow, who was equally guilty with Manns, your
petitioners believe the prerogative of mercy ought to be extended
to the latter.*

*Your petitioners, therefore, humbly pray that your Excellency
may be pleased to extend the same mercy of which, as her
Majesty's representative, you are the sole custodian, and spare
the life of this misguided, unfortunate and unhappy young man.*

Yours hopefully,

The undersigned.

For a moment Mary Manns saw a spark in her son's eyes.

'They rejected the last one,' he said, spark now gone, eyes
back to blank. 'And it is too late now in any case. Right?'

Mary Manns shook her head. 'The governor has the power
to grant you a reprieve right up until—' She stopped herself
before reminding them both of the creeping death. 'And they
let off Bow, so they have to let you off too. You were no more
guilty than him.'

The little spark returned. 'Thanks, Ma,' he said. 'I thought I
was done for.'

He summoned the courage to ask about his family.

'Your father is not well,' Mary said. 'He hasn't been out of
bed since they sentenced you.'

William Manns could not work out what had gone wrong,
what had led his son to commit a capital crime. Neither could
Mary. Henry Manns had left home four years earlier, at nineteen,
a job secured on a cattle station. He'd worked as a stockman and

in two years saved enough money to buy a bullock team and work for himself. He had never been in trouble before. Never been convicted of a crime. Never even committed one. And here he was, her son, now sitting in cuffs and chains, with her reassuring him that she could save his life. She took the letter back, kissed him on the cheek and told him again it would all be alright.

Later that morning she sat in the governor's office, begging the most powerful man in New South Wales for her son's life. *He is a good boy*, she promised. *Never committed a crime. He was drunk when he agreed to do it, that Gardiner dragging him in. We are good citizens, been in the colony for twenty-five years.*

'I also have references,' she said. 'Fifteen of them.'

Sir John Young listened to her every word. He sat patiently and attentively, no doubt moved by the mother's plea.

'Let me take the time necessary to consider what you have said and presented,' he said. 'I will have a decision for you later today.'

Mary Manns thanked the governor. He would be her son's saviour.

* * *

Sir John fronted a mass outside Government House: the press, the petitioners, the curious and – Mrs Mary Manns waiting for his reply. He delivered it, reading a carefully prepared statement.

'Ladies and gentlemen,' he began, 'I need scarcely assure you that I have given the subject of your petitions the most careful and anxious consideration, and that I deeply feel the heavy responsibility of this occasion. You are aware that I have already extended the Royal prerogative of mercy in favour of the prisoner John Bow. There are marked distinctions between his case and that of the other prisoner, Henry Manns, distinctions which, I think, cannot fail to be recognised. It is with pain, therefore, that I have to inform you that I have arrived at the conclusion that the case of the prisoner Henry Manns is not one which would justify me in exercising the Royal prerogative in his favour on my own individual responsibility.'

'No,' came the cry. 'Please ...' Mary Manns had fallen to her knees.

The governor stopped. He turned and looked towards the woman, a more heart-wrenching scene he had never seen.

'The petitions shall, however, be duly laid before the Executive Council,' he continued, 'which is summoned to meet this afternoon.'

Mary now screamed again. 'No!' she cried, knowing the decision of the Executive Council would be a death sentence.

She fainted and fell down into the mud and muck.

* * *

Darlinghurst, 26 March 1863

Whack!

Manns sat upright in bed, a cold sweat coating his skin. He looked to his left and then to his right. He saw nothing but dark.

He put his head back down and closed his eyes, exhaling. More night terrors. Old news. He once again pushed death distant, sending him back into the dark. *Go to sleep.* He began to drift ...

He sprang back up and looked into the dark, squinting hard before shaking his head. The Grim Reaper was in his room, scythe raised and ready to strike. He shook his head again. He was now fully awake, fully aware.

Today is the day that I die.

He slowly slid along the hard mattress until his back touched the wall. He was numb, mind closed but eyes open, death staring him in the face.

Whack!

This time he didn't move. He didn't even blink.

'Manns,' said the guard, whacking on his cell door. 'Visitors.'

He remained silent and still. Exit guard, enter priest.

'I am Archdeacon McEnroe,' said the father, 'and this is Reverend Father Therry and Reverend Father Dwyer. We will be with you until the end, and the Lord will be with you if you would like to confess to your sins.'

He nodded, Jesus his last hope. The priest took his confession and then sat with him, holding his hand.

'Henry Manns,' said an officer as the clock struck 9 am. 'It is time.'

Manns turned his head and looked down at the floor.

'Manns,' the officer said, louder this time.

'No,' Manns said. 'Please ... No. I don't want to ...'

Archdeacon McEnroe placed his arm around the inmate. 'Henry,' he said, 'you will find your peace with our Lord. And now he gives you his strength.'

Manns stood before pushing his hands forward, knuckles facing the sky.

'Get on with it,' he said.

And with that he was cuffed, chained and led onto the cold stone floor of the corridor. He turned and looked back at his cell and wondered if anyone had ever left such a place wishing they could go back, even to its rancid air, rotting mattress and dysentery running riot.

* * *

Manns walked into the yard, head down, flanked by the priests. He ignored what stood in the centre of the yard – the stairs, the platform and the rope – looking only at the cobblestones under his feet. Hooded, the executioner stood in wait.

A small crowd had gathered: press, police and even some of the public, a morbid few allowed in for the swinging show.

'Henry Manns,' said the clerk, 'you have been sentenced to be hanged by the neck until you are dead. You will now be consigned to the executioner, who will carry out the sentence of the law.'

Manns, still shadowed by the priests, slowly made his way towards the gallows. Life was now a game of inches. He bought himself another minute, no more. The archdeacon said another prayer as Manns was handed over to the executioner: 'Almighty and merciful God,' he intoned, 'who hast bestowed upon mankind saving remedies and the gift of everlasting life, look graciously upon us Thy servants and comfort the souls which Thou hast made, that, in the hour of their passing, cleansed from all stain of sin, they may deserve to be presented to Thee, their Creator, by the hands of the holy angels. Through Christ our Lord. Amen.'

The executioner extended his finger, pointing towards the steps that led to the top of the scaffold, about twenty feet above the ground. Manns obliged.

'Any last words?' the executioner asked. No more inches, no more time.

Manns nodded before shuffling his way to the front of the platform. Stage set, he delivered his final line: 'I would just like to thank all the people for the kindness they have showed to me,' Manns said. 'Those who petitioned for my life and were willing to show me mercy, I thank you. And I am sorry to anyone that I have hurt. I pray for you all and you all pray for me too. I will now face my final judgment.' He turned and looked towards the executioner. 'I'm ready,' he said.

The executioner reached for the rope hanging from the overhead beam and put the noose around Manns' neck while he stood silent and still. And then Manns looked at the world for the last time before the hangman produced the white cotton hood and slipped it over his head.

Goodbye colour. Goodbye light. He greeted the eternal darkness.

The executioner looked over towards the clerk as the archdeacon began another prayer, words to soothe the spectators as much as the condemned. The clerk, flanked by the governor of the gaol, looked at his watch: 9.20 am. He nodded.

The hangman pulled back on a metal lever, the simple mechanism ripping away a bolt beneath the trapdoor under Manns' feet.

Crack!

Wood smashed into wood, the trapdoor flying open with such force that it smacked into the underside of the platform. The rope snapped taut as Manns fell six feet before the noose ripped at his neck. His body bounced and shook as the rope stopped his fall. And then he screamed.

Manns should have been dead. The drop should have broken his neck. It hadn't. His limbs stiffened and then they shook. He began to convulse, a hopeless struggle against the inevitable. It would soon be over. He would be choked.

But the struggle continued. One minute. Two minutes. Three minutes.

The crowd began to gasp and groan.

'Is this right?' asked an onlooker as Manns continued to shudder and shake.

Four minutes. Five minutes.

'What's wrong?' asked another.

The clerk was becoming agitated, looking at his pocket watch and shaking his head. Manns continued to moan, shaking and kicking in his agony. And then he started to cough, the violent hacks full of blood.

Six minutes. Seven minutes.

The crowd groaned and hissed as the white hood was sprayed red. Manns continued to convulse.

'Put him out of his misery,' said a spectator.

Eight minutes. Nine minutes.

The clerk looked to the prison doctor. 'What the hell is going on?' he asked.

'The rope,' the doctor said. 'It slipped when he fell. It's caught him around the chin, not around the neck.'

Ten minutes. Eleven minutes.

Manns was now bleeding from his eyes, the white hood fast turning red. He gurgled, his throat filling with blood.

Twelve minutes. Thirteen minutes.

'For mercy's sake,' yelled one of the reporters gathered to record the execution, 'do something!'

Fourteen minutes. Fifteen minutes.

Dr West finally moved in to examine Manns, still shaking and struggling. 'Get the hangman,' he yelled.

The executioner had retreated as soon as he had drawn the bolt.

Fifteen minutes. Sixteen minutes.

The hangman returned. 'Lift him up,' he said. 'We need to lift him so I can adjust the rope.'

Seventeen minutes.

Four prison guards were ordered to the gallows. They lifted the still-convulsing Manns as high as they could while the executioner waited on a low ladder.

'That's it,' the hangman said, the rope now slack. He pulled at the noose, dripping in blood, and repositioned it around Manns' neck.

Eighteen minutes.

'Drop him,' the executioner ordered.

The guards let go, the fall no more than two feet. Manns' body resumed its fight, flailing about between heaven and earth.

Nineteen minutes.

He was slowly strangled, the rope now firmly around his neck. The violent convulsions soon became shudders, and then, after twenty minutes of horror, his movement was reduced to a twitch.

Finally he was still.

Henry Manns was pronounced dead at 9.41 am, his execution having taken a horrifying twenty-one minutes. The spectators were left stunned.

Manns' body was cut down and placed in a coffin made of cheap pine and reclaimed nails. At 10.30 am it was carried outside, four prison guards heaving it into the back of a hearse cart.

'Move,' one of the guards yelled to the crowd that had gathered outside for the spectacle. 'Let them through.'

The crowd slowly parted and left a path for the hearse to take Manns' body through the city streets.

'Whoa,' the driver commanded, his horses obeying and slowing to a stop as they arrived at the Packhorse Inn. The box was pulled off the back of the cart and dumped unceremoniously on the floor.

'Oh my boy,' wailed Mrs Manns. 'What have they done to you?' She looked at the driver. 'Get him out of that thing,' she ordered.

With some help, the driver pulled Manns out of the pine prison box and placed him in the coffin Mrs Manns had bought with her savings.

She broke down when she saw the bruises and the blood. Her son hadn't been executed. He had been murdered.

Manns' body was delivered to Campbelltown the next day by train. Mrs Manns had failed to have her son's sentence commuted but she had won the battle to have him put in a proper grave. While most bushrangers were thrown into unmarked graves on unconsecrated ground, Manns was buried next to his brother and sister, in St John's Cemetery.

Chapter 13

THE GANG

Sandy Creek, 14 March 1863

Sir Frederick Pottinger was like a man possessed as he galloped towards the hut, heels digging into his horse and burning torch in his hand.

'This way, men,' he signalled to his army of officers lying in wait. 'Let's put an end to this once and for all.'

Pottinger was at his wits' end. He'd been shouted at on the street, ridiculed in the press and even bashed outside police headquarters, but he was going to have the last laugh. He was going to end Ben Hall.

To make things worse, Pottinger had been berated for being absent at the escort trials while a band of bushrangers robbed the Pinnacle police barracks near Forbes. On 6 March the barracks had been ransacked, unseen men stealing guns, ammunition, handcuffs and uniforms. A complete and utter embarrassment.

How could anyone rob a police station?

Four officers should have been protecting the barracks, a small but significant structure that housed guns, gear and guards. But three officers had gone into Forbes on a supply run, and the remaining officer was at the pub. He had been invited to stay at the hotel by a young lady who claimed she was scared of bushrangers. The lady, Mrs Feehily, just happened to be related to Dan Charters, Hall's best mate.

'That bloody Hall,' Pottinger had said, when told of the crime. 'Have you brought him in? He has set this whole thing up. Lured that stupid bastard out and just waltzed in and took the lot.'

The officer in charge of the investigation had shaken his head. 'No,' he said. 'He claims he was staying with friends at the time of the crime.'

'And you believe him?' Pottinger had asked incredulously.

'No,' said the officer, 'but his story has been corroborated. We have no evidence against him.'

'We will see about that,' Pottinger had snarled.

Hall had beaten Pottinger twice, escaping charges for the robbery of the drays and the escort heist. But this time Pottinger wasn't going to arrest him. He was going to ruin him.

Soon Pottinger was at Hall's hut. He didn't bother knocking on the door.

'Burn it,' he ordered. 'Burn it to the ground.'

* * *

Hall watched on from the safety of the scrub as his house went up in flames.

'Don't,' said John O'Meally, grabbing Hall by the arm. 'Too many. We don't stand a chance.'

Hall wanted to charge. To jump on his horse and storm across the field. He wanted to jam the butt of his shotgun into Pottinger's shoulder and squeeze the trigger. He wanted to kill them all. Shoot every last one of them dead.

Hall had already lost all his stock, the last of his cattle found dead when he was finally released from the Forbes lock-up for his alleged involvement in the escort robbery. He had lost his share in the station too, his licence now belonging to Forbes publican John Wilson. His gold still buried, Hall had spent all his money on his legal bills and could not pay the lease. All he had left was his hut.

He watched on with O'Meally as the last thing he owned burnt down to nothing.

'They've taken it all,' Hall said. 'Every last bit of it.'

Hall had given up on a reunion with Biddy. His latest arrest had confirmed that he would never reclaim his wife. And, in fact, he had accepted that. But he still held out hope for Henry. He had thought he would get him back. But not now. No cattle, no station and now no home.

Hall looked at O'Meally. 'We warned them,' he said.

And he had. Just two weeks earlier he had pleaded to be left alone. Told them what would happen if they continued to push, prod and hound.

'I'm innocent,' Hall had said, holding a gun to Sub-Inspector John Oxley Norton's head. 'I didn't rob the barracks. Why are you blokes always coming after me?'

Norton was shaking. Moments before he had attempted to kill Ben Hall. Having come across the man Pottinger wanted for the barracks job in the company of John O'Meally and Patsy Daley, he had demanded they stop. But they had refused and made a run.

Bang!

Billy Dargin, the black tracker accompanying Norton, had taken aim and fired. The shot had missed and the bushrangers had vanished.

'Shit,' said Norton. 'Whatcha do that for? There are only two of us. What if they come back?'

And come back they had.

'Bail up, you bastards,' came the cry just two miles down the road.

Boom!

O'Meally fired his shotgun.

Bang! Bang! Bang!

Norton fired off three shots too.

Bang! Bang! Bang!

From behind his horse, the meaty rump his cover, he had fired three more.

But then: *Click!* He was out of ammunition.

'Don't kill me,' Norton pleaded when Hall forced him from behind his horse. 'Please.'

Dargin had taken off, leaving him facing three wanted men.

'I'm not going to kill you,' Hall said. 'Or anyone else. I just want to be left alone. For Christ's sake, your bloke just shot at me. For what? I haven't done a thing.'

Norton was still shaking. 'I am just following out orders,' Norton said. 'Just doing my job.'

Hall laughed. 'Orders?' he echoed. 'Pottinger, right?'

The trooper nodded.

'That bloke has it in for me,' Hall said. 'I just want to be left alone. I am no threat to him. And do you know a Holster?'

Again Norton nodded. 'He is the copper that came from America.'

Hall lowered his gun. 'Well I have heard that he will shoot me if he gets the chance,' he said. 'You can tell him I will kill him if he tries. He won't be as lucky as you.' Hall waved his gun. 'Off you go,' he said. 'Tell 'em to back off.'

And Norton did, later recounting the entire episode in court. The newspapers splashed with the latest 'Police Embarrassment'.

For Pottinger, it was waving a red rag in front of a bull. 'That's it,' he'd yelled. 'Let's end this. Hall is going down. Whatever it takes.'

Fresh troops assembled, the best trackers by his side, he had jumped on his horse.

'Let's bring them in,' he ordered.

Three days into the hunt they found tracks leading away from the scene of the ambush.

'Here,' the tracker said.

They followed them, a day later coming to a rarely used mine called Pinnacle Reef where the tracks stopped dead. The mine looked deserted, just a couple of huts, a shaft and a water well.

'Have a look in that mine,' Pottinger had ordered.

An officer walked over and stuck his head down the shaft. 'I think someone is in there, boss,' he said.

Pottinger steamed towards the shaft. 'Come out now,' he ordered. 'We have you surrounded, Hall. I am only going to ask once.' He was met by silence. 'Alright, gentlemen,' he yelled, 'set it on fire.'

'Stop,' came the cry. 'I'm coming out.'

Patsy Daley was soon standing in front of Pottinger, hands out, ready to be cuffed.

Who the fuck is this?

'Where is Hall?' Pottinger demanded. 'Tell me or you will swing.'

Daley refused to give up Hall. Even though he was a newcomer, a Johnny-come-lately, he stayed silent and told Pottinger to do his worst. Not even two weeks in the lock-up at Forbes had made him talk.

So Pottinger grabbed his torch and his men.

'There is nothing left,' said Hall as he watched the last thing he owned engulfed by flames. 'All I have is my horse and my gun.'

And with that the Ben Hall Gang was officially formed, the most notorious and prolific bushranging band in history.

* * *

Young, 21 June 1863

Ben Hall was getting a taste for crime. He and his gang had walked into a store in Cootamundra and taken two hundred pounds worth of goods, not a shot fired or a question asked. They had also robbed Herbert's Red Shirt Store after finding the shop unlocked and unmanned. The gang helped themselves to new boots, shirts, jackets and belts. Too easy.

They also robbed a sub-inspector, relieving the second-in-charge of police of his watch, saddle and bridle. Sub-Inspector Shadforth was then made to walk back to town, Hall cutting his horse and sending it into the bush.

In all, the gang, which included Johnny Gilbert, Ben Hall, John O'Meally and now Fred Lowry, John Dunn and John Vane, had committed eight armed robberies since Hall's house had been burnt to the ground. They had terrorised Lambing Flat, Forbes and everywhere in between. They were now the most infamous criminal outfit in the colony. Nobody would dare oppose them. Or at least that is what Gilbert, the escort robber, thought. He was getting bolder with each crime.

* * *

'Bail up,' came the cry, Gilbert barking the now familiar order at the travel-weary miner. 'Pull up and let's see what you have.'

Gilbert was today part of a two-man gang, Hall and O'Meally up to strife of their own.

'Bail up,' Fred Lowry added. 'You heard the man.'

Lowry had escaped from Bathurst Gaol in February and quickly gone about finding the best and baddest bushranging gang.

John McBride, a tough old miner, looked at the two men, guns raised and aimed at his head. He looked down towards his saddle, his gold and money in a bag. And then he pulled out his gun.

The prospector fired two shots before taking cover behind a tree. He had his biggest ever score in his saddle, his future and his fortune. He wasn't going to give it up without a fight.

He fired off another three shots, one of them putting a hole through Lowry's hat. His five-shooter was spent. And then the bushrangers returned serve, blasting off all nine of their rounds.

'Ahhh!' screamed McBride. 'I'm hit.' He looked down towards his leg, seeing blood and bone. One of the shots had ripped a hole in his thigh. He was also out of ammo. 'Here,' he shouted as he threw away his gun. 'I'm unarmed.'

Gilbert and Lowry did not need an invitation. Guns drawn, they approached the miner.

'You a trap?' Gilbert asked.

The miner shook his head. 'No,' he said. 'Why would you ask that?'

Gilbert reached down and pulled the miner's discarded revolver from the ground. 'Because this is a Colt Navy,' he said. 'That is what the traps use.' Also, Pottinger had recently implemented an innovation that would have the bushrangers on edge. Admitting a police uniform was unsuitable for the bush, the inspector had issued a decree that allowed officers to conduct operations while 'plainly dressed'.

'No,' McBride said. 'Look in my saddle. I have gold. I am a miner.'

Gilbert nodded and went off and got the gold. He also went through the wounded man's pockets.

'And I'll take this too,' Gilbert said, waving the revolver in his hand. 'Just in case.'

They left the man under a tree. John McBride died the next day. Having not been found for hours, he had almost bled to death when he was stumbled upon by a couple of travellers. He was dead by the time he arrived at Burrangong hospital.

Gilbert and Lowry stuck up another group of travellers the very same day, and Gilbert was also spotted waving the dead man's Colt around in a pub a couple of days later.

Hall was not impressed when he heard of the death for he knew there would be no turning back now. There would be no pleas or deals. No surrender. If caught, they would hang. And they would be coming for them with all they had.

* * *

Young, 21 June 1863

John Barnes could not believe his luck. Just on his way to visit his son, the shopkeeper turned to find himself facing Johnny Gilbert and John O'Meally.

'Bail up!' came the shout.

Barnes knew the two faces very well. They had already robbed him twice. First, two months earlier, when a gang of four had burst into his Cootamundra store and cleaned him out, and again three weeks later. Barnes had even written a letter to the *Yass Courier*, slamming the efforts of the police to stop the unprecedented wave of crime.

'Get off your horse,' Gilbert shouted.

The shopkeeper remained still. Defiant.

'You bastard,' shouted O'Meally. 'If you stir, I will put daylight through you.'

Barnes gritted his teeth. *Not again. Not this time.*

And then he made a decision that would cost him his life.

'No,' he said, grabbing the reins and kicking his horse. He made a dash, attempting to stop robbery number three.

'You bastard,' O'Meally shouted again as he began his chase. 'I warned you!'

Barnes never stood a chance against O'Meally on a race-quality horse.

A local farmer, Alexander Mackay, heard the gunfire and walked from his home to see what the hell was going on. He saw a man being chased, another man shooting at him. And then the attacker fled.

Mackay rushed towards the man, who was now slumped on his horse. The rider fell.

Barnes was dead by the time Mackay got to him. The shopkeeper had hit his head on a log during the fall and split his skull. The coroner later pulled three bullets from his body.

Now O'Meally was a killer too. The gang was armed, and not only dangerous but murderous.

* * *

Goimbla, 19 November 1863

'Fucking John Vane,' O'Meally snorted as the three members of the Hall gang rode towards Goimbla Station, a property close to Eugowra. 'He is going to dog us all in.'

News had reached the Hall gang that new recruit Vane had turned himself in. He had presented himself at Bathurst police station, surrendering with the help of a priest. He had no doubt been enticed by the offer of leniency that he and the gang had seen the day before, slapped up on the front of a store:

Colonial Secretary's Office,

Sydney, 26 October 1863

£4,000 REWARD

FOR THE APPREHENSION OF JOHN GILBERT,

JOHN O'MEALLY, BENJAMIN HALL and JOHN

VANE

and £100 REWARD for accomplice.

WHEREAS the above named persons are charged with the commission of numerous and serious offences, and have hitherto eluded efforts to apprehend them, it is hereby notified that the Government will pay a reward of £1,000 for such information that will lead to the apprehension of each of the offenders named.

The Government will also pay a reward of One Hundred Pounds for such information that will lead to the conviction of any person or persons for harbouring, assisting or maintaining any of the above named offenders.

All such information communicated by any person charged with the commission of an offence will entitle his case to favourable consideration by the Crown, and will in all cases be regarded by the Police Authorities as strictly confidential; and in the event of payment of any of the rewards above offered, the name of the recipient will not be disclosed.

The above rewards are offered in lieu of all others previously payable by the Government for the apprehension or conviction of the offenders above named.
WILLIAM FOSTER

Hall laughed at O'Meally. 'What's he going to tell them that they don't already know?' he asked. 'We will hang regardless. Whatever he says will make no difference. Forget about him — we are already the most wanted men in the colony.'

Not just the most wanted but also the most violent and prolific, the gang going on the longest crime spree in the history of the British Empire. Since the beginning of the year, the now world-famous Hall gang had committed thirty-seven robberies, been involved in five shoot-outs and murdered three men.

They had also lost one of their own, Fred Lowry going down in a hail of bullets during a shoot-out with police near Goulburn.

'And what are they going to do?' Hall asked. 'Shoot at us?'

Now O'Meally laughed. Gilbert too.

The gang had been chased by police just five days earlier when their camp had been spotted by a group of troopers and they were forced to flee. The trio were fast losing the law when they got stuck in the mud.

'Oh Christ,' Hall said, his horse almost slowing to a stop. 'Bog.'

Hall's horse was stuck. The police were closing in.

'Go,' he ordered, looking at O'Meally and Gilbert. 'Get out of here. I will fend for myself.'

Hall's long-time friends refused. O'Meally grabbed the beast by the bridle and pulled while Hall struck the horse in the rear with a bayonet.

'Almost out,' Gilbert observed. 'But quick, they are coming.'

The horse was soon free and the gang again charged on, but the police were close enough to open fire. And they had, one after another, emptying their guns. The breech-loading rifles, however, were notoriously inaccurate, and every shot had missed.

'Go,' Hall ordered. 'Let's get out of here while they reload.'

And again the gang escaped.

* * *

'Fuck Vane,' Gilbert said now as they closed in on Goimbla Station. 'Let's settle this score first. One at a time.'

The men rode towards the setting sun with vengeance in mind. David Campbell, the owner of the station, had been running his mouth.

'So this bastard has been out looking for us,' O'Meally said. 'Out with his gun telling everyone he is going to bring us in.'

Hall nodded. 'Let's see if he is a man of his word,' he said. 'See if he wants to get up on a pedestal and talk tough now.'

Hall had been hearing stories of Campbell for a couple of months. At first he had laughed when he'd heard about the cattle farmer who had stood on a stool in a Forbes pub and told everyone he was going to be the man who stopped Ben Hall.

Yeah, you and everyone else.

And he'd shrugged when he'd heard the same man had barged into a public meeting at Bathurst Town Hall. 'The police are useless,' he'd apparently said. 'It is up to us. The people. I will stop Hall and his gang. I will gather the men and do what the police cannot.'

But when he heard this Campbell and a posse of armed men had gone into the bush, guns raised and yelling, 'We are going to kill Ben Hall,' well, he shrugged no more. Instead he gritted his teeth and made a promise. *I'll pay this man a visit someday.*

And that day was today, a local dumping Campbell in it.

'You know that Campbell?' he'd asked Hall. 'The bloke who is telling everyone he's going to kill you? He lives just down the road.'

Hall hadn't shrugged this time either, just nodded and loaded his gun. 'Where does he live?'

* * *

Hall, Gilbert and O'Meally came to the top of a hill.

'There,' Hall said, pointing down into a gully. 'He must be a rich bastard.'

Hall was looking upon two structures, the first a hut with a thatched roof but solid and sturdy all the same. The second building was new. And it was big. A modern house with a tin roof built alongside the hut.

'That is good land,' said Gilbert. 'And look at all those cows.'

They marched down into the valley and towards the house. At the bottom of the hill the scrub cleared and they could now see that the dwelling was big enough to house fifty men. With a couple of guns stuck out a window they would be sitting ducks, but no one in this gang even considered the possibility. They were fearless and focused, untouchable.

Hall brazenly dismounted near the front door of the new house while O'Meally and Gilbert stayed on their mounts, shotguns pointed at whatever might greet Hall. Ben didn't knock, not right away. He slowly walked around the verandah, adding weight to each step, making sure his boots were slapping the floor. The house did not stir. Not a movement, not a sound. So Hall started stamping, crashing his left foot into the wooden planks first then his right.

Hall waved his right arm, giving O'Meally and Gilbert their signal, and with that they dismounted and walked to the front door. Hall crouched as they approached the door, rifle resting on his leg.

Gilbert knocked on the door once, then harder, but the house remained silent. Hall nodded, his chin touching his rifle as he moved his head.

Whack! It was O'Meally this time, smashing his foot into the door.

'Oww!' he shouted, the door holding while he bounced backwards.

And then all hell broke loose.

First it was the sound of glass smashing, then of slug hitting wall.

'Get down!' Hall shouted. 'Take cover.'

More shots were followed by the smash of another window breaking, but this time it was courtesy of a shotgun blast.

* * *

Campbell had been ready and waiting. A rider had come to his house an hour before with a warning, the bush telegraph evidently working two ways.

'Surrender,' Hall shouted from outside, 'we have you surrounded.'

Campbell shook his head before ordering his men to fire.

'Ahhh!' came a cry. 'I'm hit!'

Campbell lowered his gun and turned to his left. 'No!'

The property owner's younger brother was holding his shoulder and about to fall to the floor.

Bang!

Glass exploded next to Campbell's head. He turned and fired again.

'Surrender,' came the call. 'This is your last chance.'

Two shots tore up the wooden floor beside him and for the first time Campbell felt fear. He turned and looked towards his brother, whose arms dropped as he bled onto the floor.

Campbell didn't care for saving himself, but his brother? He was about to surrender. And that's when his wife came from nowhere, scooped up the gun dropped by her brother-in-law and fired a shot out the smashed window. With that Campbell also turned and returned fire.

* * *

No longer crouching but standing and shooting, Hall was stunned. *Who the hell is this guy?*

He wanted a square up. But he didn't want this. He issued another warning.

'Surrender,' he yelled. 'Stop shooting and come out. This is a fight you can't win.'

The shots kept on coming.

So Hall turned to O'Meally. 'Burn it down,' he said.

Gilbert had already provided the fuel, stacking bales of hay against the house. He poured pure alcohol over the tinder.

Vrooomp! The flames erupted into the night. Hall, O'Meally and Gilbert lowered their guns and backed away. Now that the fire was raging, Hall stopped and thought.

How many inside? Will they get out? What have we done? They had unleashed a beast that could not be tamed. A horse could be heard screaming as the flames jumped to the barn. The beast soon roasted alive.

The posse backed off, a picket fence soon all that was shielding them from the fast-rising flames.

Bang! 'You fucking bastards,' came the cry after the shot. 'I'll send you all to hell.'

O'Meally looked towards the noise and saw a silhouette moving through the blazing light of the flames. The ball hit him in the neck, the picket fence providing no protection, just a canvas to catch his blood.

'John,' Hall cried. 'John, are you hit?'

O'Meally remained silent.

Hall crawled over to his mate. 'John,' he said again, more urgently this time.

O'Meally was leaning against the fence, his neck gushing blood.

'Fuck!' Hall shouted.

O'Meally was dead in another moment.

'Is he okay?' shouted Gilbert as he covered off the man coming out of the flames. 'Ben?'

Hall turned and shook his head. He grabbed O'Meally and hugged him, blood streaming.

'We've got to get out of here,' Gilbert said. 'We've got to go.'

Hall put O'Meally on the ground on his back, face up to the sky. More shots filled the air.

'Come on, Ben,' Gilbert pushed. 'It will be us next.'

Hall ignored both the bullets and Gilbert. 'Rest in peace,' Hall said as he closed O'Meally's eyes, bloody hands smudging his mate's face.

Hall reached into the dead man's pockets, removing his wallet and a chain. Hall couldn't bring his body with them but he wanted something to give to O'Meally's family. He had to give them something.

Hall and Gilbert began their retreat, but Hall suddenly stopped.

'I can't leave him here,' Hall said. 'I have to take him home. I need to give his father more than a wallet and chain.'

Hall went back for his mate. With guns still firing, he heaved O'Meally onto his back and restarted his retreat.

'Leave him,' shouted Gilbert. 'You'll die trying to save a dead man.'

And Gilbert was right, Hall soon reduced to dragging the body.

'Until we meet again,' Hall said, before finally abandoning his mate.

* * *

While Hall and Gilbert would mourn O'Meally, few else would. The bushranger had killed at least two people – John Barnes and Adolf Cirkel – and may have been responsible for more deaths. The official autopsy ruled O'Meally died of a single shot to the throat from a large-calibre bullet. The death was ruled a 'justifiable homicide'.

O'Meally was buried in a shallow grave not far from where he was killed, in a cornfield on the outskirts of the station. His family came and exhumed the body a week later before burying him at a site unknown.

Mrs Campbell later wrote a letter to her mother detailing the extraordinary attack. 'You will be anxious till you hear direct of our safety,' Mrs Campbell wrote.

It is indeed owing to the great mercy of God that the lives of William and David were spared. So many people have been here taking notes that I doubt not you will read a truthful account in the papers. I will not therefore weary you with another.

We had no time to fear. The most dreaded part was the burning of the house and stable. You cannot imagine my agony as those flames were towering above us. Had the wind been blowing towards the house then all would have been gone. I was in deadly fear of it catching us at this point that I rushed out onto the road until the danger passed.

Mr Campbell had ventured out to the spot where he had aimed at the man. He found a gun and a hat but not the man for his mates had dragged the body for some distance. At this point we thought the man was just wounded and were afraid he would come back for his things.

A short while after we heard some rustling in the bushes and were concerned that the bushrangers were lying in wait of an ambush. David stationed the men at various points around the station where they kept watching until morning. I went to bed at about three o'clock and was woken up by the arrival of police the next morning.

They found the body and I cannot describe to you the state of my feeling when I heard of it – heard that the unhappy man had been shot by the light of the fire which he had helped raise – for at the moment he fell the country around was as light as day.

It appears the ruffians retreated to one of the huts where they were cursing and swearing in a most fearful manner that they would get revenge. And I am sad to say that a female servant heard one of them say that they regretted not shooting the woman, which I suppose was me. But thankfully his comrade told him to hold his tongue and not say such dreadful things.

William is alright now, despite receiving a charge of slugs in his breast, which resulted in four wounds in all.

Hall and Gilbert never came back.

Mr and Mrs Campbell were given bravery awards and the public raised over a thousand pounds to help reimburse them for the damage caused in the attack. The government also issued them with the five hundred–pound reward for killing the murderer O'Meally.

O'Meally proved a local attraction for some time, publicans displaying hair they claimed had been cut from his corpse.

* * *

Sandy Creek, 13 February 1864

The fire hissed and spat. Hall turned towards the flames, the heat hitting his face. The fire reminded him of what he was trying to forget. *Goimbla. O'Meally. Dead.*

Suddenly his mind was flooded with thoughts of burning barns, guns and a dying mate. He grunted and turned away again, grabbing his bottle of gin and taking a swig. With a violent movement he threw away the empty bottle, the glass shattering against the trunk of a tree, and closed his eyes.

Is this it? Is this my life? It was never supposed to be like this …

Eventually the night took him, the bushranger finally passing out. When he woke, his horse was sniffing at his head.

'Shoo,' he said, swiping at it. 'Get.'

The morning summer sun hit him like a sledgehammer. And then the birds started: crows, magpies and a lone kookaburra. The noise pounded his aching head. *O'Meally. Dead.*

Hall needed a distraction. He reached into his waistcoat, pulled out a little locket and flipped open the lid, polished silver sparkling in the sun.

Biddy.

There she was, stunning in sepia. And for a moment he was back in 1860. He was a stockman. He had a hut and a farm. He had a wife and a child on the way. Oh how he wished he could go back.

But he couldn't. Biddy had moved on. She was in love with James Taylor.

Fucking Taylor. Hall snarled.

Taylor. The drunk.

Hall had been told that Taylor was an alcoholic, the former trap spending his wage on gin. He looked back down at the photo.

Why? Why him?

Hall couldn't save Biddy. But he could save his son.

* * *

'Shit,' Taylor yelled. 'It's Hall.'

Biddy looked out the window.

'Go,' she commanded. 'Get out of here.'

Taylor steamed out the door, half dressed and half drunk, and ran across the field.

Mounted high on his horse as he approached the house, Hall watched Taylor sprint towards the scrub. He laughed as the drunkard stumbled into the bush.

Coward. Pathetic.

But he didn't chase. Hall wasn't there for Taylor. Nor was he there for Biddy.

'Ben,' yelled Biddy from the verandah. 'What are you doing here? You can't be here. What do you want?'

Hall dismounted and walked towards his wife.

'Henry,' he shouted. 'Henry, come out here. It's Ben Hall. Your father.'

Biddy rushed at Hall.

'Father?' she yelled. 'Father? What right do you have to call yourself his father? He doesn't even know who you are.'

Biddy was right. But Hall did not care.

'Henry,' he shouted again. 'Come here.'

The boy edged his way out of the house and looked at his father warily.

Hall rushed past Biddy and embraced his son. 'I'm sorry it has been so long. I'll make it up to you.' He picked up Henry and put him on his horse.

'No,' screamed Biddy. 'No, you can't!'

Hall was already behind Henry on his mount.

'Ma!' cried Henry. 'Ma, what's happening?'

Hall dug his heels in and his horse turned.

'Henry,' Biddy screamed as she ran behind them. 'No, Ben, please!'

But Hall wasn't listening. He wasn't stopping. He had what he came for. Biddy slumped when she finally gave up the chase, breaking down in the middle of a field.

'Jim,' she shouted. 'Jim, help!'

But Taylor didn't come. Terrified, he kept himself hidden in the bush.

* * *

Hall forcibly took his son, Henry, from the Sandy Creek home of James Taylor and Biddy Hall after being told the former police officer was mistreating his son. In a desperate act from an increasingly desperate man – with O'Meally dead, Gilbert now in Victoria, and the cops chasing him down – Hall thought he could finally become a father to his boy. He quickly realised he couldn't.

'William,' Hall said, the bushranger and the boy arriving at his brother's house soon after the kidnap, 'I need you to raise my boy.' Hall handed his brother a bag of money. 'Make sure he never wants for anything,' he said.

James Taylor and Biddy Hall issued William Hall with a summons for the illegal detention of the child. But the case never got to court, William handing over both the child and the money.

'That money is for the kid,' William said, looking at Taylor. 'Not grog.'

Taylor, of course, drank his way through every last penny.

Chapter 14

THE FUGITIVE

Apis Creek, 2 March 1864

Gardiner was in the stockroom when Kitty called out.

'Francis,' she shouted. 'Some men need your help.'

The outlaw turned shopkeeper put down his rapidly filling notepad. Business had been good and he was out of almost everything.

Gardiner walked into the shop and dusted his hands on his apron before extending an arm.

'G'day, mate,' he said before shaking the stranger's hand. 'Name is Francis, Francis Christie. What can I do you for?'

The scruffy-looking man, clothes stained with dirt and beard in need of a trim, regarded Gardiner for a moment.

'I'm camped just down the road with a couple of my mates,' he said. 'We are on our way to the Peak Downs diggings to try our luck. But one of the lads has come down ill. Dysentery. I was hoping to buy some oatmeal to give him a good feed and get him on the mend.'

'We are out of oatmeal,' Kitty snapped, suspicious of the stranger. 'As I told you.'

Gardiner put his hand gently on Kitty's shoulder. 'Now, Mrs Christie,' he said. 'We can't let a poor sick fella go hungry.' He looked at the prospector and smiled. ''Tis true we are out of oatmeal,' Gardiner said. 'We are just about out of everything right now and I'm sending out an order this afternoon. But I think we have a little in the kitchen.'

'That's for us,' Kitty said, looking at Frank. 'That's not for sale.'

Gardiner nodded. 'That's right,' he said. 'It's not for sale but we can spare a little and give it to this gentleman for free. And maybe he will come back another day when we are well stocked and make us rich.' Gardiner laughed whole-heartedly from the belly.

'Oh, I'll be back,' the man said, now laughing too. 'That is for sure.'

* * *

The man walked back into his camp, oatmeal in hand, grin on his face.

'It's him,' he said, dumping Gardiner's gift on the ground. 'It is bloody Frank Gardiner, alive and in the flesh.'

His mate stood tall, no sign of supposed sickness. 'How do you know for sure?' he asked.

'I just do,' came the reply. 'It's him.' He kicked the oatmeal that Gardiner had given him into the fire.

'We need to be sure,' said the third man in the group. 'We can't fuck this up.'

'Righto,' said the first man, unkempt beard and dirty clothes. 'I'll go back in a while. I'll buy a drink and find out some more.'

* * *

'Back so soon?' Gardiner asked the scruffy miner, now in the hotel built next to his store.

Gardiner ran both the store and the hotel, although his business partner, Archibald Craig, held the licence to the pub. Gardiner didn't want the name Christie on any official records.

'Yeah, thought I would buy you a drink,' the miner said. 'My mate's already on the mend. Now I'll repay you for your kindness and start making you those riches you foretold.'

Gardiner smiled and poured two drinks, one for the stranger and one for himself. All seemed well, and then came the questions.

So you're from New South Wales? Whereabouts? Ever been to Forbes? When did you get here?

Gardiner would not have thought much of the questions a month ago. But now, well, he was on edge. A man who knew Francis Christie when he was Frank Gardiner had chanced his way into the very same bar a month ago.

'By Lord, look who it is!' the interloper had said.

Glancing sideways, Frank had drawn a finger to his lips and shaken his head surreptitiously.

'Howdy, stranger,' he'd replied, recognising the man he used to sell stolen horses and cattle to in Forbes. 'Come on over here.'

Thankfully, the man now calling himself Mr Smith had got the idea. Tucked away in a corner, away from prying eyes and ears, Gardiner explained himself before making an offer.

'You can't tell anyone,' he said. 'That was my old life. I have gone straight. I have a woman and a business and that is all I need.'

He told him he had become a respectable citizen, a confidant to the president of the Australian Joint Stock Bank and a personal friend to the gold commissioner, Thomas John Griffin.

'For Christ's sake, they are thinking about making me a justice of the peace,' Gardiner continued. 'No one can ever know who I am – and I will pay to make sure.'

Mr Smith, real name Mark Brown, had raised an eyebrow. He was an ex-convict who had served time with Gardiner on the hell called Cockatoo Island.

'How much?' Smith asked. 'Just out of curiosity and all.'

'I will give you double the reward,' Gardiner snapped.

Smith, by then working as an auctioneer in Rockhampton, had shaken Gardiner's hand and given him his word – after Gardiner gave him the cash, of course. Gardiner thought his secret was safe, but now here was another stranger, buying him a drink and asking him questions about Forbes.

Gardiner gulped down his last swig.

'That will have to do me, friend,' he said. 'Got to get back to it or I will never make my fortune. And the drink is on me.'

* * *

Detectives Daniel McGlone and James Pye and Mounted Trooper Wells, all of the New South Wales police, had been sent to Rockhampton to investigate a claim that Gardiner was living in North Queensland. There had been rumours before, but never enough to warrant a search. Not until Mark Brown, alias Mr Smith, had come forward and sworn by way of statement that his old Lambing Flat 'butcher' mate was living his life as a store owner in Apis Creek. Even with Smith's statement, it was considered a long shot. The decision to send three men nine hundred miles north was not made lightly. The trip would be both time-consuming and expensive. But twenty-four days after leaving Sydney on the steamship *Balclutha*, here was McGlone, the scruffy miner, coming back from the Apis Creek hotel with a gigantic grin plastered across his face.

With darkness falling fast, his 'mining' mates were warming themselves by the fire.

'It is Frank Gardiner,' beamed McGlone, bursting his way into the circle. 'It's Frank fucking Gardiner.'

Pye played devil's advocate, flames reflecting on his face. 'Did he tell you?' he asked. 'Did he admit it?'

'No,' McGlone said. 'But I looked at his scars. Chin. Forehead. Hand. It's Gardiner. You have my word.'

McGlone slapped Wells on the back, the force of the friendly blow charged with so much excitement that the mounted trooper dropped his mug, tea splashing into the fire.

'It's Frank fucking Gardiner,' McGlone shouted again. 'Boys, we have our man. We are going to be the most famous coppers in the colony. The brave men who got the colony's most wanted man.'

And now they needed help.

'Let's go and see the native troopers,' McGlone said. 'We need as many men as possible. We can't risk buggering this up. We don't want to become the next Pottinger, do we now?'

Putting the billy on for a fresh tea, Wells laughed. 'For God's sake, no,' he said. 'So let's make it an early night.'

'Early night?' McGlone responded incredulously. 'We will go see those trackers right now. We can't give Gardiner a chance. What if he smells a rat? Maybe I spooked him already.'

This time Wells spilled his own tea. 'Fine,' he said, giving up and emptying his mug. 'Let's do it then.'

The trio rode down the road to a property where the lieutenant of the native police lived. Established in 1837, the native police were a cheap and brutal paramilitary force used by the government to enforce the colony's will. Uniformed and armed with carbines, they policed native populations, mostly under the command of a white lieutenant. The makeshift force was also used to back up the regular police.

McGlone was surprised to find this lieutenant was Aboriginal.

'We have found Frank Gardiner,' he started. He filled Lieutenant Brown in on his plan and ordered him to gather his troops.

'So tomorrow it is,' McGlone smiled.

* * *

Apis Creek, 3 March 1864

Gardiner watched as the man sharpened his axe.

'That's thirsty work,' Gardiner said, looking at the piles of uncut logs. 'First one is on me.'

The axeman grinned. 'That sounds like a good deal,' he said. He stopped sharpening, something catching his eye along the road. 'What do we have here?' he asked, looking at the men approaching. 'Some fresh meat. You better take all their money before they get to the mine because they won't be leaving with any. No gold left.'

Frank looked over and saw the scruffy miner from yesterday heading his way on horseback. He had two others with him.

Gardiner had not slept well the night before. His encounter with the stranger and all his questions had left him unsettled. But it was probably nothing. He had been wary of every stranger he had met since that damn Mark Brown had stumbled into his hotel. Gardiner squinted into the rising sun, watching the trio's approach. They were coming straight towards him.

Gardiner took a step back as the miner dismounted.

'We are heading off,' said McGlone, approaching with an outstretched hand. 'Just wanted to thank you for your hospitality and introduce you to my mates.'

Gardiner looked at the men and then their horses, packed, loaded and ready to leave. He suddenly felt stupid for his unease and shook the miner's hand.

'This is James,' the man said, pointing at the bigger of the two with him. 'And that is John,' he continued, pointing at the other one.

Gardiner nodded and smiled. And suddenly they all turned and looked behind them down the road.

'What's that racket?' asked the man who had been introduced as James. 'Are those bloody blackfellas singing?'

Gardiner took a step back and studied the approaching group of men singing on horseback. He relaxed. Just the native police.

'They're in good voice today,' he said.

Gardiner wasn't surprised to see the native police approaching, nor to hear them singing. This mob liked a song and they loved a drink. They were no threat to Gardiner or any other white.

Suddenly Gardiner was on the ground, grabbed from behind and dragged to the dirt.

'Cover him off,' McGlone screamed as he pinned Gardiner down with his chest. 'Mark him. He is a desperate man.'

Those singing blackfellas had been a threat after all – now their twelve guns pointed at Gardiner on the floor.

'You put that down,' screamed Pye, looking to the woodcutter and his axe.

He dropped it without a sound.

'Frank Gardiner,' McGlone barked as Wells produced chains and cuffs, 'you are under arrest. We are taking you into custody for having committed sundry highway robberies under arms in New South Wales. Do you have anything to say?'

Gardiner didn't. Australia's most feared outlaw did not even say a word. He didn't fight. Didn't resist. He was busted, and this time he wouldn't even bother offering a bribe.

'No,' cried Kitty Brown, bursting onto the street. 'No, you have got the wrong man. My Francis has done nothing. Leave him be.'

Frank lifted his head up from the dirt to look at Kitty. 'Hush,' he said, 'I am not going to fight, my love.'

Kitty started to cry. 'I won't leave you, Frank,' she said.

Next McGlone had Gardiner's business partner, Archibald Craig, in chains. 'For aiding and abetting a wanted criminal,' McGlone barked.

'Criminal?' Craig whimpered as the cuffs went on. 'Francis? Mr Christie? No. You have the wrong man.'

'No,' McGlone said, 'you have the wrong name. This man here is Frank Gardiner.'

Craig went white.

With Gardiner and Craig secured and the native police still pointing guns at their heads, the three New South Wales troopers searched both the shop and pub. They found gold, jewellery, guns, ammunition and more than two thousand pounds in cash, leaving them certain that they had their man.

The most audacious, successful, longest and richest run of any criminal in the colony's history had come to an end. Gardiner's fifteen-year stint as the King of the Road, starting with the theft of a horse and ending with the biggest gold robbery in history, was over. He had escaped from gaol, survived shoot-outs and ordered murderers. He had held hostages, bribed police and burnt down properties. He had been responsible for more crimes than any man that ever lived until Ben Hall took over with his gang.

And now he was cuffed and chained. A bushranger busted.

* * *

Rockhampton, 6 March 1864

Francis Gardiner was back in a cell. He didn't expect to be getting out anytime soon.

'Sorry, mate,' Gardiner said to Craig. 'I never meant for you to get caught up in any of this.'

Archibald Craig, respected business owner and law-abiding citizen, was hunched in a corner. He rested his head against the cold stone and his bum on the damp cell floor.

'All this,' Gardiner stopped and pointed at the bars and locks, 'well, I left it all behind. I gave up my old life and started a new one. The person who committed those crimes doesn't exist anymore.'

Craig managed to reply. 'Those blokes with the guns might argue that point,' he said. 'Reckon a jury might too.'

Gardiner shrugged and joined his former partner on the ground. Australia's most prized convict was utterly exhausted. The trip from Apis Creek to Rockhampton had taken three days. He had been forced to ride on a horse with his hands cuffed and his feet chained. The native police had joined the three coppers from New South Wales for the trip.

'Shoot him if he tries anything,' was the order from McGlone. 'We will bring him in dead or alive. Doesn't matter which.'

Kitty Brown joined Gardiner for the journey, living up to her vow to never leave his side. She promised to get the best lawyer money could buy.

'This will not stand,' she told the police. 'He will be set free by the end of the week.'

Craig's friend Cuthbert Featherstone also joined the party, utterly outraged by the charges laid against his long-time friend. He too vowed to fight for his mate and engage the best legal minds in the land.

'You will be out of here soon,' Gardiner promised, looking Craig square in the face.

'I'll swear you didn't know who I was. You have done nothing wrong. This will all be over?'

He stopped, hearing a familiar cry. 'Kitty? Kitty, is that you?'

It was. Kitty Brown, alias Kitty Christie, was being shoved into a cell alongside his.

'Frank,' she yelled. 'They are putting me in a cell. I have been arrested.'

'She has done nothing,' Gardiner bellowed. 'Let her out. Let her out now or there will be hell to pay!'

McGlone had gone to the hotel Kitty had checked into as soon as the party arrived in Rockhampton. She had paid for a week's accommodation but expected she would have to fork out more.

'Would you like to come and see Frank?' McGlone had asked. 'You can visit him now if you like.'

Kitty agreed; she needed to talk lawyers and tactics. But it was a trick. She was arrested as soon as she walked into the station, charged with assisting and concealing a bushranger.

Gardiner broke down, the toughest outlaw in the colony weeping as they shoved his love into a cold, lonely cell.

* * *

Brisbane, 13 March 1864

Gardiner stepped off the steamer called *Queensland* a relieved man. He smiled as the Brisbane sun hit his face. He hadn't been released from custody; in fact, he had been sentenced to stand trial for all his crimes. He was cuffed, chained and about to be shipped to Sydney to face the colony's next biggest-ever trial.

And I will probably be hanged …

But still he smiled.

'I told you it would be alright,' Gardiner had said to Kitty, moments after the Rockhampton court had set her free. 'It will all be fine now. Forget about me. Go and live your life.'

The court had ruled there was no evidence to charge Kitty and she'd been released after spending just one night in gaol. Mr Craig was set loose too, the court apologising for the mistake before sending him on his way.

But Gardiner, well, Gardiner was going to Sydney. The King of the Road would be locked up in a single cell at Australia's worst gaol and prosecuted for everything and anything the police could make stick.

Detective McGlone testified as to his heroics at the committal trial.

'I came here from Sydney after receiving some information some time ago,' McGlone said. 'I came accompanied by Detective Pye and Mounted Trooper Wells. From Rockhampton we proceeded to Apis Creek, a place about a hundred miles from here, on the Peak Downs Road. At Apis Creek I saw the prisoner in a store. I saw him when I arrived. I understand the store was owned by him. I did not arrest him on the instance

I saw him. I arrested him the following morning after seeking the assistance of Detective Pye, Trooper Wells and Lieutenant Brown of the native police. I arrested him on the road outside his store and then took him into custody. I informed him of the charge and secured him safely until I could bring him here. I charged him with various robberies, including the escort robbery at Eugowra in 1862. I arrested him in the usual way, fairly. He was knocked down and was laid on his back, quietly and secure.'

Yes, the escort robbery. Gardiner was sure he would hang, but still he seemed strangely at peace. He was polite to the police, abiding in every possible way. *Yes, sir. No, sir. Of course, sir.* He thanked the magistrate. He even smiled.

I have lived a long life, considering. Done it all. Could have been worse.

At thirty-four, Gardiner was the oldest surviving bushranger in Australia. He had been living on borrowed time ever since Pottinger had fired point-blank at his head and the gun had misfired.

Bushrangers died young. Matthew Brady dead at twenty-six. And of course, Henry Manns dead at twenty-three and John O'Meally dead at twenty-two.

And then he was actually given reason to smile.

'What's going on here today?' Gardiner asked as he stepped off the steamer and onto the dock. 'Why are all these people here?'

The trap laughed. 'To see the famous Frank Gardiner,' he said. 'Why else?'

Gardiner was given a hero's welcome, thousands flooding the docks, clapping and cheering his name. McGlone was stunned, expecting all the applause to be for him. Kitty wasn't.

'The people love him,' she said. 'He robbed the likes of you in the name of them.'

But McGlone was going to get his applause, if not from the public then from his boss. He sent a telegraph back to police headquarters in Sydney.

Brisbane, 13 March
Captain McLerie, Inspector General of Police
I have arrived here with Francis Christie, alias Clarke, alias
Gardiner. I have no doubt but he is the man. I arrested him
on the third instant at Apis Creek. He corresponds with his
description in the Police Gazette *and his portrait. Mrs Brown*
is with him, and there is no doubt about her identity. She
is coming with us, but not in custody. She will follow her
paramour. She and Frank Gardiner's partner were [sic] *arrested*
by me, but were [sic] *discharged by the Rockhampton bench.*
I shall arrive with Gardiner safe in Sydney about Saturday. I
left Rockhampton on the 10th, and arrived here today at noon.
Gardiner is lodged safe in the gaol here. No steamer here for
Sydney yet, but one is expected. Will let you know when I
leave for Sydney. If Richards is required to identify Gardiner, he
is making lemonade on the Wentworth diggings.

* * *

Kitty Brown knocked on doors and waved around cash for the next three days. With Gardiner locked up in Brisbane's gaol while waiting for the steamship *Telegraph* to take him to Sydney, Brown planned his defence. First she raised some money, selling her and Frank's share in the shop and hotel to Craig for five hundred pounds. Then she hired a lawyer.

Kitty was standing in the gaol three days later.

'Frank, you are getting out,' she beamed. 'We have just come from court and the judge has ruled the arrest was unlawful. You are to be set free.'

The Brisbane lawyer appointed by Brown had applied for a writ of 'habeas corpus', claiming Gardiner was being held in custody illegally because he was arrested without a warrant. He also argued Gardiner had been remanded without a previous warrant or any evidence of criminality, that the magistrate had acted without respect to the remand and no remand period had been stated. And on 16 March, Justice Alfred James Lutwyche of the Moreton Bay Supreme Court had sensationally agreed and he ordered Gardiner to be released.

'Let's go home, Frank,' Kitty said.

Gardiner shook his head.

'Frank?' Kitty frowned. 'What's wrong?'

'I'm not going anywhere,' Gardiner said. 'They will arrest me again as soon as they get a warrant.'

Kitty sat stunned. 'No,' she said. 'Let's go. We can go on the run.'

Gardiner shook his head once more. 'Not again,' he said. 'I'm done with that life. It's time to face up to what I have done. You need to move on.'

'I won't,' Kitty cried. 'I love you, Frank.'

Early the next morning, Gardiner was escorted onto the *Telegraph* under the cover of darkness, police determined to deny him a farewell to match his welcoming. He was locked in a solitary cell. Gardiner arrived in Sydney twenty-four hours later and again the authorities transferred the prisoner in the darkness of night. He was slapped in leg chains and taken from Darling Harbour to Darlinghurst Gaol, the beauty of the Sydney's waterway replaced by a brick-and-bar hell.

Chapter 15

THE ACCUSED

Darlinghurst, 20 May 1864

'Prisoner stand,' came the order, the clerk yelling over the crowd.

Gardiner, with his hair freshly cut and his beard closely trimmed, rose. He shuffled his way to the front of the box.

Could be worse. Could be much worse.

'Francis Christie,' the clerk continued, courtroom quelled, all eyes on the most famous man to ever stand in an Australian court dock, 'alias Francis Gardiner, alias Francis Clarke, on the sixteenth day of July 1861, at the Fish River, in the colony of New South Wales, you are charged with feloniously and unlawfully wounding one John Middleton, with intent to murder and kill.

'How say you? Guilty or not guilty?'

Gardiner stood tall. 'Not guilty,' he intoned.

The gallery, packed, every seat taken, men standing in the aisles, cheered.

'Order,' bellowed Justice Edward Wise. 'Order in the court. Silence.'

The roar became a hum.

'Silence,' he warned again, 'or I will find you in contempt of court.'

All chatter stopped. The former King of the Road took his seat, nodding towards the jury who would decide his fate.

Could have been worse. Could have been much worse.

And Gardiner was right. The man responsible for the longest and most successful stealing spree in history before his protégée Ben Hall took over had only been charged with a single crime. He was being tried for shooting at two police officers at Fish River, east of Oberon, in 1861.

In a major embarrassment for the New South Wales police, detectives could not find enough evidence to prosecute Gardiner for the crime for which he was most famous, the Eugowra escort robbery. Despite a desperate attempt to bring the leader of the bushrangers to justice, police had failed in their bid to find enough evidence to justify a trial.

Charters had refused to help. Already pardoned for his crime, the once flashy stockman now lived as a recluse, the testimony that saw Manns executed forcing him to change his name to Thompson. Charters had pinned the whole crime on Gardiner during the two most public trials in Australia's early history. But now he told them he couldn't remember who was involved. His memory had failed.

Facing ridicule should they not be able to charge Gardiner with the crime everyone knew he had not only perpetrated but masterminded, the police went into the depths of Darlinghurst to find a famous inmate or two.

Fordyce laughed in their faces when he was asked to testify against Gardiner, even when they offered him a deal that would see his sentence reduced. Bow did the same, his hatred for Charters still fresh, the feeling of being betrayed never having gone away.

But they had to get Gardiner for something. Australia's most famous criminal was in chains and cuffs, the police who tracked and apprehended the notorious fugitive had been hailed as heroes, the arrest touted as the end of the outback outlaw. They couldn't just cut him loose.

A full contingent of detectives were put to work, the police going through every one of Gardiner's alleged crimes. But their evidence amounted to little, with either no witnesses being willing to talk or Gardiner having committed the crimes disguised. The best they could get him for was shooting a trap. At least for now ...

Robert McIntosh Isaacs, no stranger to packed courts and chaos after representing the escort robbery four, stood as Gardiner's defence lawyer.

'Your honour, a small matter before we start,' he said. 'There is an issue regarding an amount of money illegally taken from my client after his arrest.' Isaacs explained how the police had seized a number of notes and coins from Gardiner at Apis Creek. 'There is no evidence that these were the proceeds of crime,' he said, 'and no warrant was produced and no legal reason given since. My client earned the said money legitimately through his business.'

Justice Wise sighed. 'Very well,' he said. 'Return the money.'

The clerk collected the evidence and walked over to the dock, handing Gardiner a pile of cash.

'Hold on a moment,' Gardiner said. 'I'll have to check it is all there.' He began to count out loud.

One pound. Two pounds. Six pounds.

He was in no hurry.

Ten pounds. Fourteen pounds. Fifteen pounds.

The crowd was amused.

Eighteen pounds. Thirty pounds. Forty pounds.

Eventually he got to a hundred and twenty.

'Yep,' he said. 'All here. Every last shilling.'

'Order,' the judge shouted, the crowd enthralled by the entertainer. 'Silence. Now can we proceed?'

A familiar face took to the floor, James Martin QC, the other lawyer who had defended the escort robbers. But Martin was not defending this time, the legal eagle now attorney general of New South Wales.

'Prosecution begin,' said Justice Wise.

Martin nodded before outlining his case.

'If a man shoots at another man,' Martin said, 'without the threat of being robbed, assaulted or killed, such a man would be guilty of murder should that man die. And if a man shoots a police officer dead while attempts are being made to apprehend him, well, that is murder too. Only through the grace of God did an officer not die when the prisoner opened fire in a cowardly attack on officers, who were executing their duty to the Crown. This is a simple case of attempted murder. Two officers of the law will tell you that the prisoner attacked them, firing first, while they were approaching to apprehend him. That Gardiner opened fire, shooting as they approached, and unloaded every round of his gun in an attempt to kill. I trust you will bring the prisoner to justice.'

And then the depositions began.

'Calling John Middleton!' the clerk called.

The burly officer took the stand. 'I was a policeman in July 1861, stationed at Tuena about twenty miles from the Fish River,' Middleton said. 'Mr Beardmore, the police magistrate at Carcoar, told me in May 1861 to apprehend Frank Gardiner – the prisoner – for robbing the Cooma mail. Mr Beardmore told me he could trace to the prisoner a certain ten-pound note, which had been stolen from the Cooma mail.'

Middleton cracked his neck.

'On the sixteenth of July 1861, I went with trooper Hosie to Fogg's at Fish River,' the officer continued. 'We were dressed in police uniform and arrived at the hut between ten and eleven in the morning. Hosie took down the rails of the fence and I went up towards the hut. I dismounted and left my horse at another fence about six yards from the hut. As I approached the hut, Mrs Fogg came to the door. She threw up her arms and went back into the hut. I also went in and saw another door opposite the entrance. There was a person entering the second door.

Middleton looked at Gardiner, the prisoner unmoved.

'Fogg was in the front room with his wife and children and he passed out of the house as I entered,' Middleton said. 'A voice behind the screen cried out as I approached, "Don't come in here – I am armed, I'll shoot you," or words to that effect. I raised the screen and as I looked in a shot was fired. I raised the screen again, presented my piece and fired. At the same instant the same man fired at me and shot me in the mouth. I drew back to reload my pistol and then found that my hand was shot.'

Gardiner shook his head.

'I went out the main door again,' Middleton continued, 'and saw Hosie and sent him around the back to try to get in. He came back to the front again and was entering the hut when he was shot, and the prisoner then came out of the house holding a pistol by the barrel. He made at me and Hosie caught him from behind. We struggled and after much difficulty the prisoner submitted to being handcuffed.'

The witness paused, making sure he got the next bit right.

'The prisoner was then struck by me with a pistol,' Middleton said. 'I hit him during the scuffle and then Hosie struck him with a whip. I then went away for assistance to remove the prisoner.'

Middleton looked down towards his right hand, rubbing it with his left.

'Dr Rowlands saw me afterwards and examined my wounds,' Middleton continued. 'I had also received a gunshot wound in the leg and another to my hand. I was eight days laid up with fever. There was no one at the hut armed but the prisoner, Hosie and myself. I did not go round the back of the house at all.'

Martin gave his witness a nod as Isaacs rose. The veteran defender of bushrangers began by asking the officer what he was wearing at the time of the botched arrest.

'I wore ordinary police uniform,' Middleton said. 'Our uniform plus I had leggings over my trousers.'

'Were you wearing a poncho?' Isaacs asked.

'I can't recall,' came the reply.

Isaacs jumped in. 'I put it to you that both you and Trooper Hosie were wearing ponchos as you approached,' Isaacs said. 'You had full-length ponchos over your police uniform and your heads were hooded. There was nothing that could have identified you as police. Isn't that right?'

Middleton was dumbstruck. 'Uh,' he mumbled, 'I can't recall whether we were wearing ponchos or not.'

Isaacs continued. 'And you did not identify yourself as police?' he asked. 'Or make an offer for the prisoner to surrender?'

Middleton shook his head. 'There was no time,' he said. 'There were shots fired.'

'Shots? So who shot first? You? Hosie? Gardiner? Or was it simultaneous?' Isaacs probed.

'The first shot was fired by the prisoner,' Middleton said. 'My pistol did not go off simultaneously with or before the first shot was fired. The prisoner's second shot and my first were almost simultaneous.'

'Are you sure?' Isaacs asked.

'Yes,' came the reply.

Isaacs turned up the heat. 'Had you been drinking?' he asked. 'Is that why you did not ask for him to surrender and why you missed with every shot you fired?'

The witness shook his head. 'I had not previously called

upon him to surrender,' Middleton said, 'and I was perfectly sober. The shots just went over his head.'

Job done, Isaacs cut the line and let the frightened fish free.

'Calling Detective Hosie,' shouted the clerk.

The Crown's second and only other witness of substance was sworn in. He went through the sequence of events before and during the shooting, his evidence a perfect match with his partner's. He then described Gardiner's escape.

'The prisoner was sitting on a sort of table,' Hosie said. 'He was handcuffed. I was sitting opposite him. Then the prisoner suddenly sprang on me, and we struggled through the house.

'At last I got the prisoner's handcuffs over a post, but he got away again, and rushed towards the river. So I followed him, and he aimed at me with a sapling which he picked up, pretending it was a gun. I subsequently fired at him but missed. I rushed him and struck him with my pistol. The blow cut his head.'

The gallery was enthralled. *What a bumbling idiot. They let him escape twice? Shot at him because he was holding a stick?* Worse was to come.

'I took him up to the house,' Hosie said, 'and asked Mrs Fogg to sew up his wounds. I then persuaded Mr Fogg to get a horse for the prisoner so we could transport him back to the station. Then we started from the place.'

Escaped twice? Make that thrice …

'After some distance the prisoner was rescued from me by another bushranger,' Hosie said reticently. 'The man rushed out of the bush and said, "Let the prisoner go." I told Fogg to let go of the reins of the prisoner's horse, and then the prisoner went away with his rescuer into the bush.'

Next up was Carcoar's police magistrate, the man said to have ordered the arrest. He simply declared he did not issue a warrant.

Isaacs shook his head when asked if he would like to question the witness. And with that the prosecution was done. Gardiner smiled.

That all you got? That's the case? The word of two fools?

'Calling Mary Fogg,' the clerk shouted, summonsing the first witness for the defence.

Gardiner smiled some more. Isaacs got straight to the point.

'So who fired that first shot?' Isaacs asked. 'Did you see Gardiner holding a gun and shooting at the man coming towards the door?'

Mary Fogg replied fast, not needing time to consider her response.

'I did not see Gardiner until Middleton pushed me in the doorway,' Mrs Fogg said. 'No shot was fired before that of Middleton.'

'So did Gardiner even have a gun? Did he threaten to shoot?'

The questions continued.

'The police came up and Gardiner walked into the back room,' Mrs Fogg said. 'He said nothing. I saw no revolver in his hand. I did not hear Gardiner say that he would shoot or any words to that effect.'

The court gasped at the woman's next statement. 'After Middleton fired I said, "My God, if you are going to fire, let me out with the children,"' Mrs Fogg said.

'And did they announce themselves as police?' Isaacs questioned.

'It was not until I saw the handcuffs that I knew the men to be policemen,' Mrs Fogg continued. 'I wanted to dress Middleton's wounds, but he went away. All three men were wounded.'

The prosecutor was silent as his case fell apart. Gardiner was smiling some more.

'Calling James Barney,' barked the clerk.

The next witness for the defence took the stand, the man a guest of the Foggs' at the time of the arrest. He threw further doubt on Middleton's account.

'I swear that Gardiner did not yell to the approaching men that he was armed,' Barney said, 'or that he would shoot if anyone came near. All I saw of the encounter was Middleton coming up to the door and firing a shot.'

The courtroom buzzed as the last witness left the stand.

'Silence,' Justice Wise yelled, his patience well and truly tried. He then gave the floor to the defence.

'Dismiss anything you may have heard about Gardiner,' Isaacs said as he worked the room, 'and only consider the facts of this case as told to you in this court. Frank Gardiner is not on trial for the escort robbery. And he is not on trial for anything else you have heard or read. Don't consider what that miscreant Dan Charters may have said in a previous trial because he is not here today and that robbery is not a question for you to decide.'

He only had eyes for the jury now.

'This man is being trialled for shooting at police while they were attempting to apprehend him,' Isaacs said. 'But how could he shoot at police when he did not know they were police? It has been clearly established in this court that the officers' uniforms were covered, that they did not announce themselves as police, and that they did not offer the prisoner a chance to surrender.'

Isaacs paused, his eyes still firmly on the men who would decide Gardiner's fate.

'So with two armed riders approaching the house,' Isaacs continued, 'strangers wearing ponchos and holding guns, who would blame the prisoner for shooting in self-defence?'

He let the jury consider the question.

'But that is not what happened,' Isaacs said. 'According to testimony it was Middleton who indeed fired the first shot, rushing into the house and ignoring a plea from a desperate mother to let her remove her children. It is now up to you to weigh up the facts and determine whether the prisoner is guilty of shooting at a police officer with intent to murder. And it is your duty to consider this charge, the only charge that has been alleged, or none at all.'

Isaacs turned and walked triumphantly back to his seat. Case closed. Job done.

'Attend only to the evidence you have heard here,' Justice Wise directed, looking at the jury. 'The notoriety of this prisoner should have no bearing on your judgment. This is a single offence that must be proved beyond a reasonable doubt. I trust you will do your duty manfully and fearlessly. Consider the evidence and make your decision just.'

Justice Wise retired the jury at 4.45 pm, but he did not close the court. This move ensured the smile didn't leave Gardiner's face.

This has got to be good. He is expecting a quick decision.

And so was everyone else in the court, not moving an inch. They sat and waited. No one wanted to miss the verdict.

'The jury has reached a decision, your honour,' said the clerk, returning to the court at 6.25 pm.

The silence was broken and the crowd anticipated a sensation.

'Order,' Justice Wise said. 'I will not tolerate this kind of behaviour in my court. I am on the verge of charging an onlooker with contempt.'

Silence returned as the jury walked back in.

'All rise,' said the clerk, with the courtroom now composed.

Here we go. Let this end. I'm coming back, Kitty.

Gardiner stood up and placed his hands around the iron bars of the box. He looked calm, no sweating or shaking.

'Gentlemen of the jury,' the court clerk asked, 'do you find the prisoner at the bar guilty or not guilty?'

The foreman stepped forward. Gardiner gripped the bars tightly.

'Not guilty, your honour,' he said.

Yes!

Gardiner had to refrain from punching the air. The gallery showed no restraint, the declaration of innocence cueing a courtroom celebration the likes of which had never been seen. Men clapped, cheered and raised their fists. They jumped up and down. Some even danced.

'Silence in the court!' Justice Wise shouted. 'Order in the court.'

The roar continued.

'Silence!' Justice Wise yelled, even louder.

Still madness, back-slapping and handshakes.

The judge let loose, his gavel smashing wood before he sprang to his feet.

'Clerk,' he barked. 'Him!'

Wise was pointing at a young man, clapping and cheering just like everyone else.

'Him,' the judge barked again. 'Bring him before me.'

The boy, no older than sixteen, went white.

'No,' he cried as the clerk grabbed him. 'Please, I'm sorry.'

The clerk ignored the protest and dragged him by the arm before the judge. The court was finally silent.

'Young man, I am committing you to Darlinghurst Gaol for contempt of court,' Justice Wise shouted. 'I am shocked, inexpressibly shocked, at this disgraceful and unseemly exhibition within the walls of a court of justice on so solemn an occasion as this. The people of New South Wales are disgraced by such a demonstration of joy at the jury's verdict acquitting this prisoner. Things have come to a shocking state.'

The young man began to cry. 'Please,' he sobbed, 'I am sorry. I just got carried away. Please forgive me. My father is a magistrate. I meant no disrespect.'

The judge paused. 'Is this true?' he asked, looking towards the bar table.

It was. The Crown solicitor vouched for the boy. So did Isaacs.

'My boy,' the judge continued, 'I am truly sorry for you. Let me warn you, let me beseech you, of giving way to such feelings as your actions now just gave evidence to. I am pained beyond belief to think a young lad like you should have joined in on a disgraceful and humiliating exhibition that has just outraged the dignity of this court. You are discharged. But let this be a solemn, and final, warning.'

Gardiner watched on, the distraction prolonging his wait.

Come on. Get on with it. Send me home.

The judge turned and faced him.

'Your honour,' James Martin suddenly barked.

Gardiner froze. *What now?*

He suddenly felt sick.

'We will be charging the prisoner with further offences,' Martin said. 'We ask that the prisoner not be released.'

No! Kitty ...

Gardiner could feel his heart break.

'Very well,' Wise said. 'The prisoner is to be held in custody pending further charges.'

Gardiner smiled no more.

* * *

Darlinghurst, 5 July 1864

Nor was Gardiner smiling when he stood to face his latest charge.

'Francis Christie,' the clerk barked, 'alias Francis Gardiner, alias Francis Clarke, on the tenth day of March 1862, at Little Wombat in the colony of New South Wales, you are charged with robbery of Alfred Horsington while under arms. How say you? Guilty or not guilty?'

Gardiner stood tall. 'Guilty,' he said.

Could be worse.

'Francis Christie,' the clerk barked again, 'alias Francis Gardiner, alias Francis Clarke, on the tenth day of March 1862, at Little Wombat in the colony of New South Wales, you are charged with robbery of Henry Hewitt while under arms. How say you? Guilty or not guilty?'

Gardiner remained tall. 'Guilty,' he said.

Let's see what I get.

Gardiner had simply shrugged when Isaacs had told him of the charges he was about to face. The defence counsel had walked his way into the stinking depths of Darlinghurst Gaol, where Gardiner had by then been a prisoner for almost four months, to break the news.

'Well, they were going to get me for something,' he said. 'Might as well be this.'

Could be worse. It's only a robbery.

'Are they all giving evidence?' Gardiner asked.

Isaacs had nodded.

Gardiner had been the only man identified when he, O'Meally, Gilbert and John McGuiness had held up Horsington and Hewitt at gunpoint. Gardiner and his gang ambushed the pair on the road that ran from Lambing Flat to Young. Wearing no disguise and holding a gun, Gardiner was the one who had shouted 'bail up'. He was also the one who had taken 189 ounces of gold from Hewitt and 253 ounces from Horsington.

Now he would be brought to justice.

Five years? Ten at worst?

'I will plead guilty,' he had said to Isaacs, 'and maybe that will be the end of it. They will have me for something. That should be good enough for them.'

Isaacs had agreed.

The courtroom was again packed with professionals, punters and paupers. They gasped and groaned when Gardiner made his first plea. And they oohed and aahed when he made his second.

Wearing her lucky hat, the same one she had worn throughout the first trial, all three days, Kitty Brown cried. Gardiner looked around for his sweetheart after confessing to his crime. His broken heart tore some more when he saw her, all lucky hat and tears.

Chief Justice Sir Alfred Stephen, the big gun brought in for this trial, noted the prisoner's plea. And then the formalities began, witnesses were called, arguments heard. Gardiner was numb throughout. Guilt decided, he hardly listened, the defeated man instead watching the pain of his lover. Kitty was a wreck throughout.

It could be worse, my love. It is only robbery. I won't hang. I'll see you again.

Finally the proceedings were over. Gardiner was ready to rise.

Let's have it then. Five years? Ten?

'I have been informed that there is another indictment on file for a much more serious charge,' the judge said.

Gardiner froze. Kitty cried out.

'For the sake of convenience I will fix trial for next Thursday. In the meantime I will read over the depositions of these two cases but I shall not pass sentence until the result of the other trial.'

Gardiner was stunned.

It is worse.

Kitty cried some more.

* * *

Darlinghurst, 7 July 1864

Gardiner smashed his fist into the prison table after learning of the charge that threatened to see him hang.

'Horseshit,' he yelled. 'They can't do that.'

But they had.

In a piece of legal manoeuvring that would outrage many in the colony, Gardiner had been charged with a variation on the same crime that he had been found innocent of just forty-eight days before. With the Crown looking to send a message to the lawless colony – out of control and an international disgrace, said many – Gardiner was charged with shooting not at John Middleton but at his partner, Trooper William Hosie. And instead of charging him with just shooting with intent to kill – a capital crime – they were now also charging him with intent to do grievous bodily harm. They wanted him to hang but they had also hedged their bets with a charge that could see him locked up for life.

There would be no technicalities this time. Apparently it didn't matter whether or not he'd been shooting at police, whether or not he'd shot first or last. Gardiner would be got. Or would he?

'Not guilty,' Gardiner said defiantly when he returned to the all too familiar dock. He took his seat, his life in the hands of the jury.

'Calling former Trooper William Hosie,' the clerk shouted, his voice now also as familiar to Gardiner's ears as the wooden bench was to his bum.

'I was a constable in the police force on the sixteenth of July 1861,' Hosie said after being sworn in. 'I am now a gold miner. On the sixteenth of July I went in company with Sergeant Middleton to the Fish River. Middleton and myself had our police uniform and leggings and ponchos on; the ponchos reached to about the knees and were not part of the uniform. Mine was of a dark colour.

'I dismounted and took down the slip rails, and Middleton rode on whilst I led my horse through the rails. Middleton reached the house first, and I was fifty or sixty yards behind. I saw Mrs Fogg fall back as if she was alarmed when she saw Middleton dismount and go to the house. She held up her hands as if in fright as Middleton was entering the house.'

Gardiner looked confused by the trap admitting their uniforms were disguised and that they had scared the life out of Mrs Fogg.

'I was about twenty yards behind,' Hosie continued. 'Almost immediately on Middleton entering I heard two shots fired, almost in succession, one after the other. Middleton rushed back to the door and told me to go round to the back of the house. He was wounded and covered with blood. I went to the back and saw that there was no means of getting in or out of the house from the back, so I came round to the front again.

'Middleton was standing in front of the door with his whip, and he told me to look out for the prisoner. I looked in and saw the prisoner standing at a window two or three yards to the right of me.

'I had on a poncho and had a pistol in my hand. I only saw the prisoner for a minute look out of the window and he immediately dropped his head down. I said to the best of my recollection "surrender" and covered him with my pistol.'

Gardiner shook his head. *Bullshit.*

'And then I fired,' Hosie continued. 'He had a pistol and was covering me with it when I fired. He then fired and I was struck in the temple.'

Gardiner was again looking confused.

Yeah, you shot at me so I shot back. And?

'I fell down senseless,' Hosie continued. 'And the next thing I can remember was seeing Gardiner rushing out with his pistol clubbed as if going to strike someone. He was only about an arm's length away from me. Middleton was standing up with the whip in his hand. I rushed on Gardiner and we had a struggle till I got him down after Middleton had struck him with his whip.'

Gardiner shook his head again.

So I shot you in the head? Knocked you senseless? And all of a sudden you were up and taking me to the ground?

'I handcuffed the prisoner,' Hosie said. 'When he was secured he said he was sorry for what he had done. He told me that he wished I had shot him dead. When Gardiner was handcuffed, Middleton searched the house and said he was so badly wounded that he would go on for assistance. After Middleton left, I got weak with loss of blood. I asked Mrs Fogg for a drink of water. Whilst I was drinking it the prisoner made a rush at me.'

Hosie took his first big breath.

'He then rushed to go out the door,' Hosie said. 'But I held him by the chains of the handcuffs and we struggled out into the yard together. I put his arms over a post but he got away and ran off to the river.'

Hosie looked towards Gardiner in the dock.

'I called upon the prisoner to stop or I would fire,' Hosie said. 'He found that the river was flooded and so he stopped. He got a sapling and rushed at me with it so I fired at him.'

Gardiner rolled his eyes. *A sapling? What was I going to do with a blooming sapling? Tickle you to death?*

'We came together and we struggled,' Hosie said, 'and I struck him over the head with the pistol until he fell down and said he was dying.'

Gardiner was now fidgeting in the dock, teeth clenched and face full of fury. *Yeah, you were so weak with blood loss a few minutes before. Must have been a bloody miraculous glass of water.*

Gardiner looked towards the jury, hoping they weren't falling for this crap.

'I thought that I had killed him,' Hosie said. 'I put a log under his head and went for Mr Fogg. With some assistance we got the prisoner onto a horse and I left with Mr Fogg and the prisoner. When we had got about three-and-a-half miles from Fogg's, two men came and rescued the prisoner from me. I was covered with a revolver. I ordered the prisoner free; giving him up was the only chance I saw of saving my life.'

Isaacs took to the floor.

Gardiner nodded. *Rip him apart.*

'So was the wound you sustained inflicted by a gunshot from Gardiner?' Isaacs asked. 'Are you sure you didn't shoot yourself?'

Now Gardiner smiled. During his pre-trial brief he had told Isaacs what had really happened. 'The idiot's gun got caught in his big poncho when he went to draw. His gun went off and he hit the wall. If he was hit by anything it was shrapnel from his own shot.'

'I can't state positively in what way I was wounded,' Hosie said. 'I will not undertake to say it was not by the ball from my own pistol. The house was a slab hut. I was the full length of the room from the slabs when I was shot. I was struck on the temple and the prisoner was within two yards of me when he fired. I should say that it was the prisoner's ball and not mine that wounded me.'

Isaacs shook his head. 'Two yards?' he exclaimed. 'Two yards? Are you saying that the prisoner shot you in the face from just two yards away and you lived? That you survived a ball to the middle of the forehead at point-blank range? You must be made of steel.'

Hosie's eyelids snapped back. He smirked, a natural defence.

'But not only did you live,' Isaacs said, 'you also had the stamina to chase down the unwounded man and beat him in a wrestling match. You disarmed him of his riverweed and then flung one of Australia's toughest and most feared men to the ground. And then you pistol-whipped him in the head. So are you sure you were wounded so gravely? Are you sure the prisoner, apparently a famed bushranger and expert marksman, shot you in the face from just two yards? Or is it possible you shot yourself?'

Hosie's smirk was gone but his face was still blank. 'I should have thought that the prisoner's ball would have penetrated my skull,' Hosie agreed. 'Yes, I was surprised I was not shot dead. Maybe it is possible that my own bullet may have split when I fired and rebounded off the wall of the hut. Maybe that would explain it. But I did not examine the house to see if there was any evidence of the ball hitting it and rebounding.'

Isaacs took a triumphant breath. He then turned away, facing the jury first and then the crowd. He gave James Martin a wink as he returned to his bench.

Isaacs thought his job was done. *Ponchos over uniforms confirmed, not declaring yourself as the police, and goddamn it, you even said you could have shot yourself.* He took his seat and looked towards Martin. The prosecutor winked back.

Martin took the floor, completely unfazed. His arrogance unnerved Gardiner.

The rigmarole began, witnesses with nothing to say taking the stand, much like the first trial.

'And that is all for the prosecution, your honour,' Martin said. He gave his mate Isaacs another wink as he took his seat. Now it was Isaacs wondering.

He turned and looked at Mary Fogg; she was ready and waiting to be called. Hosie had already admitted that he was wearing a poncho over his uniform. He had also said they had not announced themselves as police. And who had shot first? Well, that didn't matter. This was about Hosie and not Middleton. Did he need Mrs Fogg?

'We call no witnesses, your honour,' Isaacs said. He took a moment, summoning all of his composure. 'This is no ordinary case, gentlemen,' he said, addressing the jury, the judge and the gallery. He walked as he spoke, proud and tall, this his moment to shine. 'The prisoner has already been tried for the commission of this very same offence,' he continued. 'Or at the very least an offence so identical that only a technical line of distinction can be drawn. The only difference is by substitution: the name of Middleton has been withdrawn and replaced with the name of Hosie. I say to you gentlemen that the verdict on that occasion was the right verdict and the evidence in this case is precisely similar. I ask you to respect the decision.'

Isaacs stared at the jury.

'There is another point,' he continued, 'which makes this case very peculiar. While the prisoner has been awaiting trial for an offence which put his life in peril, he has been made the subject of slanderous vituperation in the newspapers. Such comments before a prisoner's trial are unprecedented in the annals of justice. They are unfair, un-Christian, cruel and vindictive. I am sure that you gentlemen will not be influenced, terrorised or coerced into finding a verdict against the prisoner through fear of being held up to ridicule and scorn by the press. I trust you will come to the correct decision.'

He took his seat.

The chief justice began his summation.

'I take it for granted that not one of you in the jury will permit prejudices against the prisoner to weigh against him,' the judge said, 'any more than you would permit sympathy to turn to his favour. The defence points to a recent verdict in a recent trial. While the decision may have been just, the charge on that occasion was substantially, and in fact, a different one of that now before the court. Now I will ask you to retire and come back with your verdict.'

The jury left the court at 4.50 pm.

Just sixty-nine minutes after they had retired, they returned. 'All rise,' said the clerk. 'Members of the jury,' he continued, 'have you agreed to a verdict?'

The foreman stepped forward. 'We have,' he said.

'And how say you? Is the accused Francis Christie, alias Francis Gardiner, alias Francis Clarke, guilty or not guilty of feloniously and unlawfully shooting Trooper Hosie with intent to kill?'

The courtroom was silent and still. Gardiner looked at the ground.

'We find him not guilty,' he said.

There was silence no more, pandemonium erupting. The gallery clapped and cheered.

Gardiner dragged his eyes from his feet.

The clerk called for quiet before continuing. 'And how say you? Is the accused Francis Christie, alias Francis Gardiner, alias Francis Clarke, guilty or not guilty of feloniously and unlawfully wounding Detective Hosie with intent to do grievously bodily harm?'

The courtroom was silent once more. Gardiner again looked at the ground.

'We find him guilty,' the foreman said.

Gardiner's eyes stayed on the floor as the courtroom again erupted, this times with boos and catcalls. Kitty Brown broke down.

The gavel came down like thunder and the chief justice screamed for order. He soon had it.

'Continue,' he said to the clerk.

Gardiner was silent, his eyes still on the floor.

'Have you anything to say why the court should not pass sentence upon you according to law?' the chief justice asked the prisoner.

Gardiner lifted his head.

'No,' he said. 'I have nothing to say. But I have prepared a letter to present to the court.'

Isaacs produced the note and passed it to the judge. It was Gardiner's final play.

'Very well,' said Chief Justice Stephen. 'Give me a moment to examine the document.'

To his Honour the Judge,
I do not address you with the desire to impress upon you my innocence of this charge to which I have pleaded guilty, but my wish is to point out the untruths in the evidence on the part of the witnesses.

In the first place they all distinctly assert that there were four in number, whereas there were five. They also assert that three stuck up the cart containing Mr Horsington, his wife and boy, and that I alone went to Mr Hewitt.

Now it is just the opposite.

I went to the cart, the four to Mr Hewitt. Again they state that Mr Hewitt was thirty yards in the rear of the cart, whereas on the contrary, he was thirty yards in advance of the cart.

Again it was I who told them to bail up, using no other words or threats, and at the same time Mr Hewitt received a similar order from the other four men. While I was directing Mr Horsington where to turn off into the bush a shot went off from one of the four men, caused through the restlessness of the horse.

I at the time was within two or three yards of Mr Horsington and his wife. I immediately turned around and asked who fired the shot. Mr McGuiness said he fired the shot by accident. I immediately told him that he would have to leave the party as soon as he received his share. He left later that night.

I spoke loudly as McGuiness was about thirty yards away. Mr Horsington and his wife were right beside me yet they swear they heard nothing of the conversation.

They also swear that Mr Downey was a member of the party. I sincerely swear that Mr Downey was not a part of this party, on this or any other occasion.

Mr Horsington and his party also allege the offence took place on 10 March, while really it did not take place until five or six weeks later.

Had I decided to take this matter to trial I would have been able to provide an alibi for this date. I do not write this your honour to escape punishment, for on the contrary it incriminates me. I only to wish to point out the inaccuracy and had I not pleaded guilty to these charges I may have been able to escape punishment.

If I may be permitted, in praying for a merciful decision in my case, I beg to say that it is not alone on the above grounds. For the last two years I have seen the error of my ways, and I have endeavoured, with God's assistance, to lead an honest and upright life.

I have had great temptations in this time with large gold collections from the Peak Downs mines entrusted to my holding, yet I had honest resolutions and I was sufficiently strong to prevent me from doing a dishonest action. I do trust the honour to believe that I had other temptations and that I resisted them too. I have vowed to never fall into those practices again.

And now, your honour, as we must all on the last great day of judgment throw ourselves on the mercy of the great judge, so do I now throw myself upon your mercy as my earthly judge. I pray for a lenient and merciful consideration in my case.

I am, your honour, your humble servant,

FRANCIS CHRISTIE

* * *

The chief justice passed the document back to the clerk.

'Let it be noted that I have read the prisoner's letter,' he said. 'I will now respond.'

He turned and looked Gardiner in the eye.

'You're not unknown to me,' Chief Justice Sir Alfred Stephen said firmly, still staring at his face. 'I have known about you and your actions for a number of years. If you are now determined to lead a correct life you will be met with a suitable reward by your own conscience.

'But you owe a duty to society. You have shown a dreadful example to many young men and women in this colony. You have been the acknowledged captain of a band of robbers, carrying terror and rapine through many parts of this colony.

'You have by your own lawless outrages brought this community to the last stage of degradation. Everyone in England, and in the other colonies, thinks New South Wales is a den of thieves. Surely you must know you have to undergo punishment for your crimes? If you were allowed to go would you have friends to assist you? Are you still rich? What lesson would that teach you or anyone else?

'And you have not only robbed the rich but plundered the poor. And that is beside the point. I know many rich men and it is the sweat of their brow that brought them their riches. What right do you have to take it?

'Many young men owe their misfortunes to you,' the judge continued. 'That young Manns owes his death at the gallows to you, plunged into eternity because he followed you.

'This court in which you stand is the gaol to all bushranging,' the judge said. 'I am desirous of doling out a lesson that I hope the community will not forget. You are a man that many sympathise with, but I think had you perished as some of your companions have done, it may have been a wholesome lesson to the community and the world.'

And then came the sentence.

'For the offence of which you have just been found guilty,' the judge said, his voice growing louder, 'you will be kept in hard labour on the roads or other public works for the term of fifteen years, the first two of which will be served in irons.'

Gardiner dropped his head.

'For the robbery of Horsington under arms,' the judge said, 'in which you have pleaded guilty, I sentence you to ten years under hard labour.'

Gardiner shook his dropped head.

'And for the robbery of Hewitt under arms,' the judge said, 'in which you have also pleaded guilty, I sentence you to seven years under hard labour.'

Gardiner now lifted his head.

Fifteen years. Could have been worse. I can do that.

'The first sentence will include time already served and finish fifteen years from the date of your arrest,' the judge said. 'The second sentence will begin on the expiry of the first and the third will begin on the expiry of the second.'

Could have been worse? How about thirty-two years? I can't do that.

Gardiner went numb. He had effectively been given a life sentence. He would have to live to sixty-seven to ever be free, and that wasn't likely in this colony, let alone in hard labour.

The door to the dock swung open and Gardiner was ushered out.

Oh Kitty. Poor Kitty.

Gardiner looked around for his love and saw her, hysterical with grief in her lucky hat.

'Frank,' she screamed, 'I'll fight this. It's not the end.'

Gardiner shook his head.

'I love you, Frank,' she yelled. 'I'll never leave you.'

And now Frank cried too, one of Australia's toughest outlaws, shed a tear. He couldn't speak. He wanted to yell back to Kitty Brown but he couldn't muster a word. Instead he gave her a pained look and shook his head again.

'Let's go, Frank,' said the guard.

The King of the Road was taken back to Darlinghurst Gaol, which would be his home for the next thirty-two years.

Chapter 16

THE PRISON

Sydney, 14 July 1864

After throwing her lucky hat away in disgust, Kitty Brown finally got her meeting with the colonial secretary.

'What can I do for you, Mrs Brown?' Henry Parkes asked after ushering Kitty to a seat.

'I would like permission to visit Francis,' she said. 'I have so far been denied at every attempt. It has been four months since I have seen him.'

Kitty's last conversation with her lover had been on the docks of Brisbane on 13 March. The prison authorities had denied every application she had lodged; they were so numerous she had lost count. She had also gone to Henry Parkes, sending him letters and storming his office until he'd agreed to a meeting.

'I am certainly sympathetic to your plight,' Parkes said, 'but it is my understanding that you have been denied visiting rights to the prisoner because you are not legally married to Mr Christie.

It is prison policy that only immediate family and legal counsel are allowed visitation rights.'

A revelation came.

'But we are married,' Kitty said. 'We were married in Rockhampton.'

Parkes raised his brow. 'Well, this is news to me,' he said. 'Do you have documentation?'

Kitty shook her head. 'No,' she said. 'It was lost during the arrest.'

Parkes raised his other brow.

'Well, I am sure the documentation can be obtained,' Parkes said. 'If you can get the church to forward the documents we will be happy to consider a new request and it will be granted should Mr Christie prove to be your legal husband.'

Kitty sighed, knowing the documentation did not exist. She had married Gardiner in a private – and not legal – ceremony in Rockhampton. She was still legally married to John Brown.

'I'll put another application in then,' she said, hoping for a miracle. She paused. 'And then another after that and another after that. I won't stop until I can see my Frank. And as for the length of sentence,' she continued, 'it is ridiculous in its excess. Surely something can be done? He can't be locked up for that long.'

Parkes shook his head. 'The sentence is final,' he said. 'Your only avenue is to petition for a pardon.'

Kitty nodded. 'Then that is what I will do.'

* * *

Darlinghurst, 20 July 1864

'Gardiner,' the prison officer barked. 'You have visitors.'

Gardiner was sitting in the yard, soaking up some rare and welcome sunlight. He followed the guard back into the godless shadows of the gaol, the stench of shit smacking him straight in the face as soon as he entered the gloomy corridor.

'Francis,' beamed a woman as he entered the visiting room.

Gardiner looked bewildered.

'Charlotte?' he said, staring at the woman who called his name. 'And Archina?'

Gardiner was stunned. He had not seen his sisters since he was ten.

'Frank,' Archina beamed. She hurried over and gave him a hug. Charlotte followed suit.

Gardiner had been estranged from his sisters for twenty-three years. Three years after he'd left home at the age of ten, his father and stepmother moved to Victoria with his sisters, assuming he was dead.

'We moved back to Sydney after mother died,' Archina said. 'That was about seven years ago. I am married now, Frank. Married with five children.'

Gardiner was filled in on the plight of his long-lost family. He took a moment after learning his father had died the previous year.

'He became a painter,' Charlotte said. 'He painted half of Sydney after we moved here.'

Frank nodded. There were no tears for his long-forgotten father. But he started crying when Archina told him that she and Charlotte had been at the trial. Both trials, each and every day.

'We were hoping you would see us in the courtroom,' Archina said. 'We were in the gallery for the entirety of the case. But I suppose you wouldn't have recognised us even if you had.'

And then a bombshell.

'Kitty is living with us,' Charlotte said. 'She had nowhere to go so we took her in. She is desperate to see you, Frank. She wants you to know that she still loves you and always will.'

Gardiner broke down. 'Kitty?' he sobbed. 'Kitty? She is living with you?'

Charlotte nodded. 'And stop that,' she said. 'We are fighting for you. We are petitioning to have you out.'

Gardiner pulled himself together.

'Kitty,' he said. 'How is she?'

Archina produced a note.

'Not the best,' she said as she passed him the letter. 'She just got this.'

Gardiner took the letter, his hands suddenly shaking.

Mrs Brown,

I have given consideration to your latest application and I regret to inform you that it has been denied. I have passed on my decision to the Sherriff. I cannot grant you permission to see prisoner Francis Christie, alias Francis Gardiner, as you are still legally the wife of another man. I am not making this decision to be harsh but given the circumstances the request is entirely against the spirit of the regulations.

Henry Parkes
Colonial Secretary, NSW

Gardiner looked at his sister, his eyes red, lips quivering.

'She must move on,' Gardiner said. 'This will kill her. I am not getting out. She must live her life.'

But Gardiner knew she wouldn't. Kitty Brown wouldn't give up on him.

Gardiner kissed his long-lost siblings. And that is when he decided he would escape.

* * *

Darlinghurst, 30 December 1864

Gardiner looked at his hand: a pair of tens. Maybe his luck was about to change?

'I'll raise you,' he said, pushing a pile of fresh tobacco into the centre of the table.

The dealer, an inmate named Walter Cust, smiled.

Gardiner threw his cards onto the table.

'Twenty,' Cust said, glancing down at his own ten. 'That will be tough to beat.'

Gardiner looked at the pile of tobacco and matches on the table. It would be enough to last him a week.

'Turn 'em over,' Gardiner demanded. 'Let's have it then.'

Gardiner watched on as the dealer flipped the final card. He already had a ten on the table. Only an ace would see him beat.

'And it's a …' The dealer flipped the card.

'Fuck,' Gardiner shouted, staring at the ace of clubs. 'It had to be.'

The dealer pulled in his score of tobacco and matches. Prison currency.

'Don't worry,' Cust said. 'Some luck is about to come your way. That little thing we are planning is looking good.'

Gardiner and Cust had been secretly plotting an escape attempt. After his reunion with his sisters, and more so what they told him of Kitty, Gardiner had decided to get out. He could handle prison life – breaking rocks, eating cold porridge and sniffing shit – but he couldn't survive knowing his lover wouldn't rest until he was out. Cust offered him his ticket, telling him that he had people on the outside who would bribe a guard to set them free.

Escape from Darlinghurst was impossible without help. The walls could not be climbed and the stone could not be cut. But bribing a guard? That could work.

'It's all set for tomorrow,' Cust said under his breath. 'The screw can't get us from our cells but he will be able to take us out through the hospital. You will have to come down sick and get yourself moved to the hospital for the night.'

Gardiner nodded.

'I have also made all the arrangements for when we get out,' Cust continued. 'We will be hidden and looked after. What happens then is up to you.'

Gardiner had not put a foot wrong during his nine-month stint in Darlinghurst. No one would suspect anything if he faked an illness. Why would they? He had been a model inmate, quiet and unwilling to speak of his previous exploits, respected by prisoners and guards alike.

So the next afternoon he rubbed his eyes until they were red and stuck his fingers down his throat. He was taken to the hospital where Cust was already in a bed on the other side of the room. Gardiner gave him a wink when the guard's back was turned. And then he waited, and waited. Eventually he fell asleep. When he woke up it was the next morning.

He looked across to where Cust had been before he drifted off.

No!

The man with the plan was gone.

'Looking for your mate?' the guard asked. 'He's over in B Wing, in solitary. Word is he was going to escape. And word is you were going to go with him. But he isn't giving you up.'

Gardiner now felt genuinely sick.

The *Goulburn Herald* got wind of the failed escape and, despite having no evidence to link Gardiner to the attempt, named him in a report.

Mr Francis Gardiner, ex-bushranger-general, is neither dead nor dying. Since his conviction many persons have said he would never die in prison if he could make his escape, but the clever scoundrel's apparent good conduct in Darlinghurst Gaol appeared to be a complete refutation of all such insinuations. Had he not made important revelations to the government respecting bushranging and bushrangers? Was he not suffering from a deep-seated disease of the heart? Even the gaol surgeon was so completely deceived, and sympathisingly sent Gardiner to the hospital, ordering him to

*be supplied with the usual medical comforts. During the recent
disturbances Gardiner's conduct showed so marked a contrast
to that of the mutinous scoundrels who kept the unfortunate
warders constantly on the qui vive that he humbugged the gaol
officials as successfully as an English ticket-of-leave man I
read of some time ago, who, when giving advice to a notorious
housebreaker as to the easiest means of getting a ticket-of-
leave, said, 'Be sure to have the chaplain visit you as often as
possible, and on every occasion turn up the white of your eyes.'
Gardiner adopted tactics something similar. A few days ago,
when a fellow prisoner informed the gaoler that Frank Gardiner
was about to escape, the story found little credence, but the
informer backed up his story by naming a warder with whom
Gardiner was said to have made arrangements for escaping.
The warder was watched, and on his attempting to leave
the prison he was arrested and searched when, fortunately
for the public but unfortunately for Gardiner and his friends,
documents were discovered, one of which showed that the
next night Gardiner expected to be without the prison walls,
and wished his friends to meet him at 10 pm, naming the
rendezvous, and the other was a promissory note or order
for £300 for services rendered by the bearer. It is needless
to say that the warder's future services have been dispensed
with, and that Gardiner's future security will be more closely
attended to.*

Gardiner soon found out that fellow prisoner John Robinson
had given up both Cust and the officer who had been bribed,

telling another warder he had a letter Cust had written to his outside help.

Gardiner thought he would never see Kitty Brown again.

* * *

But Kitty refused to give up on Frank. She sent him letters, one after the other, pledging that she would never leave him, that she would find a way to get him out. It tore Gardiner apart.

I have to see her, just once. And then I have to tell her to move on.

So Gardiner begged. He started with the prison guards, then the governor of the gaol, and eventually the colonial secretary.

And one day the second-highest authority in New South Wales appeared in his cell.

'Mr Gardiner,' Colonial Secretary Henry Parkes said, 'I understand you would like to talk to me?'

Gardiner was stunned, Henry Parkes standing in his shit-stinking cell.

'Mrs Catherine Brown,' Gardiner said. 'My wife.'

Parkes nodded. 'Yes,' he said. 'I am aware of Mrs Brown and her relationship to you. Go on.'

Gardiner made his plea.

'I have forfeited my rights to liberty,' Gardiner said. 'I have no argument there. But do my convictions mean that I must endure a life bereft of common humanity? Should I and the love of my life be fated never to have even the poor consolation of visitation, a privilege granted to men and women whose convictions far outweigh those placed against my name?'

Then Gardiner cried. Parkes placed his hand on the prisoner's shoulder.

'Let me see what I can do,' he said.

And with a tear of his own, Parkes walked from the cell and out of the prison.

The colonial secretary summoned Kitty Brown to his office two days later. 'I will allow you to visit Francis Gardiner,' Parkes said.

Kitty cried again, this time tears of joy.

* * *

Parkes explained his decision in parliament.

'I paid a visit to Darlinghurst Gaol,' Parkes told the assembly, 'and during this visit a number of prisoners made application, through the gaoler, to see me for the purpose of making sundry requests. Among those persons was Francis Gardiner, who requested to be allowed to be visited once a month by Mrs Brown. He added that he would not have made this request only this woman had been living with him as his wife.

'I consulted with another member of the government, made inquiries of the police as to the character of Mrs Brown, and was assured by Captain McLerie, the inspector general, that she was a respectable woman. I made further inquiries, which satisfied me that this person, Mrs Brown, appeared to be permanently separated from her husband, and that she had lived since the conviction of Gardiner in the house of a person who was represented to me as a respectable married woman.

'After making these queries, I gave this special order to the principal gaoler at Darlinghurst to allow Catherine Brown to see Francis Gardiner.'

And then came the kicker.

'This order, however, is available for a single visit only and must not be allowed to alter or modify in any respect further the instructions from this office on the second instant.'

So, after a 298-day separation, Francis Gardiner would get to see his Kitty Brown. He would hug her, kiss her and profess his love. And then he would never see her again.

* * *

Darlinghurst, 5 January 1865

'Frank!' Kitty cried as Gardiner walked into the room. 'Frank!'

And there she was, the love of his life, wearing a new lucky hat and with her lips waiting to be kissed. 'Kitty!' Gardiner shouted.

He broke away from the prison guard and rushed towards his wife, leg chains rattling against the stone floor. And then came the moment he had been dreaming of, the one he'd thought would never come. The moment that would melt the heart he thought he no longer had.

He hugged his Kitty Brown.

'I love you,' Gardiner said. 'Oh, I love you.'

* * *

'Frank,' the guard said quietly and politely. 'Five minutes. Got to take you back soon. It's already been more than an hour.'

Kitty broke down. 'No,' she said. 'Please. A little longer.'

The guard shrugged.

Frank hugged his Kitty.

'Don't,' he said. 'Please. I need to know that you will be alright. I can't go on unless I know that. You have to forget about me. You have to go on. I need you to be happy. Promise me that you will be happy?'

Kitty still sobbed.

'I have something for you,' Gardiner said. He turned to the prison guard and waved him in.

'Oh,' the guard said. 'Right.'

He walked over and handed Gardiner a book.

'Here,' Gardiner said. 'For you. Now I will always be with you.'

Kitty looked down at the Bible he had passed her, leather-bound, with gold lettering.

'See,' Gardiner said, pointing down at the gold type on the front: *Catherine*. 'I printed it myself.'

Kitty turned the page. 'Oh Frank,' she said. 'It's beautiful.'

A teardrop landed next to the angel Gardiner had drawn, etched and then printed on the title page. The ink ran, the cherub forever stained with love. Catherine read the inscription: *Presented to Catherine by her affectionate Frank. 1865.*

Kitty smiled. Another tear hit the paper.

'I love you,' he said. 'I always will. But this is goodbye.'

And Frank Gardiner kissed his Kitty for the final time.

Chapter 17

THE COP

Forbes, 6 January 1865

Sir Frederick Pottinger was back behind his desk. With the January heat turning Forbes into a furnace, he thought today was as good a day as any to remain indoors. Actually, given his reputation, most days were better spent indoors.

Suddenly the door burst open, the humidity hitting him before the blast of words.

'They are at the races,' yelled Pottinger's deputy. 'They have come into Forbes. They are at the blooming races!'

Pottinger pushed away the pile of papers on his desk and jumped to his feet.

'Hall?' he asked. 'At Wowingragong? Are you bloody joking?'

'No, boss,' the officer said. 'No joke. Hall is there. They are all there.'

This was Pottinger's chance to redeem himself.

'Shall we get a squad together?' the trooper asked. 'Go down and arrest them now?'

Pottinger shook his head. 'We will get them tomorrow,' he said. 'It's a two-day event. We need to come up with a plan. I am not going to give him a chance.'

Hall had become Pottinger's obsession. McGlone had captured Gardiner, taken all the glory. He had done what Pottinger couldn't.

'What do you mean you have nothing on him?' Pottinger's superior had blasted when he said he couldn't pin the escort robbery on Gardiner. 'Nothing?'

Pottinger had cringed. 'Not without Charters,' he said.

Pottinger's once promising career had gone to crap.

Hall. I need Hall. Then I will be a hero. Finally.

The Ben Hall gang had gone on to become arguably Australia's greatest criminal outfit. In 1864 the gang had committed thirty-five robberies as they continued the most prolific crime spree that Australia would ever see. Hall had survived four shoot-outs with police. One of them involved Pottinger.

'You lost him again,' the colonial secretary had roared at Pottinger. 'How many times is that now? Four? Five?'

Pottinger had thought he had his man when he surprised Hall and his gang, now including James Gordon and James Dunleavy, on 7 August 1864. Pottinger had been tipped off that Hall was camping near Ping's station, six miles from Seventeen Mile Rush. And the tip was good. But in yet another hail of bullets, Hall and his men had escaped.

Pottinger was left fuming, embarrassed and, once again, ridiculed by all.

Goddamn you, Ben Hall. Damn you to hell.

And now here he was, in Forbes, at the races. Walking around in plain view, no disguise, and just a couple of hundred yards away from Pottinger's hut.

How dare he! I'll put a bullet in his head.

Sir Frederick came up with his plan. It would either make him or break him.

* * *

Hall stirred, the bushranger raising his head from his saddle as foliage crunched underfoot. Australia's most wanted man was camping under the stars about two miles from Forbes. The scrub provided not only cover but also an intruder alert, bush style. With the summer scorch in full swing, the ground was carpeted with dry leaves and dead grass.

Crunch. Crunch. Crunch.

Hall pulled out his revolver and aimed.

'Woohoo,' said Dunleavy. 'It's just me.'

Hall uncocked his six-shooter. 'Where the blazes have you been?' he asked, gun now back by his side.

'In town,' Dunleavy said as he sat down. 'Went to get the paper. You think I am going to the races without doing the form?'

Hall smiled as he put his head back down, the trail-worn veteran amused by the young recruit's vigour and excitement.

'Wake me up when you find all the winners,' Hall said. He closed his eyes, the heavily foliaged eucalypts providing enough cover to shield him from the first rays of the sun, whose strength suggested another scorcher.

'Are you kidding me?' Dunleavy exclaimed. 'Here, Ben, take a look at this.'

Hall rolled over. 'Sure,' he said. 'When I wake up.'

Dunleavy leaped to his feet and rushed towards Hall. He held the paper in his face.

'There,' Dunleavy said, jamming his index finger into the broadsheet so hard it threatened to poke through. 'Right there. It's Pottinger, the bastard. Look!'

The young buck now had Hall's attention. He squinted, eyes adjusting to the rush of light.

'See?' Dunleavy exclaimed.

Hall did. 'Ha!' he shouted. 'Well I'll be a monkey's uncle. Pottinger the jockey. That will do me.'

'It gets better,' said Dunleavy. 'Look at the horse he is riding on.'

Hall examined the print.

'Bushranger,' Dunleavy said. 'Bushranger? Is he taking the piss?'

Hall could not believe what he had just read. Sir Frederick Pottinger was listed to ride a horse called Bushranger in the final event of the day, a match race against a horse called Scrammy Jack.

'Yes,' Hall said, 'that is exactly what he is doing. He is taking the piss.'

Hall screwed up the newspaper and threw it on the forest floor.

* * *

Pottinger arrived at the track about midday. He had sent an undercover army to the track at sunrise.

'No sight of him, sir,' one of them said. 'We haven't seen him all day.'

Pottinger nodded. 'They will be here,' he said. 'It will be too much to resist.'

The racetrack was teeming with punters from all walks of life, all shapes and sizes. And whether a professional or pauper, they were all talking about one thing: Sir Frederick Pottinger.

That Pottinger is about to commit suicide. What a fool. This will be good. Didn't he burn down Ben Hall's house? He is dead.

The bookmakers had to stop taking bets, money flooding in for Scrammy Jack.

Can't win a race if you are shot dead.

But it was all part of Pottinger's make-or-break plan. He was counting on an ambush.

'They will come at us on the run down to the back straight,' Pottinger said. 'Hall will want to make a scene. He will probably want to race me before he shoots me, show-off that he is. But we won't give him the chance.'

Pottinger was setting up an ambush of his own, undercover traps on horses lining the track. Fully armed and mounted, they were to pounce on Hall as soon as he arrived.

'Still no sight of Hall,' a detective told Pottinger as the match race drew near. 'Nothing. And none of the punters have seen him at all.'

Pottinger remained silent as he took his saddle.

Maybe he isn't here? No, he will come. He has to. I burnt down his bloody house!

Pottinger dug his heels into his horse and tugged at the reins, the horse responding as he moved towards the start line.

Bang!

The starter fired his gun and Pottinger was away, his horse rocketing off the line and taking the lead.

A hundred yards. Three hundred yards.

Pottinger turned, first looking at Scrammy Jack, the horse and its rider two lengths back. He then looked to the rail, scenery rushing past, a blur of colour, but no sign of Ben Hall.

Five hundred yards. Six hundred.

Scrammy Jack had moved up, and was now only a length behind. But still no sign of Hall. They were coming into the bend. The final turn.

Seven hundred yards. Eight hundred yards.

Scrammy Jack and Bushranger were now nose to nose. But no Ben Hall.

A thousand yards.

Scrammy Jack crossed the line four lengths in front. Still no Ben Hall.

'Come on,' Pottinger called out as he pulled his horse up, the sprint becoming a canter. 'Come and get me, Hall!'

Pottinger waited on his mount, circling the finish line. He waited, waited and waited.

But still no Ben Hall.

* * *

Forbes, 10 February 1865

The *Sydney Morning Herald* was the first to break the story, the bombshell making the newspaper's final edition.

DISMISSAL OF SIR FREDERICK POTTINGER

The government have ordered the dismissal of Sir Frederick Pottinger from his appointment as inspector of police. The charge on which he has been dismissed was that of disobeying one of the rules of the police force in taking part in the recent public races at Forbes.

Pottinger at first thought nothing of his failed attempt to catch Ben Hall at the Wowingragong races. In fact, he assumed he would be applauded for showing initiative and originality. And then the press got hold of the story. *The Empire* ran the following article on 17 January:

BEN HALL AND GANG

On the first and second days of the races at Wowingragong, these worthies were at the back of the course, drinking and amusing themselves. It is said that when Sir Frederick Pottinger was riding one of the races, Hall remarked, 'I had a good mind to shoot him.' It is a curious thing that, although many persons well knew the bushrangers were there, the police seemed entirely ignorant of the fact. The gang will venture too much one of these fine days and will find themselves in the hole.

* * *

Inspector General John McLerie was fuming. 'Hall was at the races?' he yelled. 'At Forbes? And Pottinger was there? And he what? He rode in a race instead of arresting the British Empire's most wanted man?'

It was the latest embarrassment to his under-siege force. McLerie dispatched a letter to Pottinger immediately after reading the report.

'It being directly opposed to regulations of the department that Officers of the Police take part in any racing matters, I presume the material in the newspaper paragraph annexed is incorrect,' McLerie wrote. 'Sir Frederick Pottinger is requested to report.'

Pottinger sat down and wrote a fourteen-page report, detailing his bold, brave and original plan to catch the bushranger. He explained how he had devised the plan to draw out the bushranger and was adamant his action 'fully warranted the discretionary departure in point from the letter of the rules'.

Pottinger thought that would be the end of the matter but the press would not let it rest. His decision to ride a racehorse had become a sensation.

McLerie responded to Pottinger's report, or perhaps more to the public ridicule and lashing in the press.

'No amount of explanation can justify what occurred,' McLerie wrote. 'The reasons offered are quite inadequate to justify the disobedience of an order.'

And then McLerie ended one of the most controversial policing careers in Australian history. His peerage did not save Pottinger this time. After six years as an officer in the New

South Wales police force he was sacked. Pottinger was a hunter of bushrangers no more.

* * *

Blaxland, 5 March 1865

Pottinger could not let it go. *It can't end like this. Sacked. And Hall …*

Having already failed in England, gambled away his family fortune and tarnished his famous family name, Pottinger could not accept becoming a two-time loser. He had moved to Australia for a fresh start. To make a name for himself. To do it all on his own. And he'd been shot at, stood toe-to-toe with the colony's most dangerous criminals.

It's not over. Not yet. Not like this …

Pottinger had set out for Sydney to plead for his job.

'Whoa,' Pottinger yelled, sticking his head out of the wagon. 'Whoa!' Louder this time, the hooves relentless as the horses trotted through the Blue Mountains.

The driver pulled on the reins. 'What is it, sir?' he asked.

'Need another piss.'

Pottinger surveyed the scene, a flowing green paddock cut into the middle of an endless forest of trees.

'Plums,' Pottinger said. 'Have a look at those beauties.'

Purple, juicy and still dripping wet following a summer shower, they hung from the rows planted with military precision. Pottinger was starving.

'A little snack,' he said. 'Won't be a moment.'

Pottinger had set off for Sydney at sunrise, leaving Forbes on a mission to save himself from his latest and greatest humiliation. He'd booked a room at the bottom of the Blue Mountains, only an hour or so away now, but after a full day on the road, he couldn't resist the temptation of the fruit.

Pottinger walked into the field, his mind racing with what was ahead.

Surely they will see sense. It was only a horse race. And I could have caught Hall.

Pottinger would be in Sydney the following afternoon, a train taking him from Penrith to Sydney.

It can't end like this. It won't end like this. I will make them see sense.

Pottinger picked four plums, big, ripe and ready to eat, then turned and started back for the road.

Ah, what the hell. Breakfast too.

He turned back and grabbed again at the branch.

Five. Six. Seven.

His hands couldn't hold them all so he cradled them like a newborn in his right arm.

'Whoa,' Pottinger shouted. The coach was moving, horses spooked and hooves hitting the ground. 'Hang on,' he shouted as he chased his ride.

Still cradling his plums, Pottinger reached out with his left hand and grabbed the side of the coach. He jumped and yanked himself forward.

Then, suddenly, plums flew into the air, Pottinger was hurled from the side of the coach and smashed into the dirt, and there was a bang as his gun went off. The purple fruit exploded around him.

'Blazes,' shouted the driver, horses now stopped. 'What was that? Gunfire? Sir?'

Pottinger pulled himself from the ground.

'The plums,' he said. *Oh shit ...*

Pottinger's hand shot up to his side, and all of a sudden he was in agony. As he keeled over he looked at the ground and saw blood.

'Are you hit?' asked the driver.

Pottinger pulled his hand away from his ribs and brought it to his face. It was covered in blood, warm, wet and dripping.

'Are you alright?' the driver asked.

Pottinger pressed his hand hard into his side and pulled himself from the ground. 'There is a house over there,' he said, pointing towards a sign that read *Wascoe's Inn*. 'Looks like we will stay there.'

In a freak accident, a ball from his own pistol had torn through his flesh. Pottinger's four-barrel pistol had fallen from his waistcoat as he attempted to pull himself onto the runaway cart. The .32-calibre American Sharps firearm, loaded and locked, had hit the footrail of the wagon. The lead ball had entered his stomach at point-blank range, the soft tissue offering no resistance as the bullet rocketed up into his ribs, smashing three of the bones. The bullet came to a fleshy finish an inch from his heart.

It's nothing. Better tomorrow.

'I may need some tending to,' Pottinger said to the publican as he walked through the door of the inn. 'Just a scratch. A bandage and bed and I will be on my way tomorrow. I have an important appointment in Sydney.'

But Sir Frederick Pottinger never got to his appointment – he spent the next thirty-five days in a Sydney hospital.

'It can't end like this,' he said as they applied leeches in a last-ditch attempt to save his life. 'A disgrace. A failure. And Ben Hall ...'

On his deathbed he spoke of unfinished business. 'The escort robbery,' he said. 'Just two left. Gilbert. Hall. Bring them to justice ...'

And then Sir Frederick Pottinger, a second baronet and former police inspector of New South Wales, died on 9 April 1865, a 'hectic fever resulting from a gunshot wound to the abdomen and chest' taking his life. He was not yet thirty-four.

* * *

Randwick, 13 April 1865

In death he got what he wanted in life.

A hero, they said. *Bravest man the colony has ever seen. Only one who ever stood up to them. Gave his life for us. And he would have got that Ben Hall ...*

One of the most ridiculed men in Australian colonial history died a hero. He'd been a stranger to applause, affection and adulation while he was alive, but the tributes flowed in for Sir Frederick Pottinger when he was dead.

'In the prime of life – but thirty-four years of age – and in the midst of a career of usefulness, has died Sir Frederick

Pottinger, as genial-hearted, affectionate and charitable a man as ever lived,' wrote *Bell's Life in Sydney* on 15 April:

> *His was a triumph of usefulness not only from the fear of him by the criminals, but for his hearty sociability everywhere. His enemies, if any, were very few, his friends were legion. Good-tempered, clever, and thoroughly charitable, he gained the hearts of all …*
>
> *This lamented gentleman was buried on Tuesday morning. The cortege, consisting of the hearse, three mourning coaches, and the carriages of several of our leading citizens, moved from the Victoria Club, at half-past nine o'clock, and proceeded to the Randwick cemetery, where the last rites of the Church of England were issued.*

Chapter 18

THE EXECUTION

Billabong Creek, 4 May 1865

Frigid wind hitting his face, sun soon to set, Hall made his way through the bush. Alone, just him and his horse, he listened as hooves hit leaves. *Crunch. Crunch. Crunch.*

Hall looked left. He looked right. *I might as well have a bell around my neck ...*

He looked forward and back. Nothing. Just him and his horse. Or so he thought.

Hall was being watched. Hidden in the thick scrub near the creek, eight heavily armed men lay in wait. Six troopers. Two black trackers. Shotguns, rifles, revolvers.

'Not yet,' whispered Sub-Inspector James Henry Davidson, the replacement for Sir Frederick Pottinger. 'We watch. We wait.'

* * *

Hall had just said goodbye to his son. Splitting from Johnny Gilbert and latest recruit John Dunn, Hall had travelled back to Sandy Creek to see Henry.

'Son,' he'd said, 'you might not see me for a while. I have to go on a bit of a trip. A holiday. I don't know when I'll be back.'

Henry Hall, now six, had nodded. What this man was saying meant nothing to him.

'Henry,' Hall said, more animated now, 'do you know who I am? Do you understand what I am saying?'

Henry nodded again. 'You are Ben Hall,' he said. 'The famous bushranger. And you are my father.'

Hall hugged his son. 'I love you, Henry,' he said. 'Remember that. Whatever they say about me, you just remember that I love you. And that I am your dad.'

With a tear in his eye, Hall turned away from Henry. Biddy walked after him.

'Biddy,' Hall said, 'I am sorry.'

And then the unthinkable happened. Biddy Hall – now Biddy Taylor – gave her forgotten husband a kiss.

'No, I am sorry, Ben,' she said. 'Sorry that it has come to this. I wish it had been different. I really do.'

Hall wanted to cry. Choking back tears and unable to speak, he turned and jumped on his horse. Slapping the reins, he kicked his heels and rode into the sunset while James Taylor watched from the safety of the bush.

Out of sight, well on his way, Hall had started to sob.

Will I ever see them again? Will I see my son grow up, become a man?

Hall knew the answer.

* * *

The reign of Hall, Gilbert and Dunn in the central west of New South Wales had come to an end. Another murder, this time Dunn killing a trap, had assured their fate. The reaction from the authorities has been swift and tough. Brutal. In a bid to finally put a stop to Hall and his gang, with the latest killing the final straw, the government had passed an Act designed to end bushranging in New South Wales.

One of the most controversial pieces of legislation in the history of the British Empire was passed twenty-four days before Hall said goodbye to his boy. Called the *Felons Apprehension Act of 1865*, it authorised both police and citizens to kill an 'outlaw' on sight. Legal murder. No trial, no judge, no jury. A death sentence. The Act also provided that anyone convicted of harbouring an 'outlaw' was liable to fifteen years' imprisonment and confiscation of all land and goods. The three-thousand-pound reward for the gang was now payable whether they were caught dead or alive.

'The strenuous endeavours made in the south to capture Ben Hall and his gang seems to be telling upon them with terrible effect,' the *Sydney Morning Herald* wrote following the passing of the Act:

> *The accounts we have read of the nervousness of Hall and the watchful suspicion he shows to everyone he meets tell of the straining vigilance they are compelled to maintain in a bid to avoid capture.*

*The Felons Apprehension Act is inspiring them with terror,
and the unceasing wear upon body and mind, which they must
feel by the manner in which they are to be hunted, it would be
impossible for the vagabonds to remain at large for a much greater
length of time.*

Hall knew this reporter was right, so the Hall gang agreed to quit New South Wales. To stop the robbing. To stop the shooting. After ninety-four confirmed robberies and possibly many more, the greatest crime spree in history was over. Hall's crimes would dwarf those of the most famous robbers of them all, such as John Dillinger, Jesse James and Butch Cassidy.

'Where to?' Gilbert asked. 'Victoria? Don't tell me you are thinking of Queensland?'

Hall shrugged. 'America,' he replied. 'I don't think we will be safe anywhere this side of the ocean.'

'No,' Gilbert blasted, 'Victoria! America? No way.'

Hall shrugged again. 'Well, let's just get out of here,' he said. 'Go and see your family and friends. Whoever you have to see.'

'I'm not fucking leaving Australia,' Gilbert said.

Hall grabbed Gilbert by the neck. 'We are not staying here,' he shouted. 'We can't. Go and do what you have to and then we will meet at Goobang Mick's. Don't trust anyone. You can't trust anyone.'

Hall was right. So why did he trust Michael Coneley?

* * *

Coneley handed Hall a plate, potatoes steaming, freshly slaughtered beef stewed. The more he concentrated on acting normal the more nervous he felt.

Known to Hall as Goobang Mick, Michael Coneley had ridden to Forbes earlier that day and told the police that Ben Hall, Johnny Gilbert and John Dunn were planning to meet at his house.

'A thousand pounds each, right?' he'd asked Sub-Inspector Davidson. 'Three thousand all up?'

Davidson had nodded. 'That and you won't spend the next fifteen years in gaol and have everything you own confiscated by the Crown,' the trap replied.

Coneley had frowned. 'Okay,' he'd said. 'Well, just promise me you'll get him. Shoot him dead if you have to. He will know it was me that gave him up. He will kill me if he gets away.'

Hall took the plate, Judas handing him his last supper.

'You crook, Mick?' Hall asked. 'You look like shit.'

'Yeah, mate,' Coneley said. 'Think I've come down a bit sick. Bit of bad chook maybe? But she'll be right.'

Pull yourself together …

'Bog in,' Coneley said. 'Looks like there will be plenty left.' He turned and pointed at two plates, full and untouched. 'So where are the other two?'

Hall shrugged. 'No bleeding idea,' he said. 'They were supposed to be here hours ago. Maybe they are still farewelling some sheilas.'

They weren't. Gilbert and Dunn had been nearing Goobang Mick's hut when they'd seen two riders in the distance.

'Traps,' Dunn had shouted. 'Over there. Go!'

They'd bolted.

'Righto, mate,' Hall said. 'I'm going to hit the sack. I've set up a camp about a mile away. Best that way in case the traps come. I don't want you going down for taking me in. It's fifteen years now for taking one of us in, you know? I'll come back for brekkie, hopefully with the other two.'

* * *

Sub-Inspector Davidson had been watching Hall all night. From the moment Hall had walked into Mick Coneley's hut until he drew his very last breath, Davidson had had his eyes on the Empire's most wanted man.

Davidson had assembled a team of eight men to travel to Billabong Creek after Coneley had come forward and informed on his mate. The party included Sergeant James Condell, troopers Thomas Hipkiss, John Caban, Edward Buckley and John Boyan, and black trackers Billy Dargin and Charley.

At 10 pm, when Hall left Coneley's hut, the bushranger had walked straight past Hipkiss, Caban and Buckley, who were hidden in the scrub. They were tempted to open fire but had been ordered by Davidson to wait for daylight. The sub-inspector did not want Hall disappearing under the cover of darkness.

The army of eight, armed and ready, had reconvened after Hall had made a bed out of fallen leaves and laid down to sleep.

'We wait until first light,' Davidson said. 'We wait until he rises.'

He told Hipkiss, Caban, Buckley, Boyan and Charley to go and make camp on the other side of the clearing.

'We will push him towards you,' Davidson had said. 'Set an ambush. Just lie in wait until you hear my call.'

Davidson, Condell and Dargin had taken a position a hundred yards away from Hall. Condell and Dargin lay down on the wet ground where they stayed awake, soaked and shivering, for the next six hours. Davidson had hunched against a tree, his eyes never leaving Hall.

'He's moving,' Davidson had said as the emerging sun sent the sky pink.

* * *

Billabong Creek, 5 May 1865

The sun edged over the horizon, the virgin rays mixing with the lingering night cloud to turn the sky pink. The brilliance woke up the birds, a tawny frogmouth calling first before being joined by a kookaburra and then a magpie. Soon the bush was alive with a cacophony of sounds from birds and insects.

Hall rolled over, opened his eyes and looked up at the sky, the pink now edged by orange and framed by a brilliant blue. Hall never tired of the beauty of the bush. Although his back hurt, his clothes stank and a bug had bitten his face, the 'starlight hotel' had its upside.

He planted a hand into the dirt and pushed himself up. Time to feed his horse before going back to Mick's to feed himself.

'Shit,' Hall said, rubbing his eyes now before looking to his left and right. 'Ah,' he muttered, spotting his horse over in the field. She'd freed herself from the sloppy hitch and gone off to find the sun.

Hall stood and stretched his arms into the sky as he let out a yawn. He picked up a bridle and left the safety of the scrub to fetch his horse.

'Stand,' came the cry. 'Stand fast. Hold!'

Hall turned and saw three men armed with shotguns, rifles and revolvers storming out of the bush. They were fifty yards away and closing fast.

Hall dropped the bridle, turned and ran.

'Surrender,' came the voice again. 'Stand!'

But Hall had already taken off, the bushranger stumbling as he reached down to his belt to pull out his gun. Soon he could hear their footfall, boots crashing into brittle brown grass.

Boom!

Hall heard the noise first, then he felt the pain.

A slug had torn into his back. The force of the blast sent him stumbling. But he didn't fall. He didn't stop. He turned, only for a moment, to face his attackers.

Davidson. Condell. Dargin.

Hall recognised his hunters. He saw their faces and he saw their guns. And they were only thirty yards from him now. He ignored the pain and the hole the size of a fist below his shoulder blade, gaping and bleeding, and ran some more.

Bang!

Another bullet hit his back. He stumbled again. But he didn't stop.

Bang!

On he ran.

'Get him!' came the cry.

Hall stopped in his tracks. That shout had come from straight in front of him. He looked up and saw another five men. He had been running straight towards them.

Bang!

One of them fired, but still he didn't fall. He grabbed onto a sapling, one of a cluster of young trees sprouting in the middle of the field. While Davidson, Condell and Dargin approached from behind, the five others charged. And then the bullets came, one after another.

Finally Hall fell, the bushranger collapsing when a bullet tore through his belt, into his stomach and up into his ribs and then dying as he hit the ground. He was only twenty-seven.

But still the bullets came, lead balls ripping flesh from his now lifeless body.

'Gotcha, ya bastard,' screamed Sergeant Condell, looking down at the body of the man he was sure had robbed him at Eugowra Rocks in 1862. 'That one is for Sir Fred.'

In all twenty-five shots had been fired, five double-barrelled shotguns each firing twice, and three revolving carbines each emptied of all five rounds. And not one of those shots had missed.

'Ben Hall got a most fearful riddling,' Davidson later wrote in a letter to his father. 'I had no control over my men after that first shot. They were perfectly mad and the air was filled with yells and shouts of frantic Irishmen. Such a row I have never heard.'

Davidson searched the dead man's body and found seventy-four pounds in notes, a gold chain, a gold ring, a powder flask, two tins of percussion caps, a bag of bullets, three revolvers and a miniature portrait of a woman.

Biddy.

* * *

Hall's body was taken back to Forbes, limp and lifeless, bloodied and riddled with lead, strapped to the back of a horse. Even at 4 am, a crowd was there to meet it, fifty or so watching as the police carried the corpse into the police hut. They laid Hall's body on the floor of a room inside the barracks.

'As I entered I saw the clothes of the ill-fated man in the outward room,' a reporter wrote. 'The hat, which was low crowned, was perforated on all sides. The coat was riddled too. There were wounds to match on his body. They were too numerous to count.'

The official inquest into the death of Ben Hall declared the shooting was 'justifiable homicide'. Even though Hall had not officially been declared an outlaw – meaning the *Felons Apprehension Act* could not be applied – and even though Hall had not let off a shot – some later claimed that Hall did not even draw his gun – the twenty-five bullets fired into Hall, most at point-blank range, were declared legal.

On 7 May, two days after he was killed, possibly murdered, Ben Hall was buried in an unmarked grave at the Forbes cemetery. A headstone was not erected until 1923. *'In Memory of Ben Hall,'* it said. *'Shot 5th May 1865, Aged 27 Years.'*

Chapter 19

THE DAMNED

Tappue Creek, New Zealand, 18 January 1868

In one hand she held the Bible, leather-bound and gold-etched. In the other she held a revolver. She had grabbed both – the gun and the book – following a fight with her new husband.

'You're a drunk,' she had screamed. 'And a gambler.' She launched forward and pounded her fist into his chest. 'You are no Frank. Oh, what he would do to you. Frank would—'

And suddenly the attack had stopped.

Frank.

She had spoken the name she had been trying so hard to forget.

'I'm sorry,' she said to her husband, a man called Richard Taylor.

She had placed a kiss on his cheek and walked away.

Now she was standing on the edge of a cliff, gun in her right hand and Bible in her left.

Frank.

She looked down at the Bible, gold script perfectly etched.

Catherine.

She flicked open the cover and there it was.

Presented to Catherine by her affectionate Frank. 1865.

Kitty Brown had tried to begin again. She had married another butcher from Lambing Flat and moved to New Zealand. New country. New husband. New life. But she knew now that she still loved the same man.

A tear rolled down her cheek as she raised the gun.

'I'm sorry, Frank,' she said. 'I tried to forget.'

And then she bit the barrel.

* * *

Darlinghurst, 20 February 1868

The prison officer walked into the cell, where the inmate was up and ready for work.

'Frank,' said the officer. 'You better read this.'

Frank raised his brow.

'Righto,' he said. 'Give us a squiz.'

The officer handed the prisoner the broadsheet. Gardiner started to read.

SUICIDE OF MRS BROWN

The unfortunate woman whose name was brought before
the public some years ago, as the paramour of Gardiner, the
bushranger, appears, by information recently brought to Sydney
by a person who was present at the inquest on her remains,

to have come to a miserable end. This event happened several weeks ago. For some time before her death she was living at Tappue Creek, Thames River diggings, New Zealand, with a man who was formerly employed by a butcher on Lambing Flat.

Mrs Brown, it seems, was in the habit of carrying a pistol, and in a frenzy put the pistol to her mouth and shot herself. The man with whom she lived was suspected of causing her death, but while lying on her death-bed – and she lingered for a week after the fatal wound – she fully exonerated him, and declared that the wound was inflicted by her own hand. She also told those who attended her that she was the same Mrs Brown who lived with the bushranger Gardiner, and requested that some likenesses she had preserved of him be placed in her coffin.

Gardiner placed the newspaper on his bed.

'You want to stay in today, Frank?' the officer asked.

There was no response.

'I'm sorry,' said the guard. 'I'll leave you be.'

The guard walked out. Frank still hadn't moved. There were no tears. No screams. He was shocked, silent and still.

Gardiner did not leave his cell that day or week. In fact, he stayed on his bed for the next twelve days. Eventually he did cry, and scream. 'Kitty,' he shouted, waking the entire cell block with his painful cry in the middle of the night. 'Kitty! Why?'

Again, the heart that he thought was already shattered broke some more. The love of his life was dead, aged just twenty-four.

* * *

Darlinghurst, 30 June 1872

Gardiner never got over the death of Kitty Brown. A picture he kept in a brass locket was a constant reminder of love lost. He would open the locket and look at the one and only portrait ever taken of his sweetheart. And then he would close it.

'We will meet again,' he would say.

Gardiner had considered ending his own life in the dark days that followed the revelation. He thought he had nothing to live for. And he would have joined his Kitty in death had it not been for his sisters, Charlotte and Archina. He just couldn't put them through the hurt.

Now visiting him weekly, the pair showed him love in a place where previously there was none. And eventually they helped heal his broken heart.

'You will have a life again, Francis,' Charlotte said. 'You'll see. We are going to get you out.'

Charlotte and Archina had spent the last eight years tirelessly campaigning for Gardiner's release. They refused to give up on their long-lost brother now found. And on 3 June 1872 they were given hope when Sir Hercules Robinson became the fourteenth governor of New South Wales.

'The new governor is sympathetic, Francis,' Charlotte continued. 'We will petition him for your early release.'

And they did, the sisters collecting almost five hundred signatures before presenting Sir Hercules with their case.

Your petitioners humbly implore your Excellency's merciful consideration of their unfortunate brother's case, towards affording a remission of his terrible sentence on the following grounds.

Previous to his apprehension he was obtaining his living as a storekeeper in Queensland for nearly two years, having abandoned his former career of wickedness and had left the colony fully determined to lead an honest industry.

That only four months after his conviction there was a desperate outbreak of prisoners in the gaol, in which he took no part.

That the prisoner has always given every satisfaction to the clerk as well as to the governor of the gaol.

That the prisoner's health has already suffered so much from his long confinement as to cause him to be almost constantly under the hands of the doctor for disease of the heart and other serious symptoms.

Lastly, that your petitioners feel certain that if your Excellency be pleased to grant him a pardon, he will thus be afforded an opportunity of redeeming the past, and from your petitioners' knowledge of his character they can confidently assure your Excellency that he will never again commit himself, and from the very confident and feeling manner in which his Honour Sir Alfred Stephen has on many occasions addressed himself to the petitioners' brother and remarked upon his reformation, they hope that he will recommend the prayer of this petition to the most favourable consideration of your Excellency.

The signatures were attached, the names including famous legislator William Bede Dalley, Chief Justice Sir Alfred Stephen and Colonial Secretary William Forster.

And in an unprecedented move, Forster, the second highest authority in New South Wales, had also provided a reference.

'I am willing to add my testimony and recommendation in the case of Frank Gardiner,' Forster wrote. 'Having been referred to in a petition for the mitigation of the sentence of Francis Gardiner, as holding the office of Colonial Secretary when an outbreak at Darlinghurst Gaol occurred, I have much pleasure in testifying to the fact of Gardiner's good conduct on that occasion, as well as to his general good conduct during the entire period of his incarceration. I am glad to report this opinion so that it may operate as it ought in the prisoner's favour. And so far as these and other circumstances mentioned in the petition entitle his case to favourable consideration of the government.'

The governor replied to Forster.

'When the prisoner has served ten years his case may again be brought forward,' Sir Hercules said. 'If his conduct should in the meantime be good, I should be disposed to grant him then a pardon, conditional on him leaving the country. At present I do not concur with the petitioners that the sentence which the prisoner has undergone is sufficient for the ends of justice.'

And with that there was hope.

* * *

Darlinghurst, 7 April 1874

'I told you,' Charlotte said as she kissed her brother. 'I told you I would get you out.'

Gardiner raised his brow. 'Get me out?'

Charlotte nodded.

Frank was speechless.

'Well, are you going to say something?' Charlotte continued. 'Don't just stand there like a fool.'

Gardiner began to cry. 'You did it?' he asked. 'You really did it?'

Charlotte nodded again. Her ten-year campaign, relentless and unwavering, was finally over.

'Thank you,' Gardiner said. 'I never thought I would live to see the day.'

Gardiner's pending release was made public a month later, when a member of parliament asked Henry Parkes whether rumours of his pardon were true.

Parkes confirmed the fact. Bushranging was over. Hall was dead. Gilbert was now dead too, the last of the escort robbers never to be caught shot dead by police in May 1865, just eight days after Hall was killed.

'The governor has issued a pardon,' Parkes said. 'He will be released on the twentieth of July. After serving ten years he will be set free. But he will not be allowed to reside in the colony of New South Wales until the original term of his sentence expires.'

* * *

Darlinghurst, 20 July 1874

The prison warder tapped the bar.

'Frank,' he said. 'I'm coming in. It's time.'

This time Gardiner sprang from his bed, on his feet in an instant.

'Now?' Gardiner asked. 'But it is the middle of the night.'

The prison officer walked into the cell that had been Gardiner's personal hell for the previous ten years.

'They don't want you to be mobbed,' the guard said. 'So let's go.' The guard turned, his lantern illuminating the rest of Gardiner's cell. 'Unless you want to stay here?'

Gardiner laughed. 'Well, it is kind of cosy,' he said. 'And that smell? It grows on you after a while.' Gardiner slapped the warder on the back and laughed some more. 'Oh Christ no,' he said. 'Get me out of this godforsaken hole.'

Gardiner was taken from his cell and onto the catwalk. He could see little except what the glow of the guard's lantern revealed. He thought about all the things he had seen in this place: fights, murders, hangings.

And then he smiled; some good times too. Gardiner had met some men he would forever remember as mates. Card partners, stone-cutting buddies – hell, he even liked most of the screws. Soon the light from the lantern lit up a familiar door. The visiting rooms. His eyes suddenly welled.

Kitty.

It was the last place he had seen the love of his life. He sniffed the air, imagining the scent of her perfume. A tear rolled down his face.

He remembered the Bible. He had given it to her in that very room.

Catherine.

Gold etched into leather.

He smiled, remembering the final kiss. He wiped the tear from his face as his thoughts turned to his sisters. It was in the same room that he was reunited with them after twenty-three years. Where they kissed him, each and every week, and then, after ten years in prison, told him he would once again have a life.

'Open up,' shouted a prison officer.

Gardiner stood and watched as the gigantic iron door began to move. His heart pounded. He felt like turning and running back to his cell.

Ten years? What am I going to do? What's left for me out there?

'Francis' cried Charlotte, his sister standing on the path outside.

He rejoined the world with five steps, through the gate and under the stone arch. But still he wasn't free. Not yet.

* * *

Newcastle, New South Wales, 21 July 1874

'Please, cobber?' Gardiner said. 'Just one night? I need to say goodbye. I'm not going anywhere.'

The burly officer, one of four detectives who had escorted Gardiner from Sydney to Newcastle on the steamship *Lady Young*, shook his head.

'I can't be the bloke who loses Frank Gardiner,' he said. 'I have my orders. These chains are not to come off until you leave for China.'

Gardiner had been freed from Darlinghurst Gaol. But his pardon was conditional. He could not live anywhere in the British Empire until the full term of his sentence expired. And his chains would not be removed until he stepped off Australian shores.

'My sisters,' Gardiner said. 'I just want to thank them. I may never see them again. Please let me say goodbye.'

The detective's heart went soft. 'One hour,' he said. 'I'll give you one hour. But the chains stay on and we are coming with you.'

Gardiner spent the next hour sipping, smiling and eventually sobbing with Charlotte and Archina in a Newcastle tea house.

'I wish it had been different,' Gardiner said. 'If I had stayed a butcher—'

Archina cut him off. 'We would never have found you,' she said. 'We would never have seen you again. We were only reunited because you became who you did. Frank Gardiner, the famous bushranger. My brother. The King of the Road.'

'But all the lives,' Gardiner said. 'O'Meally, Gilbert, Manns and Ben.' He paused. 'And Kitty ....' Gardiner broke down. 'How can I ever go on?'

'You can and you will,' Archina said. 'For us. Because if you don't, we won't. We couldn't.'

'Alright,' Gardiner said. 'For you.'

He kissed his saviours, the sisters he would never see again.

* * *

The chains came off the following day.

Clink! Clank!

'That's a sound I never want to hear again,' Gardiner said, laughing.

Frank Gardiner was finally free.

Chapter 20

THE EXILE

San Francisco, USA, November 1874

Gardiner walked up onto the deck, grabbing the rail as the ship hit yet another swell.

'Land ahoy, Frank!' shouted the sailor. 'Look. Over there!'

Gardiner looked past the bow. 'Where?' he asked. 'I can't see a thing.'

Gardiner squinted, steadied and focused. All he saw was white, the fog so thick he could barely see the front of the ship. He raised a palm into the air, expecting to grab a handful.

'Ha,' laughed the sailor. 'Welcome to San Francisco. You better get used to it.'

After thirty-three days of cramped cabins, whacking waves and festering food, Gardiner had sprinted from the bowels of the *Republic* and onto the deck when he was told he was nearing his new home.

America. Finally.

He'd suffered more than a month of seasickness since boarding the steamship in Hong Kong. He should have known after the journey from Newcastle, but he would have endured worse, such was his dislike for China. It wasn't just a new world: it was a different planet. So he'd boarded the *Republic* and headed to San Francisco, a place that was apparently 'just like Sydney'.

'There,' said the sailor. 'Look.'

Gardiner saw land, shore at first then mountains. He was suddenly taken back to Wheogo. To the Weddin. Fog rushed from the peaks, a misty mountain waterfall. And then the sun broke through to reveal San Francisco Bay. And they were right.

Sydney ...

Gardiner had only seen one harbour as beautiful as this, only one that could match its size and magnificence. The similarity almost floored him. There was even an island. He shivered as he thought of Cockatoo Island, his first prison hell. But this island, almost identical in shape and size to the Sydney Harbour convict gaol, was not a gaol, not yet. The sailor told him they called it Alcatraz.

* * *

'Are you Francis Gardiner?' asked the well-dressed gentleman on the quay sporting a suit, tie and umbrella. 'Otherwise known as Francis Christie?'

'Why do you want to know?' Gardiner asked. 'And who are you?'

The man stepped forward.

'Press,' he said. 'I am the editor of the *San Francisco Chronicle*. And you are Frank Gardiner, right? The famous Australian outlaw? The Empire's very own Jesse James?'

Gardiner shook his head. 'Jesse James?' he replied. 'No, sir, I am not. I have never killed a man. But Frank Gardiner? Well, yes I am. But I am no longer an outlaw. I have served my sentence and I am here legally, and to start a new life. An honest life.'

The reporter beamed, a prospector striking gold. He reached into his bag and pulled out a pad and pen.

'So tell me, why are you here?' he asked. 'What have you done and what will you do?'

Gardiner shook his head. 'Sorry but this isn't an interview,' he said. 'Not here. Not now. Come back when my words mean something.'

The reporter came back the next day and the day after that. He finally got his interview six months later.

'Okay, shoot,' Frank said. And then he laughed. 'Bushranger joke,' he clarified. 'Go ahead.'

The reporter smiled. 'So, what are your future intentions?' he asked.

'I mean to earn an honest livelihood,' Gardiner said, smoke in hand, leaning back in his chair. 'Though I am debarred from returning to Australia, I have the good wishes of three-fourths of the people there.'

The reporter had been scribbling furiously but now pulled up his pen. 'Really?' he asked. 'Were you not Australia's most notorious criminal? A thief like they had never seen?'

'But I never committed any murder,' Gardiner said. 'And I have given more than half my earnings on the road to poor travellers, and I never robbed a poor man in my life.'

'Why did you commence such a career?' the reporter asked.

'For want of suitable employment,' Gardiner said. 'Young men can find no employment in the country districts except for herding sheep or stock riding. The latter occupation leads to horse stealing simply because you become wholly engrossed in horse flesh, and crime is so easily committed that you do not think of the consequence.'

The reporter nodded. 'But what made you rob the mails?' he asked. 'The biggest gold robbery in history.'

Gardiner took a breath. 'I don't know,' he shrugged. 'I was young at the time and spent my money as quickly as I got it. I thought it was an easy life, and that seemed an easy score. And it was, at least for a while. Soon I changed my mind and resolved at all hazards to lead a good life, and when I relinquished bushranging and went to Apis Creek, where I was apprehended, I never dreamed but I might die there at a good, honourable old age.

'I was known as Frank Christie and many thousands of pounds had been entrusted to my custody. I had a good reputation far and wide.'

The reporter pulled his head up but continued to scrawl. 'Have you a good prospect before you?' he asked.

'Yes, after ten years confinement I am glad to be free again,' Gardiner said. 'I think my Australian reputation was so good, in spite of my crimes, that my record may have reached this country. I am determined to lead an honest life, and I am quite able to fill my part in it credibly.'

The reporter smiled, gold finally struck. His story was published in the *San Francisco Chronicle* in April 1875 and reproduced worldwide.

* * *

By then, Frank Gardiner had long been a San Francisco celebrity. His arrival had made the front page of the *San Francisco Chronicle*:

> *One of the world's most famous outlaws has arrived in San Francisco. A man of apparently 45, with a full round English face, jet black beard and moustache, Francis Gardiner stepped off a steamship from Hong Kong yesterday. Gardiner, who is the mastermind behind the world's biggest gold robbery, said he was no longer an outlaw and vowed to live an honest life on our shores.*

Gardiner spent his first night in San Francisco on the street. He woke up again to white, the city flooded by another fog. He only had three things on his mind as he walked down the street.

Food. A bed. A job.

'Look,' came the cry. 'It's Gardiner. There he is.'

Gardiner turned and four men were rushing his way. He steadied for a fight.

'No, Frank,' one said. 'We are Aussies.'

And so it began …

The harbour, the weather, the sights and the smells were all like Sydney. And then Gardiner heard he really was in Sydney.

'This is Sydney Cove, Frank,' the Aussie on the street said. 'We are all from Sydney. And, mate, well, you are a bloody legend. This town is yours. Whatever you want. We're the Sydney Ducks. We run everything here.'

Gardiner had stumbled his way into a part of San Francisco known as the Barbary Coast, which in the 1840s had been known as Sydney Cove. In 1848, San Francisco had been a town of fewer than a thousand inhabitants. But then a man called James Marshall found an undisclosed amount of gold nearby, at Coloma, and in just one year the settlement became a tent city of twenty-five thousand. Soon they included an estimated eleven thousand Australians who had travelled from Sydney to San Francisco between 1848 and 1850 seeking their fortune.

These men, mostly ex-convicts, turned the tent city into a living hell. Forming a gang known as the Sydney Ducks, the ragtag swell of mostly Irish descent took charge of the city. They would later be credited as being the first gang in the United States to centralise every vice: grog, gambling, prostitution and drugs. In 1851 the government passed its first piece of anti-gang legislation, rushed through after the Sydney Ducks were blamed for the 1849 fire that had burnt half of San Francisco to the ground. Despite this, the Sydney Ducks continued to rule the waterfront between Broadway and Pacific Street. And in 1876 they decided to buy a bushranger a bar.

* * *

Barbary Coast, San Francisco, November 1876

The traveller walked into the Twilight, weary yet eyes wide open. He wasn't there for a drink. He was there for the legend.

'Is this Gardiner's joint?' he asked. 'Frank Gardiner?'

The barman grabbed a glass. ''Tis,' he said as he started to pour. 'And by order of the owner, the Frank Gardiner you ask about, every Australian has his first drink free.'

The punter smiled: a legend and a free drink. It was his lucky day. He looked around the bar. It was heaving: shouting, singing and sculling; conversation, dance and drink. He had heard that Gardiner's bar was a belter. Smack bang in the middle of Kearny Street – San Francisco's sleaziest district – it was party central. There were dance halls, concert saloons and bars. And then there were the brothels. They were everywhere.

But there was only one bar owned by a bushranger.

'Is he here?' the punter asked.

The bartender slid him his drink. 'He is,' the barman said.

'Can I meet him?' the punter asked after taking a swig for courage.

'Yes,' the barman replied. 'But not until you buy a drink. Gardiner doesn't like being robbed.' The barman chuckled as he extended his hand. 'Name's McGlone,' he said. 'Daniel McGlone. Nice to meet you.'

The punter almost dropped his drink. 'McGlone?' he echoed. 'The trap? The copper who arrested Frank?'

The barman laughed. 'Yep,' he said. 'But I ain't no trap. Not anymore.'

The punter turned, a hand suddenly on his back.

'Yeah, that's the wretch who got me,' Gardiner said. 'Put a gun in my side and told me I was nicked. Famous he said he would be. Said I was going to make him rich. And now he is working for me!'

McGlone laughed while the stranger looked on open-mouthed.

'Oh,' Gardiner continued, 'the look on his face the day he walked in here. I went for my gun, I did. I grabbed it, I levelled it, and then I went for the trigger. And then? Well, he got down on his knees. "A job," he said. "I just want a job." Ha.' He looked at McGlone. 'That's when I realised there was a fate worse than death,' Gardiner winked.

'And look, now you are making me famous after all,' McGlone smiled.

Gardiner made a gun with his hand. 'Bang,' he said. 'Should have shot you when I had the chance.'

* * *

Gardiner shouted the Australian another drink.

'So what brings you here?' he asked. 'Gold?'

The punter nodded. 'Yep,' he said, looking Gardiner firm in the face. 'But I hear all the California gold is gone. I am here to get me some Australian gold.'

Gardiner raised a brow.

'Your gold, Frank,' the tourist said. 'Tell me where it is and I will go and get it for you.'

'My gold?' Gardiner asked.

'Yeah, the gold from the escort robbery,' the visitor continued. 'All that gold they never recovered. You buried it in the Weddin, right? Tell me where and I'll go dig it up. I'll bring it back for you if you give me a share.'

Gardiner raised his brow again. 'They never did find all that escort gold now, did they?' A wry smile crept across his face. 'There must be almost ninety pounds of it. And you think it is buried in a hole somewhere?'

The Australian nodded. 'The Weddin Mountains,' the tourist said. 'You buried it there before it all went to shit.'

Gardiner laughed. 'Give this lad another drink,' he said. 'Some good American bourbon. Sorry, mate, that's the only gold I have. Buried treasure? Well, that's a myth.'

* * *

Frank Gardiner opened his second San Francisco bar in 1879. Like the Twilight, it was a roaring success. Men came from everywhere to meet the legend who had once been called the King of the Road.

'Bigger than Jesse James,' they said. 'Wilder than anything in the Wild West.'

And then in 1880 he cashed out. Suddenly sold both his bars and headed east.

'Did Gardiner go looking for gold?' a punter asked McGlone, who had kept on working at the Twilight. 'Or has he gone looking for trouble?'

McGlone shook his head. 'He isn't looking for anything,' he said. 'He left because he finally found everything he has ever been looking for.'

Gardiner's heart, once shattered and broken, had finally healed. And then it had been stolen. Gardiner married an American woman in 1880 and retired to southern Colorado. They had two children, twin boys. He lived happily on a ranch, spending his days under the desert sun.

He died in 1902, aged seventy-two, his wife and sons by his side. But before he went into his final sunset and darkness eternal, he told his wife and boys the story of a young man they called Prince of Thieves and Australia's greatest bushranger. He told them how he, gun in hand, loot stuffed into his well-worn and bulging leather saddlebag, had galloped through gum trees after losing the law.

And he told them of the treasure.

'The map is in my trunk.'

Epilogue

Mount Wheogo, February 1912

Knock! Knock!

Knock! Knock! Knock!

'Hang on,' the old man shouted. 'I'm coming. Hold your horses.'

He shuffled slowly down the corridor and opened the door.

'What's all this banging about?' asked Jack Butler, as he glared out at the two young men. 'I bloody well heard you the first time.'

'I am sorry about that, sir,' said one of the visitors. 'My name is William. And this here is Lilburn – Lyle.'

Old Jack extended his hand. 'Yanks?' he inquired. 'What the hell are you doing here? You're a long way from home.'

The one called Lilburn stepped forward and shook Butler's hand.

'Did a Mrs Catherine Brown once live here?' he asked. 'A woman who they called Kitty?'

Butler narrowed his eyes. 'Yeah, Kitty lived here,' he said. 'Her parents owned this house a long time ago. But I am here now. Have been for a while. And what do you want with my house?'

'Oh no, sir,' said William. 'We don't want your house. We were just hoping to get permission to do a little digging on your property. We are geologists representing a large company back in the US and we have come out to search for radium. We have some information that these hills here are rich with the stuff.'

Butler gave them a good once-over, looking them up and down before staring them in the face.

'Radium?' he echoed. 'What the hell is that? And what does it mean to me?'

'Oh, it's a chemical a French lady called Marie Curie discovered a few years back,' Lilburn answered. 'It may have some applications that could prove important. And you will be compensated, sir. Compensated very well if we find what we are looking for. The company we represent has plenty of money.'

So Jack Butler gave the two Americans permission to dig.

* * *

Three weeks later, Butler walked to the top of the hill.

'Lyle?' he shouted. 'William? You lads here?'

There was only silence. He had come up after failing to see the fire that had smoked and flamed for the last three weeks. Last night, nothing.

'Hello,' he shouted again.

Silence.

He found the remains of their fire, the charcoal hemmed in by blackened stone. He dragged his foot through the embers. Nothing sparked.

'Lyle?' he shouted again. 'William?'

More silence. And then he saw the hole.

'My lord,' Butler said, looking at the house-sized crater. He took another step and saw two wooden boxes, covered in dirt and smashed open. He walked over to take a closer look. They were empty.

Then he saw the tools: spades, shovels and pickaxes. The digging equipment had been thrown to the side, abandoned and left to the weather.

'Hello?' Butler shouted again, turning around in a circle.

Jack Butler never saw the two Americans again. One of his neighbours later told him he'd given the twins a lift to the railway siding at Forbes. 'No luggage,' he said. 'Nothing but a couple of hessian bags. And boy did they look heavy.

'And you know what?' he continued. 'I only gave them a lift because they reminded me of Frank Gardiner. You remember Gardiner, right? The King of the Road? Well, these two, they looked just like him. Spitting images of him, the both of them. It was the strangest thing ...'

Select Bibliography

Nick Bleszynski, *'You'll Never Take Me Alive': The Life and Death of Bushranger Ben Hall*, Random House, Sydney, 2005

George Boxall, *History of the Australian Bushranger*, Scholar's Choice, date unknown

Peter Bradley, *Ben Hall: Stories from the Hard Road*, Yellow Box Books, Sydney, 2013

John Donohoe, *Ben Hall's Treasure*, self-published, 2014

Robert Ellis, *The Life and Times of Frank Gardiner*, self-published, date unknown

Barry R. Ledger, *The Attack on Goimbla Station*, Barry Ledger, Orange, NSW, 1991

John McGuire, *Early Colonial Days: The Biography of a Reliable Old Native*, Eugowra Promotion and Progress Association, Orange, NSW, 2009

Evan McHugh, *Bushrangers: Australia's Greatest Self-Made Heroes*, Penguin Books, Melbourne, 2011

Robert Macklin, *Fire in the Blood: The Epic Tale of Frank Gardiner and Australia's Other Bushrangers*, Allen & Unwin, Sydney, 2005

Edgar F. Penzig, *The Sandy Creek Bushranger: A Definitive History of Ben Hall, His Gang and Associates*, Historic Australia Publishing Company, Lane Cove, NSW, 1985

Tom Prior, Bill Wannan, H. Nunn, *Plundering Sons: A Pictorial History of Bushrangers*, Lansdowne Press, Melbourne, 1966

Rex and Thea Rienits, *A Pictorial History of Australia*, The Hamlyn Publishing Group, Middlesex, 1969

Trevor Shearston, *Game*, Allen & Unwin, Sydney, 2013

Jane Smith, *Ben Hall*, Big Sky Publishing, Newport, NSW, 2014

Jane Smith, *Frank Gardiner*, Big Sky Publishing, Newport, NSW, 2014

Noel Thurgood, *The Gold Robbery Escort Trials*, Kangaroo Press, Kenthurst, NSW, 1988

Trudy Toohill, *The Reporting of Ben Hall the Brave Bushranger*, Wild Colonial Press, Mount Crosby, Queensland, 2016

Charles White, *History of Australian Bushranging, 1863–1880: Ben Hall to the Kelly Gang*, Scholar Select, date unknown

Acknowledgements

I'd like to thank the following people for contributing to *Australian Heist*:

Hannah Bayly, Nathan Billings, Mick Carroll, The
Eugowra Historical Society, Scott Forbes, Simone
Ford, Jess Halloran, Claire Harvey, Huskisson Beach
Tourist Resort, James Kellow, Helen Littleton,
Laura Mactaggart, Tim Morrissey, Catherine Phelps,
Jax Phelps, Peter Phelps, James Silver and Lara Wallace.

All of you helped me tell this incredible tale. Hopefully we will get to do it all again ...